CLASSICS
OF
ANCIENT
CHINA

SUN-TZU

THE ART OF WARFARE

LAO-TZU: TE-TAO CHING
A NEW TRANSLATION BASED
ON THE RECENTLY DISCOVERED
MA-WANG-TUI TEXTS,
TRANSLATED, WITH AN
INTRODUCTION AND COMMENTARY,
BY ROBERT G. HENRICKS

SUN-TZU
THE ART OF
WARFARE

THE FIRST
ENGLISH TRANSLATION
INCORPORATING
THE RECENTLY DISCOVERED
YIN-CH'ÜEH-SHAN TEXTS

TRANSLATED,
WITH AN INTRODUCTION AND
COMMENTARY, BY
ROGER T. AMES

ROBERT G. HENRICKS,
SERIES EDITOR

BALLANTINE BOOKS • NEW YORK

A Ballantine Book
Published by The Random House Publishing Group

Translation and new text
copyright © 1993 by Roger T. Ames

Published in the United States by Ballantine Books, an imprint
of The Random House Publishing Group,
a division of Random House, Inc., New York, and simultaneously
in Canada by Random House of Canada Limited, Toronto.

Grateful acknowledgment is made to Wing Tek Lum
for permission to reprint "Chinese Hot Pot" from *Expounding
the Doubtful Points* (Bamboo Ridge Press) by Wing
Tek Lum, Copyright © 1987 Wing Tek Lum.

Library of Congress Cataloging-in-Publication Data
Sun-tzu, 6th cent. B.C.
  [Sun-tzu ping fa. English]
  Sun-tzu : the art of war : the first English translation incorporating
the recently discovered Yin-ch' üeh-shan texts / translated, with an
introduction and commentary, by Roger T. Ames. — 1st ed.
    p. cm.
  Includes bibliographical references and index.
  ISBN 0-345-36239-X
  1. Military art and science--Early works to 1800. I. Ames, Roger T.,
1947– . II. Title.
U101.S95 1993b
355.02–dc21   92-52662
                                                                    CIP

www.ballantinebooks.com

Text design by Holly Johnson

Manufactured in the United States of America

First Edition: January 1993

For Jason

CONTENTS

Sun-tzu: The Art of Warfare: A Translation

ACKNOWLEDGMENTS

These are exciting days for the study of classical China. Over the past few decades, students of early China, encouraged by the continuing discovery of textual materials lost for millennia, have been working to bring this culturally formative period into sharper focus.

Owen Lock, a China specialist and also editor-in-chief of Del Rey Books (an imprint of Ballantine Books), has followed these developments closely, and has been keenly aware of their significance for understanding the cultural origins of the longest continuous civilization in human history. *Classics of Ancient China*, the series of which this volume, *Sun-tzu: The Art of Warfare*, is a part, has been created by Owen as a means of bringing this revolution to the attention of a broad reading public. His careful attention to this book at every stage, his detailed comments on draft manuscripts, and his informed enthusiasm for the subject itself have made the project enjoyable and exciting from the outset, and I am most grateful to him.

Robert G. Henricks, with his translation of *Lao-tzu: Te-tao ching*, inaugurated this series, and by the sustained quality of his scholarship has set a high standard for us all. He, like Owen, read the manuscript, and gave me comments that have made it a better book. I have relied on another author in our series, Robin D. S. Yates, who has been ever generous with his advice on military technology.

In Beijing, I benefited from personal conversations and from the important publications of Wu Jiulong (Wu Chiu-lung) and Li Ling. In Shenyang, the consummate scholar Zhang Zhenze (Chang Chen-tse) shared his work and his warmth.

I would also like to thank Tian Chenshan of the Center for Chinese Studies at the University of Hawaii, who worked closely with me on the preparation of the critical Chinese text. Several of my colleagues gave their time and their thoughts in reading different generations of the manuscript: I am grateful to Michael Speidel, Tao T'ien-yi, Elizabeth Buck, and Daniel Cole.

The *Chuang-tzu* tells us that none of us walks alone; each of us is "a crowd," a "field of selves." D. C. Lau, Angus Graham, Yang Yu-wei, Eliot Deutsch, David L. Hall, Henry Rosemont, Jr., and Graham Parkes—and my family: Bonnie, Jason, Austin, and Cliff—have all crowded around as I collected myself and did this work, and I have spent a lot of time with each of them. If an expression of gratitude could ever be at once sincere and selfish, it is so for me on this occasion.

Roger T. Ames
Honolulu

INTRODUCTION

THE "NEW" SUN-TZU

The *Sun-tzu*, or "*Master Sun*," is the longest existing and most widely studied military classic in human history. Quite appropriately, it dates back to the Warring States period (c. 403–221 B.C.), a formative phase in Chinese civilization when contributions in literature and philosophy were rivaled in magnitude and sophistication only by developments in an increasingly efficient military culture.

Over the course of the preceding Spring and Autumn period (c. 722–481 B.C.), scores of small, semiautonomous states had joined in an ongoing war of survival, leaving in its wake only the dozen or so "central states" (*chung-kuo*) from which present-day "China" takes its actual Chinese-language name.[1] By the fifth century B.C., it had become clear to all contenders that the only alternative to winning was to perish. And as these rivals for the throne of a unified China grew fewer, the stakes and the brutality of warfare increased exponentially.

During this period, warfare was transformed from a

gentlemanly art to an industry, and lives lost on the killing fields climbed to numbers in the hundreds of thousands. Itinerant philosophers toured the central states of China, offering their advice and services to the contesting ruling families. Along with the Confucian, Mohist, and the Legalist philosophers who joined this tour was a new breed of military specialists schooled in the concrete tactics and strategies of waging effective warfare. Of these military experts, history has remembered best a man named Sun Wu from the state of Wu, known honorifically as "Sun-tzu" or "Master Sun."

A major reason why Master Sun has remained such a prominent force in the military arts is the military treatise *Sun-tzu: The Art of Warfare (Sun-tzu ping-fa)*, that came to be associated with his name early in the tradition. Over the centuries, a library of commentaries has accrued around the text, and it has been translated into many, if not most, of the world's major languages.

Although there are several popular English translations of the *Sun-tzu*, several of which are discussed below, there are reasons why a new translation and study of the text is necessary at this time. The *Sun-tzu* offered here in this *Classics of Ancient China* series differs markedly from previous editions in several important respects.

In 1972 a new text of the *Sun-tzu* was uncovered in an archaeological find in Shantung province, containing not only large sections of the thirteen-chapter work that has come down to the present day, but also portions of five lost chapters of the *Sun-tzu*. All of these materials, previously unavailable to the student of the *Sun-tzu* text, were entombed as burial items sometime between 140 and 118 B.C.

This archaeological discovery means several things.

The English translation of the thirteen-chapter core text contained in Part I of this book has been informed by a copy of the *Sun-tzu* over a thousand years older than those on which previous translations were based. Prior to the excavations at Yin-ch'üeh-shan, the most recent text on which translations could be based had been a Sung dynasty (960–1279) edition. The supplemental five chapters that have been translated below as Part II and which in length are about 20 percent of the thirteen-chapter core text, are entirely new, and provide us with additional insights into both the content and the structure of the original text.

Part III of this book contains another window on the *Sun-tzu* provided by traditional encyclopedic works and commentaries containing references to the *Sun-tzu* dating back as early as the first century A.D. In length, this section adds more than 2,200 characters—over a third of the thirteen-chapter text. The encyclopedic works as a genre were generally compiled by gathering citations from the classical texts around specific topics such as the court, animals, plants, omens, courtesans, and so on. One recurring encyclopedia topic has been warfare. Ancient commentaries written by scholars to explain classical works have also on occasion referred to the *Sun-tzu*. To this new, expanded text of *Sun-tzu* I have added Part III. It contains materials from the encyclopedias, and from some of the earliest commentaries, that have been ascribed directly to Master Sun. Now that we can have greater confidence that the *Sun-tzu* was a larger, more complex text, there is good reason to believe that at least some of these attributions are authentic. One factor that had previously brought these materials into question was a difference in style: The thirteen-chapter text is narrative prose while the encyclopedic citations are, by and large, in dialogue form. Now that we have confirmed "outer" commentarial chapters of the *Sun-tzu* that are also structured as dialogues and that share many stylistic features with the encyclopedic citations, our reasons for being suspicious are less compelling. Although the authenticity of any one of these passages is still impossible to determine, the general correspondence between passages found in the reconstructed *Sun-tzu* and those preserved in the encyclopedias suggest that many of the citations might well be from the lost portions of this text.

I also have included in Part III a few fragments from a 1978 archaeological find in Ch'ing-hai province dating from the first or second centuries B.C. Six of the strips uncovered refer explicitly to "Master Sun," suggesting some relationship with the *Sun-tzu*.

In addition to working from the earliest text of the *Sun-tzu* now available and translating newly recovered portions of the *Sun-tzu*, I have tried to underscore the philosophic importance of this early work. Most accounts of the *Sun-tzu* have tended to be historical; mine is cultural. In the Introduction that precedes the translations, I have attempted to identify those cultural presuppositions that must be consciously entertained if we are to place the text within its own world view. In our encounter with a text from a tradition as different from ours as is classical China's, we must exercise our minds and our imaginations to locate it within its own ways of thinking and living. Otherwise we cannot help but see only our own reflection appearing on the surface of Chinese culture when we give prominence to what is culturally familiar and important to us, while inadvertently ignoring precisely those more exotic elements that are essential to an appreciation of China's differences. By contrasting our assumptions with those of the classical Chinese world view, I have tried to secure and lift to the surface those peculiar features of classical Chinese thought which are in danger of receding in our interpretation of the text.

In addition to the role that philosophy plays in enabling us to distinguish the classical Chinese world view from our own, it has another kind of prominence. We must explain the intimate relationship in this culture between philosophy and warfare: We need to say why almost every one of the early Chinese philosophers took warfare to be an area of sustained philosophical reflection and how the military texts are themselves applied philosophy.

This edition of the *Sun-tzu* seeks to satisfy the needs of the China specialist as well as those of the generalist. To this end, a critical Chinese-language text of the *Sun-tzu* has been reconstructed from the available redactions of the work on the basis of the most authoritative scholarship available, and included with the translation. This critical text is based upon the collective judgment of China's leading scholars in military affairs. For the generalist who seeks a better understanding of the text within its broader intellectual environment, I have provided the aforementioned philosophic overview.

Given the long and eventful history of the *Sun-tzu* itself, its introduction to the English-speaking world has been very recent and rather undistinguished.[2] In spite of some illuminating criticisms by D. C. Lau (1965) about the quality of the Samuel B. Griffith translation (1963), one would still have to allow that Griffith's rendition of the *Sun-tzu* and his commentary on various aspects of the text was a quantum improvement over what had gone before and to date has been our best effort to capture the text for the English-speaking world. The first prominent English translation by Captain E. F. Calthrop (1908) was indeed so inadequate that the vitriolic and undignified assault that it provoked from the well-known sinologist and translator Lionel Giles, then an assistant curator at the British Museum, discolors the reasonable quality of Giles's own attempt. While the Giles translation of 1910 is somewhat compromised by his unrelenting unkindnesses to poor pioneering Calthrop, it is still a scholarly first run on a difficult text and has the virtue of including a version of the *Sun-tzu* in Chinese.

Not much happened in the half century between Giles and Griffith. The strength of Griffith's work is that it is the product of a mature and intelligent military man. Samuel B. Griffith rose to the rank of Brigadier General in the United States Marine Corps, and wrote extensively and well on military matters from the battle of Guadalcanal to the Chinese People's Liberation Army. The many practical insights provided by Griffith's commentary are invaluable, and the quality of his translation is superior to Giles's and to recent popular attempts such as the Thomas Cleary translation (1988), informed as the latter is by neither practical military wisdom nor scholarship.

Finally, I have used the occasion of this publication to introduce the reader to recent Chinese archaeological excavations—especially those beginning at Yin-ch'üeh-shan in 1972—in acknowledgment of the importance of these discoveries for rethinking the classical period in China. From these sites we have recovered a cache of textual materials, including everything from new redactions of extant classics to works that have been lost for thousands of years. In many ways, each of these excavations captures one historical moment from centuries long past, and allows us, with imagination, to step back and steal a glimpse of a material China that has not otherwise been available to us. And from these ancient relics and textual materials we are able to reconstitute one cultural site to test our theories and speculations about a world that is no more.

ARCHAEOLOGY: A REVOLUTION IN THE STUDY OF EARLY CHINA

For students of culture concerned with the formative period of Chinese civilization and its early development, the discovery of lost textual materials, reported to the world in China's archaeological journals since the resumption of their publication in 1972, has been nothing short of breathtaking. The texts that have been recovered are of several kinds.

One category of documents is that of extant texts. The texts in this grouping are important because they have been spared the mishandling of those perhaps well-intentioned but not always well-serving editors and scribes responsible for a two-thousand-year transmission. For example, the December 1973 excavation of the Ma-wang-tui Tomb #3 in Hunan dating from c. 168 B.C. has yielded us two editions of the *Lao-tzu*[3] that predate our earliest exemplars by five hundred years.

D. C. Lau's recently published revision of his *Lao-tzu* translation based on a study of the Ma-wang-tui texts is an effective demonstration of the value of these new documents in resolving textual problems that have plagued commentators for these two thousand years.[4] And with Robert G. Henrick's *Lao-tzu: Te-tao-ching* in this same *Classics of Ancient China* series, the careful textual work goes on. In addition to the *Lao-tzu* and the *Sun-tzu: The Art of Warfare* included here in this second volume of the series, portions of the *Book of Changes (I Ching)*, *Intrigues of the Warring States (Chan-kuo ts'e)*, and *The Spring and Autumn Annals of Master Yen (Yen-tzu ch'un-ch'iu)* have also been unearthed, and are undergoing the same kind of detailed analysis. It has even been reported that a partial text of the *Analects* was recovered at a Ting county site in Hopei province in a 1973 find, but at this writing the material has not yet been made available to foreign scholars.[5]

Another category of document that has been recovered is that of extant texts that have long been regarded by scholars as being apocryphal; that is, works of doubtful authorship and authority. Portions of the military treatises *Six Strategies (Liu-t'ao)* and *Master Wei-liao (Wei-liao-tzu)*, found in the cache of military writings in Tomb #1 of Yin-ch'üeh-shan, belong to this group. Of course, the discovery of these texts in a tomb dating from c. 140 B.C. is ample evidence of their vintage. There is also the collection of *Master Wen (Wen-tzu)* fragments found at the Ting county site that, by virtue of the important differences between the authoritative recovered text and the altered received *Master Wen*, promise to relocate this work centuries earlier than previously thought.[6]

A third important classification of texts is works concerning astronomy and prognostication that have hitherto been entirely unknown to us. The *Wind Direction Divination (Feng-chiao-chan)* and *Portent and Omen Divination (Tsai-i-chan)* documents, and the calendrical register for 134 B.C. recovered from Yin-ch'üeh-shan Tombs #1 and #2 are examples of this kind of material.

A fourth category of textual materials is that of works we have known about by name, but which in substance have been lost to us for the better part of two millennia. Undoubtedly the most important finds in this category are the four treatises collectively referred to as the *Silk Manuscripts of the Yellow Emperor (Huang-ti po-shu)*—Ching-fa, Shih-liu-ching, Ch'eng and Tao-yüan—that precede the second copy of the *Lao-tzu* on the cloth manuscripts recovered from Ma-wang-tui #3,[7] and the *Sun Pin: The Art of Warfare*[8] found in Yin-ch'üeh-shan #1. Annotated translations of both of these works are in progress, and are scheduled to appear in this same *Classics of Ancient China* series.

In addition to these works that are new to us in their entirety, there are also lost portions of extant texts that themselves have been transmitted in some edited or otherwise abbreviated form. For example, the *Sun-tzu: The Art of Warfare* from Yin-ch'üeh-shan, in addition to containing over 2,700 characters of the received thirteen-chapter text, approximately one third of its total length, also includes five chapters of supplemental materials that we have not seen until now. In this same find, there are also some forty-two bamboo strips that look like lost portions of the *Master Mo* (*Mo-tzu*).

The value of these newly discovered documents for extending and clarifying our knowledge of early Chinese civilization cannot be exaggerated. And the prospects of new finds are very good indeed, especially since several important locations are already known to us—for example, the late–third century B.C. tomb of the First Emperor of the Ch'in dynasty. While work on these known sites proceeds slowly, with scholars awaiting those advances in technology necessary to maximize preservation of the contents of the tombs, many other finds are being uncovered by accident in unrelated construction projects. Because of the impact that this archaeological material is having and is bound to have on the scholarship of classical China, a continuing familiarity with developments in this area has become an essential element in the training of every China classicist. Having said this, the nature of the material, the painstaking work necessary to recover and analyze it, and the real possibility of new discoveries at any time makes the work available on these documents necessarily tentative. For this reason, the present book is and can only be a progress report—an update on one particularly important find. The mission of our *Classics of Ancient China* series is to continue to make the substance of these finds available to the Western reader.

THE EXCAVATION AT
YIN-CH'ÜEH-SHAN

Of the various archaeological excavations published to date that have brought this new textual material to light, the two most important at this writing are the Western Han (202 B.C.–A.D. 8) tombs at Ma-wang-tui in Ch'ang-sha, Hunan, discovered in late 1973, and those at Yin-ch'üeh-shan near Lin-i city in Shantung. Portions of *Sun-tzu: The Art of Warfare*, the focus of this study, were recovered in the latter excavation in 1972.

After the initial find, the Yin-ch'üeh-shan Committee devoted some two years of research to the 4,942 bamboo strips and strip fragments on which the texts were written before making the preliminary results of this work known to the world in February 1974. For details of the early reports, a catalog of the contents of these tombs, and the best efforts of contemporary scholarship to date the tombs and identify the occupants, see the appendix.

Perhaps the most significant and exciting textual material uncovered in Tomb #1 is the additional text of the extant *Sun-tzu: The Art of Warfare* and the large portions of the long-lost *Sun Pin: The Art of Warfare*.

The contemporary archaeologist Wu Chiu-lung, in a 1985 revision of the earlier 1974 report, summarizes the overall content of the bamboo strips in the following more general terms.[9]

The Han strips from Tomb #1 can largely be divided into those of which we have extant traditional texts and those where the texts have been lost. Since the text provided by the Han strips and the extant text are often dif-

13

ferent, it is not always possible to keep the two categories clearly separate. In the first category of extant texts there are:

1. *Sun-tzu: The Art of Warfare (Sun-tzu ping-fa)* and five chapters of lost text

2. *Six Strategies (Liu-t'ao)*—fourteen segments

3. *Master Wei-liao (Wei-liao-tzu)*—five chapters

4. *Master Yen (Yen-tzu)*—sixteen sections

In the second category of lost texts, there are:

5. *Sun Pin: The Art of Warfare (Sun Pin ping-fa)*—sixteen chapters

6. *Obeying Ordinances and Obeying Orders (Shou-fa shou-ling)*—ten chapters

7. Materials on discussions of government and discussions on military affairs—fifty chapters

8. Materials on *yin-yang*, calendrics, and divination—twelve chapters

9. Miscellaneous—thirteen chapters

In addition, there are many leftover fragments, and the process of reconstruction goes on.

The 1985 first volume of the Yin-ch'üeh-shan Committee's anticipated three-volume set includes reconstructed texts for all of the documents 1–6 listed above; the remaining materials will be made available with the promised publication of volumes II and III.

From Tomb #2 we have a calendar for the first year of the *yüan-kuang* reign period (134 B.C.) of Emperor Wu (r. 141–87 B.C.) of the Western Han. It contains a total of thirty-two strips. The first strip records the year, the second strip lists the months, beginning with the tenth month and continuing until the following ninth month—a total of thirteen months. Strips three to thirty-two then record the days, listing the "stem and branches" designations for the first to the thirtieth day of each month. Together, these thirty-two strips constitute a complete calendar for the year.

There are varying opinions among scholars as to the dating of the texts themselves. From the archaeological evidence (see Appendix), we can estimate that Tomb #1 dates from between 140 and 118 B.C., and Tomb #2 dates from between 134 and 118 B.C. However, the dates at which the texts were transcribed would, of course, be earlier than the tombs in which they were buried, and the dates at which they were first compiled, earlier yet.

One potential clue as to the dates of the copied texts is the custom of avoiding the characters used in the emperor's name in texts transcribed during an emperor's reign. The Western Han, however, was not strict in its observance of such imperial taboos. The names of emperors Hui, Wen, and Wu all occur on the strips, and there are even instances of the less common characters of Empress Lü and Emperor Ching. The most that can be said is that these texts from Yin-ch'üeh-shan seem to observe the taboo on the first emperor of the Han dynasty, Liu Pang (r. 206–194 B.C.), avoiding the character *pang*, and using *kuo* (which also means "state") instead, with one exception in the supplemental strips of Chapter 4 of *Sun Pin: The Art of Warfare*, "T'ien-chi Inquires About Battlefield Defenses," which might have been an oversight.

The contemporary scholar Chang Chen-tse concludes that the strips must actually have been written during the dozen years Liu Pang was on the throne.[10] Other scholars are more cautious, insisting the taboos are inconclusive evidence. Wu Chiu-lung, for example, discounts the taboo factor, and instead compares the style of writing with other recent finds.[11] On this basis, he estimates the Yin-ch'üeh-shan texts were copied in the early years of the Western Han dynasty sometime during the period covered by the reigns of Emperor Wen (who ascended the throne in 179 B.C.), Emperor Ching, and the beginning years of Emperor Wu (who began his reign in 141 B.C.).

THE "ONE OR TWO 'MASTER SUNS'" DEBATE

Although fragmentary, the sizable portion (over one third) of the transmitted *Sun-tzu: The Art of Warfare* that was unearthed at Yin-ch'üeh-shan is the same in general outline as the received standard Sung dynasty edition: *Sun-tzu with Eleven Commentaries (Shih-i chia chu Sun-tzu)*. This is significant because it demonstrates that by the time this text was copied sometime in the second century B.C., the thirteen-chapter "classic" of *Sun-tzu* had already become fixed as a text. Where the recovered text differs from the received Sung dynasty edition, it is usually more economical in its language. It frequently uses characters without their signifiers or with alternative signifiers, and homophonous loan characters have often been substituted for the correct forms—familiar features of those early writings that have been unearthed—suggesting perhaps a lingering resistance to the standardization of the characters promoted by the Ch'in dynasty (221–206 B.C.) some years earlier, and,

16

further, the prominent role of oral transmission in the tradition. Where the Sung dynasty edition of the thirteen-chapter *Sun-tzu* is generally a fuller and more intelligible document, the opportunity to challenge problematic passages with a text dating from a full millennium earlier adds important new evidence for reconstructing a critical text. The other extraordinary value of the Yin-ch'üeh-shan text lies in the sixty-eight pieces constituting five partial chapters that had previously been lost. A version of one of these chapters, translated below in Part II as [An Interview with the King of Wu], was possibly reworked by Ssu-ma Ch'ien (c. 145–86 B.C.) into his biographical account of Master Sun. These additional sections are representative of the kinds of commentarial literature that would accrue over time around a classic once it had found its canonical form.

Sun Pin: The Art of Warfare, although only a partial and fragmentary text, still compares in length to the thirteen-chapter *Sun-tzu*. In the earliest published reports of the archaeological dig at Yin-ch'üeh-shan in 1975, the thirty fragmentary chapters identified as the *Sun Pin* contained some 8,700 characters. The *Sun-tzu*, for the sake of comparison, is approximately 6,000 characters. The revised sixteen-chapter text of the *Sun Pin* published in 1985 still provides sufficient detail to give us a reasonably clear picture of a work that has been known only by title for nearly two thousand years.

The fact that these two texts were recovered at the same time from the same tomb helps to resolve a question that has hovered over the two militarist treatises for centuries. Until this archeological find, only the core chapters of one of the two texts had been available—the thirteen-

17

chapter *Sun-tzu: The Art of Warfare*. Over the centuries all manner of speculation has arisen with respect to the authorship and even authenticity of the work, and particularly concerning its relationship to the second militarist text, *Sun Pin: The Art of Warfare*.

From the historical record, it is clear that scholars of the Han dynasty distinguished between the two military figures and their treatises, and that the debate among scholars as to whether there was one "Master Sun" or two (or one *Sun-tzu* text or two) is a post–Han dynasty phenomenon that arose after *Sun Pin: The Art of Warfare* was lost.

The *Historical Records* (*Shih-chi*), completed in 91 B.C., contains a biographical account that clearly separates Sun Wu (c. 544–496 B.C.), a contemporary of Confucius at the end of the Spring and Autumn period in the service of the state of Wu, and his descendent, Sun Pin (c. 380–316 B.C.), a contemporary of Mencius who flourished during the middle years of the fourth century B.C. in the employ of Ch'i.[12] In the biographies of these two persons who were separated by nearly two centuries, the *Historical Records* mentions both the *Sun-tzu: The Art of Warfare* in thirteen chapters (the same number of chapters as our extant Sung dynasty text), and *The Art of Warfare* attributed to Sun Pin. The latter text eventually disappeared from sight until portions of it were recovered in 1972.

Further, the "Record of Literary Works" (*Yi-wen chih*) of the *History of the Han Dynasty*, a catalog of the imperial library completed during the first century A.D., records the existence of two distinct texts:

1. *Sun-tzu of Wu: The Art of Warfare* in eighty-two

chapters and nine scrolls of diagrams. Yen Shih-ku's (581–645) commentary states: "This refers to Sun Wu."

2. *Sun-tzu of Ch'i: The Art of Warfare* in eighty-nine chapters and four scrolls of diagrams. Yen Shih-ku comments: "This refers to Sun Pin."

In addition to this specific historical information, there are further references to the two figures in the late Warring States and Han dynasty corpus. In spite of the fact that these sources often refer to both men as "Master Sun" ("Sun-tzu"), we are usually able to distinguish between them. For example, in the *Intrigues of the Warring States* (*Chan-kuo ts'e*), edited by Liu Hsiang (77–6 B.C.) in the late first century B.C., and throughout Ssu-ma Ch'ien's *Historical Records* as well, there are references to "Master Sun" that, from context and historical situation, can only refer to Sun Pin.[13] In the *Spring and Autumn Annals of Master Lü* (*Lü-shih ch'un-ch'iu*), probably completed c. 240 B.C., reference is made specifically to Sun Pin: "Sun Pin esteemed strategic advantage [*shih*]." This passage is glossed by the late Eastern Han commentator, Kao Yu (fl. 205–212), who states: "Sun Pin was a man of Ch'u [*sic*] who served as a minister in Ch'i working out strategy. His eighty-nine chapters deal with the contingencies surrounding strategic advantage [*shih*]."[14]

From the many Ch'in and Han dynasty references to these two texts, it would seem that at least until the end of the Eastern Han (A.D. 220), both texts were extant and were clearly distinguished by scholars of the time. Since the *History of the Later Han* (*Hou-Han-shu*), compiled over the third to fifth centuries A.D., does not include a catalog of the court library, the next logical place to expect a record of the two texts is the "Record of Classics and Documents" (*Ching-chi chih*) in the *History of the Sui Dynasty (Sui-shu)* compiled in the seventh century.[15] The total absence of any reference to *Sun Pin: The Art of Warfare* in the *History of the Sui Dynasty* together with the fact that Ts'ao Ts'ao (155–220), enthroned as King of the state of Wei (220–265) during the Three Kingdoms period, makes no mention of it in his commentary on the core thirteen chapters of *Sun-tzu: The Art of Warfare*, suggests rather strongly that *Sun Pin: The Art of Warfare* disappeared sometime between the last years of the Eastern Han dynasty in the third century, and the beginning of the Sui dynasty in the sixth century.

In spite of the many references and allusions to the two distinct texts in the Ch'in and Han dynasty literature, from the southern Sung dynasty (1127–1279) down to the present, prominent commentators such as Yeh Shih, Ch'en Chen-sun, Ch'uan Tsu-wang, Yao Nai, Liang Ch'i-ch'ao, and Ch'ien Mu have questioned both the authorship and the vintage of *Sun-tzu: The Art of Warfare*. Doubt concerning the historicity of Sun Wu was certainly reinforced by the fact that the *Commentary of Master Tso (Tso-chuan)*, one of China's oldest narrative histories, which dates from the turbulent fourth century B.C. and which otherwise evidences great delight in recounting military events, never refers to him at all. Some of these later scholars have questioned the historicity of the strategist Sun Wu; others have claimed *Sun-tzu: The Art of Warfare* perhaps originated with Sun Wu, but was edited and revised by his mid–fourth-century descendant, Sun Pin. Some have even suggested that Ts'ao Ts'ao, canonized as the "Martial King," compiled *Sun-tzu: The Art of Warfare* on the basis of earlier works before appending his own commentary.

The unearthing of these two texts in the same Han dynasty tomb at Yin-ch'üeh-shan goes some way to resolving the "one or two 'Master Suns'" dispute. Firstly, there are unquestionably two distinct texts, both extant in the second century B.C. Secondly, the discovery supports the traditional opinion that there were in fact two "Master Sun's"—Sun Wu and Sun Pin—and further lends credence to those historical records that offer such an opinion.

There is a real danger here, however, of pursuing the wrong questions and, in so doing, losing sight of what might be more important insights. We really must ask, for example: What do we mean by the *Sun-tzu* as a text, or even "Sun-tzu" as a historical person? The quest for a single text authored by one person and a preoccupation with historical authenticity is perhaps more a problem of our own time and tradition. There is a tendency on the part of the contemporary scholar to impose anachronistically our conceptions of "text" and "single authorship" on the classical Chinese artifact and, by doing so, to overlook the actual process whereby a text would come into being. This is a particular concern in dealing with cultures where oral transmission was a significant factor and in which authorship tended to be cumulative and corporate.

I am suggesting that works such as the *Sun-tzu* might have emerged more as a process than as a single event, and those involved in its authorship might well have been several persons over several generations. This Yin-ch'üeh-shan find reveals what I take to be a historical moment in the process. There is a redaction of the core thirteen-chapter

Sun-tzu that certainly predates the imperial editing of the text undertaken by Liu Hsiang at the end of the first century B.C., and which corroborates the several early references to a thirteen-chapter work. The fact that Sun Wu is referred to honorifically as "Master Sun" (translating the *"tzu"* in "Sun-tzu" as "Master") is evidence the text was not written by Sun Wu himself, and is also an indication the text was compiled and transmitted by persons who held Sun Wu in high regard as a teacher and as an authority on military matters. We can be quite sure this thirteen-chapter document was not composed by Sun Wu, and was probably the product of some later disciple or disciples, probably several generations removed from the historical Sun Wu. The text itself is at the very least a secondhand report on what Master Sun had to say about military strategy.

In Part II, "The Questions of Wu" chapter refers directly to the events surrounding the dissolution of the state of Chin that climaxed in 403 B.C. to begin the Warring States period. Even though this chapter belongs to the "outer" text of the *Sun-tzu*, which we must assume to be later commentary, to have Master Sun rehearsing the incidents that followed from the collapse of Chin places this discussion well into the fourth century B.C. at the earliest. It is clearly an anachronism.

There is also a revealing discrepancy between the Sung dynasty edition of the *Sun-tzu* and the Han strips version that might be of some significance in dating the actual compilation of the text. The last paragraph of Chapter 13 in the Sung dynasty edition reads:

Of old the rise of the Yin (Shang) dynasty was because of Yi Yin who served the house of Hsia; the rise of the Chou dynasty was because of Lü Ya who served in the house of Shang. Thus only those far-sighted rulers and their superior commanders who can get the most intelligent people as their spies are destined to accomplish great things.

The same passage in the Han strips version can be reconstructed as:

[*The rise of the*] Yin (Shang) dynasty [*was because of Yi Yin*] who served the house of Hsia; the rise of the Chou dynasty was because of Lü Ya who served [*in the house of Shang*]; [*the rise of the state of . . .*] was because of Commander Pi who served the state of Hsing; the rise of the state of Yen was because of Su Ch'in who served the state of Ch'i. Thus only those far-sighted rulers and their superior [*commanders who can get the most intelligent people as their spies are destined to accomplish great things*].

While we have no information on the Commander Pi who served the state of Hsing, we do know that Su Ch'in was a Warring States military figure and statesman who, flourishing in the early years of the third century B.C., lived more than a century and a half after the historical Sun Wu.[16] Since Su Ch'in, in fact living a generation removed from

Sun Pin, belongs to an era long after the historical Sun Wu, reference to him in this passage would, on the surface, suggest that the *Sun-tzu* is a text from the hand of a much later disciple or disciples. Alternatively (and this is the opinion of many, if not most, contemporary scholars), this passage in the Han strips text is a later interpolation.

In the introduction to his translation of the *Sun-tzu*, Samuel Griffith identifies several anachronistic references within the text itself that in sum push the date of the text well into the Warring States period: allusions to the scale of warfare, the professionalization of the soldier, the separation of aristocratic status and military rank, the deployment of shock and elite troops, the suggestion that rank-and-file troops as well as officers wore armor, the widespread use of metal currency, and so on.[17] For the most part, Griffith's arguments that *Sun-tzu* was compiled sometime in the period 400–320 B.C. are persuasive. The two references to the crossbow in the *Sun-tzu* that Griffith takes to be anachronistic, however, are probably not an issue. In their recent study of early military technology, Joseph Needham and Robin Yates have concluded that the crossbow was probably introduced into China by non-Han peoples in the middle Yangtze region as early as 500 B.C.[18]

On the basis of the Yin-ch'üeh-shan find, we can speculate that the eighty-two chapter *Sun-tzu*, a text including both the "inner" thirteen-chapter core and the "outer chapters" represented by fragments recovered in this archaeological dig, is assuredly a composite work—the product of many hands and many voices that accrued over an extended period of time. The role of oral transmission cannot be discounted. The nature and economy of the written text suggest its contents might have originally been discussion notes, copied down, organized, and edited by several generations of students, as was the case in the compilation of the *Analects of Confucius*. These materials were probably gathered together, collated, and subjected to a process of editorial refinement important for economical transmission—that is, a deletion of redundancies and marginally relevant references, the removal of historical detail that might bring the antiquity of the text into question, and so on. The main structural difference between the *Sun-tzu* and the *Analects of Confucius* is that the *Sun-tzu* is by and large organized thematically, while the order of the *Analects* is more random, with passages only sometimes being grouped—loosely—around a discernible theme or idea. The arrangement of the *Sun-tzu* is more linear, sequential, and thematic than the *Analects*, a characteristic increasingly in evidence in the texts compiled in the late fourth and third centuries B.C.

Another formal characteristic of the *Sun-tzu* that recommends a later rather than an earlier dating is the sustained dialogue structure of the newly recovered "outer" chapters. This distinctive feature suggests that these chapters were composed considerably later than the core thirteen-chapter text.

The overall congruencies between the Yin-ch'üeh-shan *Sun-tzu* and our received thirteen-chapter redactions suggest strongly that, by the time of the entombment of this text, the core text of *Sun-tzu* had already been edited into something closely resembling its present form, and thus had already become "fixed." Given the early Han dynasty date of this copy, this canonization of the *Sun-tzu* is what one would anticipate, following as it does the same pattern as other important pre-Ch'in works. In his examination of the *Lao-tzu*, D. C. Lau identifies the century between the writing of the *Master Han Fei* (c. 240 B.C.) and the compilation of the *Master of Huai Nan* (140 B.C.), as the time in which the *Lao-tzu* settled into its present form. Lau offers the following explanation for the congealing process that seems to have occurred at this particular historical juncture:

> It seems then that the text [the *Lao-tzu*] was still in a fluid state in the second half of the third century B.C. or even later, but by the middle of the second century B.C., at the latest, the text already assumed a form very much like the present one. It is possible this happened in the early years of the Western Han Dynasty. There is some reason to believe that in that period there were already specialist "professors" (*po shih*) devoted to the study of individual ancient works, including the so-called philosophers (*chu tzu*), as distinct from the classics (*ching*). . . . This would cause the text to become standardized. . . .[19]

In 213 B.C., the Ch'in court at the urging of the Legalist counsellor, Li Ssu, decreed that all existing literature representing the writings of the various philosophical schools, and particularly the Confucian classics, be turned over to the governors of the commanderies to be burned. The "burning of the books," as this event has come to be called, might well have made the reclamation of the classical corpus a priority item for the newly established Han dynasty a few years later.

At Yin-ch'üeh-shan, in addition to the core thirteen-chapter text, however, representative fragments of five commentarial chapters were also found that are very different in structure and style. We can speculate that these extensions of the core chapters were probably appended by later generations in the Sun clan lineage (*chia*) to explain and elaborate what the passage of time had made increasingly unclear. These "outer" chapters of the text were again probably authored by the disciples and descendants of Sun Wu, but at some greater distance in time from the Master than the core chapters.

The central militarist (and later, Legalist) tenet that there are no fixed strategic advantages (*shih*) or positions (*hsing*) that can, in all cases, be relied upon to achieve victory, must be considered when we decide what kind of coherence we can expect from what was a growing body of work. Consistent with the stated principle that each situation must be taken on its own terms, different periods with different social, political, and material conditions would require different military strategies to be effective. The military philosophers, like any school that continued over time, would necessarily have to reflect changing historical conditions in the articulation of their doctrines. Reference to a specific historical site and occasion softens the otherwise more rigid demands of theoretical abstractions and categorical imperatives.

On the basis of the shared tenet that different circumstances require different strategies for success, we can make the claim that even where the *Sun-tzu* and the *Sun Pin* seem clearly to contradict each other, they are still entirely consistent. For example, *Sun-tzu* is explicit in discouraging the strategy of attacking walled cities:

Therefore the best military policy is to attack strategies; the next to attack alliances; the next to attack soldiers; and the worst to assault walled cities. Resort to assaulting walled cities only when there is no other choice.[20]

Sun Pin, on the contrary, regards siege as a viable strategy.[21]

In what at present are regarded as supplemental chapters to the core text, the *Sun Pin* even recommends assaulting "female" fortifications.[22] The distinction between "male" and "female" fortifications is illustrated in the following terms:

A walled fortification situated in the midst of a low-lying swamp which, even without high mountains or deep valleys around it, is still surrounded on all sides by crouching hills, is a male fortification, and cannot be attacked. [*A walled fortification in which*] the troops have access to fresh, flowing water [*has a vital water supply, and cannot be attacked*]. A walled fortification which has a deep valley in front of it and high mountains behind is a male fortification, and cannot be attacked. A walled fortification within which there is high ground while beyond its walls the land falls away is a male fortification and cannot be attacked. A walled fortification within which there are crouching hills is a male fortification, and cannot be attacked.

When troops on the march in setting up camp for the night are not in the vicinity of some source of water, their morale will flag and their purposes will be weakened, and they can be attacked. A walled fortification which has a deep valley behind it and no high mountains on its flanks is a weak fortification and can be attacked. [*An army camped*] on the ashes of scorched land is on dead ground, and can be attacked. Troops who have access only to standing pools of water have dead water, and can be attacked. A walled fortification situated in the midst of broad swamplands without deep valleys or crouching hills around it is a female fortification, and can be attacked. A walled fortification which is situated between two high mountains without deep valleys or crouching hills around it is a female fortification, and can be attacked. A walled fortification which fronts a high mountain and has a deep valley to the rear, which is high in front but falls away to the rear, is a female fortification, and can be attacked.

This seeming inconsistency between *Sun-tzu* and *Sun Pin* is understandable if we factor into our assessment developments in military technology that made siege more effective, and the development of walled cities as centers of wealth and commerce that made siege more profitable.

Chariots, ineffective against high walls, were a central military technology for Master Sun; a cavalry equipped with crossbows was an innovation important to Sun Pin. Do we conclude that we have competing opinions here, or can such seeming inconsistencies be adequately explained by the assertion, shared by both texts, that different situations require different strategies for success?

Somewhere in this process of the eighty-two-chapter *Sun-tzu* being composed, transcribed, edited, and transmitted to succeeding generations, the *Sun Pin* emerges as a second text that, while seeming to belong to the *Sun-tzu* lineage, at the same time achieved an increasingly significant degree of distinction and, in due course, independence. The differentiation of *Sun Pin* from the then still-growing *Sun-tzu* corpus was at least in part due to the military successes of Sun Pin himself that became an integral part of the historical record and set his textual materials off from the earlier *Sun-tzu*. Having achieved this relative independence, *Sun Pin: The Art of Warfare* then probably followed the pattern of the *Sun-tzu: The Art of Warfare* in first becoming "fixed" as a core text, and then accruing a commentarial tradition around itself. The *History of the Han Dynasty* reports that the *Sun Pin* comprised eighty-nine chapters, probably a mixture of "inner" core chapters and later commentarial appendixes.

The sixteen-chapter *Sun Pin* that has been reconstructed from the Yin-ch'üeh-shan find differs from the more consistently theoretical *Sun-tzu* by beginning from chapters that report on specific historical incidents. It then generalizes from these battles and strategy sessions to outline certain basic tenets of military theory. In the Yin-ch'üeh-shan Committee's first report on the *Sun Pin* (1974), it had reconstructed the *Sun Pin* text in thirty chapters. In the committee's 1985 review of these materials, one reason given for reducing the thirty-chapter text to sixteen is that some chapters that are not demonstrably *Sun Pin* might well belong to the "outer chapters" of the *Sun-tzu*. The line separating the two texts is, at best, often unclear. In fact, it is possible that the lineage of authors who contributed to the *Sun-tzu* might well have included Sun Pin himself, and some of the materials that came to constitute the *Sun Pin: The Art of Warfare* might have, at one time and in some form or another, been part of the "outer chapters" of the *Sun-tzu*. Indeed, the entire body of textual materials might, under different circumstances, have been revised and edited to constitute the one *Sun-tzu*. Instead, the materials were divided to become the two separate treatises on warfare, the *Sun-tzu* and the *Sun Pin*.

How else has the Yin-ch'üeh-shan archaeological dig shed light on the early years of the Han dynasty? In addition to the value of the Han strips in assessing the historicity of the classical corpus, they are an important resource for investigating the changing forms of written Chinese characters, especially during the early years in which the clerical form (*li shu*) was being institutionalized. The strips also offer up new loan characters, and new insights into rhyme patterns current in the formative period of Chinese civilization.

Perhaps the most important consequence of the Yin-ch'üeh-shan find is not the specific resolution of the "two Master Suns" debate, but a more general principle: That is, we must take the process of textual "growth" into account and give greater credence to the traditional dating of these early works. In addition to the *Sun-tzu* and *Sun Pin*, we have recovered portions of other texts previously dismissed as apocryphal. The fact that the fragments of the *Master Yen, Master Wei-liao,* and *Six Strategies* all have text very similar to the received redactions suggests a greater respect is due traditional claims of authenticity.

SUN WU AS A HISTORICAL PERSON

According to the biography in the *Historical Records*, the first comprehensive history of China completed in 91 B.C., Sun Wu was born in the state of Ch'i (in the area of present-day Shantung province) as a contemporary of Confucius (551–479 B.C.) at the end of the Spring and Autumn period, and came into the employ of King Ho-lu of Wu (r. 514– 496 B.C.) as a military commander. He gained an audience with King Ho-lu who, after having read the thirteen chapters of the *Sun-tzu: The Art of Warfare*, summoned him to court. Putting Sun Wu to the test, the King requested that Sun Wu demonstrate his military skill by conducting a drill using the women of his court. An alternative version of this same story was reclaimed in the Yin-ch'üeh-shan dig, and has been translated below in Part II as "[An Interview with the King of Wu]." This must be one of the best-known anecdotes in Chinese military lore:

> The King . . . dispatched 180 of his court beauties from the palace. Sun Wu divided them into two contingents, placed the King's two favorite concubines as unit commanders, and armed them all with halberds. He then instructed the women, "Do you know where your heart, your right and left hands and your back are?" The women replied, "We do indeed." "When I say 'Front'," he said, "face in the direction of your heart; when I say 'Left,' face in the direction of your left hand; when I say 'Right,' face in the direction of your right hand; when I say 'Back,' face in the direc-

tion of your back." The women agreed. Having set out the various drill commands, he then laid out the commander's broad-axe, and went through and explained his orders several times. Thereupon, he drummed for them to face right, but the women just burst into laughter.

Master Sun said, "Where drill orders are less than clear and the troops are not familiar enough with the commands, it is the fault of their commander." Again going through and explaining his orders several times, he then drummed for them to face left. Again the women just burst into laughter.

Master Sun addressed them, "Where the drill orders are less than clear and the troops are not familiar enough with the commands, it is the fault of their commander. But where they have already been made clear and yet are not obeyed, it is the fault of their supervising officers." He then called for the beheading of the right and left unit commanders.

The King, viewing the proceedings from his balcony, saw that Master Sun was in the process of executing his two favorite concubines, and was appalled. He rushed an attendant down to Master Sun with the command, "I am already convinced of the Commander's ability in the use of the military. If I don't have these two concubines, my food will be tasteless. It is my wish that you do not behead them."

Master Sun responded, "I have already received your mandate as Commander, and while I am in command of the troops, I am not bound by your orders." He thereupon beheaded the two unit commanders as an object lesson.

Appointing the next two in line as the new unit commanders, he again drilled them. Left, right, front, back, kneel, stand—at every turn the women performed with the precision of the square and compass, and did not dare to utter a sound. Master Sun thereupon sent a messenger to report to the King, "The troops have now been properly disciplined. Your Majesty can come down to inspect them. Do as you like with them—you can even send them through fire and water!"

The King of Wu replied, "The Commander may return to his chambers to rest. I have no desire to descend and review the troops."

Master Sun said, "The King is only fond of words, but has no stomach for their real application." At this, Ho-lu knew Master Sun's ability at military affairs, and ultimately made him his Commander. That Wu crushed the strong state of Ch'u to the west and occupied its capital at Ying, intimidated Ch'i and Chin to the north and rose to prominence among the various states, was in good measure due to Master Sun's military acumen.[23]

Elsewhere in his *Historical Records*, Ssu-ma Ch'ien records Sun Wu's counsel to King Ho-lu in the campaign against the state of Ch'u.[24] Following Sun Wu's advice, the state of Wu was able to occupy the Ch'u capital within six years. Evident from these historical reports is the fact that Sun Wu was not only a military tactician, but also a very capable strategist who was able to lead his state to victory.

Although the details of Sun Wu's life are for the most part lost, the place of his *Sun-tzu: The Art of Warfare* as *the* fundamental work in classical military literature is unassailable. The military chapters of the *Book of Lord Shang*, a Legalist text dating primarily from the third century B.C.,[25] are heavily indebted to material adapted from the *Sun-tzu*.[26] The *Master Hsün's* "Debate on Warfare" treatise is in fact a very specific Confucian assault mounted by Master Hsün (c. 320–235 B.C.) against those prevailing military concepts and attitudes clearly drawn from the *Sun-tzu: The Art of Warfare*.[27] The Legalist Han Fei, a student of Master Hsün, reports on the popularity of the *Sun-tzu: The Art of Warfare* in a world that had been scorched with centuries of unrelenting military strife: "Everyone in the realm discusses military affairs, and every family keeps a copy of the *Master Wu* and the *Sun-tzu* on hand.[28] The "Military Strategies" treatise in the *Master of Huai Nan*, certainly one of the most lucid statements on early military ideas, evidences an intimate familiarity with the *Sun-tzu: The Art of Warfare* and builds upon it. From the centuries leading up to the founding of imperial China, over its two-millennia-long career, and during the decades of unprecedented military intensity in the twentieth century, the *Sun-tzu: The Art of Warfare* has maintained its status as the world's foremost classic on military strategy.

THE RECONSTRUCTED SUN-*TZU:*
THE ART OF WARFARE

The 1985 volume of the Yin-ch'üeh-shan Committee's re-construction of the *Sun-tzu* divides it into two parts. Part I includes the remnants of the thirteen-chapter edition (over 2,700 characters) with representative text from all of the chapters except Chapter 10, "The Disposition of the Terrain" (*ti-hsing*); Part II comprises five additional chapters unknown to us previously, one of which relates the story found in the *Historical Records* biography of Master Sun where Sun Wu disciplines the concubines of King Ho-lu of the state of Wu.

There are also six fragmentary segments of wood that, when pieced together, constitute a table of contents for the scrolls of bamboo strips containing the core *Sun-tzu* text.

From appearances, the bamboo manuscript was divided into two portions, with a table of contents and a character tally for each one. From what remains of the table of contents, we can still identify eight chapter titles of what, from all appearances, was a list of thirteen. This would suggest the table of contents of the *Sun-tzu* was the same then as our present Sung dynasty edition, although there seem to be discrepancies in the order of the chapters. The comparative similarity between the recovered text and the traditional text means that *Sun-tzu* was not edited into its present thirteen chapters by later commentators such as Ts'ao Ts'ao (155–220) or Tu Mu (803–852) as traditionally thought, but had this arrangement much earlier.

Part II's five newly recovered chapters, a total of over 1,200 characters or some additional 20 percent of the received text, have a commentarial relationship to the thirteen-chapter core. "The Questions of Wu" chapter records a dialogue between Master Sun and the King of Wu on the state of Chin and on governmental policies. Although this dialogue format is not found in the existing thirteen-chapter text, it is familiar from the long citations of *Sun-tzu* preserved in the T'ang dynasty (618–907) encyclopedic work on laws and institutions, the *T'ung-tien*, translated below in Part III of the present volume.

"The Yellow Emperor Attacks the Red Emperor" chapter begins with the "Master Sun said . . ." formula, and seems related in content to Chapter 9, "Deploying the Army" (*hsing chün*), which also alludes to the Yellow Emperor's victory over the emperors of the four quarters.

"[The Four Contingencies]" chapter further elaborates on sections of Chapter 8, "Adapting to the Nine Contingencies"; the fragments of "The Disposition [of the Terrain] II" seems related in content to Chapter 9, "Deploying the Army," and to Chapter 11, "The Nine Kinds of Terrain."

These chapters are all appended to the present text because, like much of the materials attributed to *Sun-tzu* recovered from other sources in the early corpus and the later encyclopedic works, they too elaborate on and explain the core thirteen-chapter text.

As we saw above, the "Record of Literary Works" (*Yi-wen chih*) of the *History of the Han Dynasty* lists in the category of "Military Strategists" the *Sun-tzu of Wu: The Art of Warfare* in eighty-two chapters and nine scrolls of diagrams. This certainly refers to a larger compilation than the familiar thirteen-chapter text. In the commentary of Chang Shou-chieh (fl. A.D. 737) to the biography of Master

Sun in the *Historical Records*, he comments: "The Ch'i-lu of Juan Hsiao-hsü of the Liang dynasty (502–556) lists the *Sun-tzu: The Art of Warfare* in three scrolls. The thirteen-chapter text is the first scroll, and there are also a second and a third scroll."[29] It is possible that the last two scrolls were comprised of explanatory chapters that included among them the lost text recovered on these bamboo manuscripts.

The contemporary scholar Li Ling, in describing the compilation of the eighty-two-chapter *Sun-tzu*, compares it to the original inner and outer books of the *Mencius*.[30] Our present *Mencius* was edited by the Han dynasty commentator Chao Ch'i (d. A.D. 201), who expunged four "outer books" that he took to be the spurious work of a later age rather than the authentic work of Mencius. Ch'ing dynasty (1644–1911) collections have been made of passages attributed to Mencius but not contained in our present text, which might be remnants of those lost "outer" books.

Another analogous compilation is the *Master Kuan* (*Kuan-tzu*) (compiled c. 250 B.C.). Although more explicitly commentarial, the chronologically later "explanatory" (*chieh*) chapters of the *Master Kuan* serve a function similar to that of the "outer chapters" of the *Sun-tzu*.

It is most unlikely that the eighty-two-chapter *Sun-tzu* was one text by a single author. A plausible story is that the expository thirteen-chapter *Sun-tzu* differed substantially in date, content, and structure from the later outer books. Following the editing of the father-and-son Han dynasty bibliographers, Liu Hsiang (77–6 B.C.) and Liu Hsin (d. A.D. 23), the inner thirteen-chapter core and the outer chapters were brought together in the eighty-two-chapter text. The military strategist and scholar Ts'ao Ts'ao (155–220) wrote commentary only on the thirteen inner chapters, and subsequently, the outer chapters, supplementary to the inner chapters, were lost. Much of what has been preserved of the outer chapters recovered from the Yin-ch'üeh-shan (*Sun-tzu: Part II*, below) and from the later encyclopedic works and Ta-t'ung county archaeological finds (*Sun-tzu: Part III*, below) does differ in style and content from the thirteen inner chapters, although most of these materials bear a recognizable commentarial relationship.

ANALYSIS OF *SUN-TZU:* *THE ART OF WARFARE*

WISDOM AND WARFARE

Discussion of military affairs is pervasive in early Chinese philosophical literature. This in itself is a fair indication of the perceived importance of warfare as a topic of philosophic reflection in China, a concern that is not paralleled in Western philosophical literature. It is a seldom-advertised fact that many if not most of the classical Chinese philosophical works contain lengthy treatises on military thought: the *Master Mo, Master Hsün, Master Kuan,* the *Book of Lord Shang,* the *Spring and Autumn Annals of Master Lü,* the *Master of Huai Nan,* and so on. In addition, other central texts such as the *Analects, Mencius, Lao-tzu, Master Han Fei,* and the recently recovered *Silk Manuscripts of the Yellow Emperor* contain extended statements on military thought. In fact, in the imperial catalog included in the *History of the Han Dynasty,* the military writers are listed under the "philosophers" (*tzu*) classification.[31] It might be fair speculation to say that, in the philosophical literature of the classical period, a text would be perceived as less than complete if the conversation did not at some point turn to an extended discussion of military strategies and even tactics.

This abiding interest in military affairs is a particularly curious situation for a culture in which warfare is neither celebrated nor glorified, and in which military heroism is a rather undeveloped idea. When it comes to social status, the warrior in China did not have the benefit of having Greek and Roman forbears.[32] Even in those Chinese treatises that deal exclusively with military affairs, we generally find the same paternalistic concern for the welfare of the people familiar to us from the Confucian literature, and an explicit characterization of warfare as an always unfortunate last resort. There is no self-promoting militarism.

The question that emerges, then, is this: Given the general disparity in status between civil and martial virtue in the Chinese tradition, how do we explain the intimate, even interdependent relationship between the occupations of philosopher and warrior assumed by the early Chinese thinkers?

The military experience, early and late, was important in the culture. Armies up to the late Spring and Autumn period were still constituted by aristocratic families living in the vicinity of the capital, and ordinary people played a relatively minor role in the actual fighting. The merchant class was also largely excluded. The armies would be led personally by representatives of the ruling families and by high-ranking ministers of royal blood who would be educated from an early age in both civil and military arts.

Even with Confucius, whose death in 481 B.C. usually marks the end of the Spring and Autumn period, it is clear from the profile preserved in the *Analects* by his disciples that he was trained for both a literary and military career.[33]

During the increasingly more frequent and brutal conflicts of the Warring States period, a real separation emerged between the civil and the military, with mercenaries from lower classes selling their talents to the highest bidder. Warfare moved from an honorable occupation to a profession,[34] and the numbers of those slaughtered on the battlefield and in the reprisals that sometimes followed increased from the hundreds to hundreds of thousands.[35]

The simple explanation for the relationship between philosophy and warfare is that military strategy, like any of the other "arts" (culinary, divinatory, musical, literary, and so on), can be used as a source of metaphors from which to shape philosophical distinctions and categories.[36] Further, military campaigns—particularly at that juncture in Chinese history when political survival was on the line— were a critical preoccupation in which the full range of human resources, including philosophical sensibilities, could be profitably applied. The resolutely pragmatic nature of classical Chinese philosophy resists any severe distinction between theory and application and, as a consequence, philosophizing in this culture is not merely theoretical—it entails practice, "doing." Hence warfare, to the extent that it is philosophical, is necessarily applied philosophy.

Such speculations are undoubtedly part of the answer. But is it simply that military practices can provide grist for philosophical reflection, and philosophy can be applied as some organizing apparatus for military action? Such surely is the case, but the relationship runs deeper. I want to suggest that beneath the rather obvious divergence in subject matter between the cultivation of wisdom in one's person and the cultivation of victory on the battlefield, there is an identifiable correlativity: There is a peculiarly Chinese model of "harmony" or achieved order (ho) both fundamental to and pervasive in the classical culture that is pursued by philosopher and military commander alike.

There is a more concrete way of reformulating this question about the intimate relationship between wisdom and warfare that underscores this shared sense of an achieved harmony. How can we explain the clear assumption in this classical Chinese culture that the quality of character which renders a person consummate and exemplary in the various roles of social, political, and cultural leader will also serve him equally well in the role of military commander? We might recall two relevant Confucian precepts:

1. The exemplary person is not a functionary (ch'i).

2. The exemplary person pursues harmony (ho), not sameness.[37]

What it means to be exemplary, then, is not determined by what function one serves or by what specific skills one possesses, but by one's character. The assumption is that persons of superior character will be exemplary in whatever occupation they turn their hand to—an assumption that is alive and well today. We need only recall the way in which cultural and political leaders are portrayed in the contemporary expression of the Chinese tradition. Mao Tse-tung,

42

as a familiar recent example, was profiled for public view as a great statesman, a poet, a calligrapher, a military strategist, a philosopher, an economist—even an athlete swimming the Yangtze river. It is the ability of the leader to achieve "harmony," however it is defined, that is signatory of what it means to be a person of superior character, whether this harmony is expressed through communal leadership or through military prowess.

To understand the close relationship between warfare and philosophy in classical China, then, we must look to the dynamics of an underlying and pervasive conception of harmony (*ho*) that, for the classical Chinese world view, grounds human experience generally.

THE CLASSICAL CHINESE WORLD VIEW: THE UNCOMMON ASSUMPTIONS

In Chinese there is an expression, "We cannot see the true face of Mount Lu because we are standing on top of it." Although virtually all cultural traditions and historical epochs are complex and diverse, there are certain fundamental and often unannounced assumptions on which they stand that give them their specific genetic identity and continuities. These assumptions, extraordinarily important as they are for understanding the culture, are often concealed from the consciousness of the members of the culture who are inscribed by them, and become obvious only from a perspective external to the particular tradition or epoch. Often a tradition suspends within itself competing and even

conflicting elements that, although at odds with one another, still reflect a pattern of importances integral to and
constitutive of its cultural identity. These underlying
strands are not necessarily or even typically logically coherent or systematic, yet they do have a coherence as the
defining fabric of a specific and unique culture.

Within a given epoch, even where two members of a
tradition might disagree in some very basic ways—the
Confucian and the follower of Master Sun, for example—
there are still some common assumptions more fundamental than their disagreements that identify them as members
of that culture and have allowed meaningful communication, even where it is disagreement, to occur.

Looking at and trying to understand elements of the
classical Chinese culture from the distance of Western traditions, then, embedded as we are within our own pattern
of cultural assumptions, has both advantages and disadvantages. One disadvantage is obvious and inescapable. To the
extent that we are unconscious of the difference between
our own fundamental assumptions and those that have
shaped the emergence of classical Chinese thought, we are
sure to impose upon China our own presuppositions about
the nature of the world, making what is exotic familiar and
what is distant near. On the other hand, a clear advantage
of an external perspective is that we are able to see with
greater clarity at least some aspects of "the true face of
Mount Lu"—we are able to discern, however imperfectly,
the common ground on which the Confucian and the follower of Master Sun stand in debating their differences,
ground that is in important measure concealed from them
as unconscious assumptions.

While it is always dangerous to make generalizations about complex cultural epochs and traditions, it is even more dangerous not to. In pursuit of understanding, we have no choice but to attempt to identify and excavate these uncommon assumptions, and to factor them into our understanding of the Chinese tradition broadly, and in this instance, into our assessment of the Chinese art of warfare. The differences between the classical Chinese world view and those classical Greek, Roman, and Judaeo-Christian assumptions that dominate and ground Western traditions are fundamental, and can be drawn in broad strokes in the following terms.

SOME CLASSICAL WESTERN ASSUMPTIONS: A "TWO-WORLD" THEORY

We can call the world view that by the time of Plato and Aristotle had come to dominate classical Greek thinking a "two-world" theory. Later, with the melding of Greek philosophy and the Judaeo-Christian tradition, this "dualistic" mode of thinking became firmly entrenched in Western civilization as its dominant underlying paradigm. In fact, this way of thinking is so second nature to us in the Judaeo-Christian tradition that we do not have to be professional philosophers to recognize ourselves reflected in its outline. A significant concern among the most influential Greek thinkers and later the Christian Church Fathers was to discover and distinguish the world of reality from the world of change, a distinction that fostered both a "two-world theory" and a dualistic way of thinking about it. These thinkers sought that permanent and unchanging first principle that had overcome initial chaos to give unity, order, and design to a changing world, and which they believed makes experience of this changing world intelligible to the human mind. They sought the "real" structure behind change—called variously Platonic Ideas, natural or Divine law, moral principle, God, and so on—which, when understood, made life predictable and secure. The centrality of "metaphysics" in classical Greek philosophy, the "science" of these first principles, reflects a presumption that there is some originative and independent source of order that, when discovered and understood, will provide coherent explanation for the human experience.

There were many diverse answers to the basic question: What is the One behind the many? What is the unity that brings everything together as a "*universe*"? What—or Who—has set the agenda that makes human life coherent, and thus meaningful? For the Jewish prophets and scribes, and later for the Christian Church Fathers, it was the existence of the one transcendent Deity who through Divine Will overcame the formless void and created the world, and in whom truth, beauty, and goodness reside. It is this One who is the permanence behind change, and who unifies our world as a single-ordered "universe." It is this One who allows for objective and universal knowledge, and guarantees the truth of our understanding. Because this One is permanent and unchanging, it is more real than the chaotic world of change and appearances that it disciplines and informs. The highest kind of knowledge, then, is the discovery and contemplation (*theoria*) of what is in itself perfect, self-evident, and infallible. It is on the basis of this fundamental and pervasive distinction between a permanently real world and a changing world of appearance, then, that our classical tradition can be said to be dominated by a "two-world theory."

Another way of thinking about this "two-world" theory that has its origins in classical Greece begins from a fundamental separation between "that which creates" and "that which is created," "that which orders" and "that which is ordered," "that which moves" and "that which is moved." There is an assumption that there exists some pre-assigned design that stands independent of the world it seeks to order. The contrast between the real One—the First Cause, the Creator, the Good—and the less-real world of change, is the source of the familiar dualistic categories that organize our experience of the world: reality/appearance, knowledge/opinion, truth/falsity, Being/Nonbeing, Creator/creature, soul/body, reason/experience, cause/effect, objective/subjective, theory/practice, agent/action, nature/culture, form/matter, universal/particular, logical/rhetorical, cognitive/affective, masculine/feminine, and so on. What is common among these binary pairs of opposites is that the world defined by the first member is thought to stand independent of, and be superior to, the second. This primary world, defined in terms of "reality," "knowledge," and "truth," is positive, necessary, and self-sufficient, while the derivative world described by the second members as "appearance," "opinion," and "falsity" is negative, contingent, and dependent for its explanation upon the first. After all, it is reality that informs and explains what only appears to be the case, and allows us to separates the true from the false, fact from fiction. On the other hand, appearances are shadows—the false, the fictive. And like shadows, at best they are incidental to what is real; at worst, not only are they of no help to us in arriving at clear knowledge, they obscure it from us. Because the secondary world is utterly dependent on the first, we can say that the primary world is necessary and essential, the "Being" behind the "beings," and the secondary world is only contingent and passing. There is a fundamental discontinuity in this world view between what is real and what is less so.

It is because the first world determines the second that the first world is generally construed as the originative source—a creative, determinative principle, easily translatable into the Judaeo-Christian Deity, that brings both natural and moral order out of chaos. Hence, our early tradition tends to be both *cosmogonic*, meaning it assumes some original act of creation and initial beginning, and *teleological*, meaning it assumes some final purpose or goal, some design to which initial creation aspires. God created the world, and human life is made meaningful by the fact that God's creation has some design and purpose. It is from this notion of determinative principle that we tend to take explanation of events in the world to be linear and causal, entailing the identification of a premise behind a conclusion, a cause behind an effect, some agency behind an activity.

Perhaps a concrete example will help bring this dominant Western world view into clearer definition. The way in which we think about the human being serves this need because in many ways humanity is a microcosm of this

48

"two-world" universe. In this tradition, we might generalize in the following terms. A particular person is a discrete individual by virtue of some inherent nature—a *psyche* or soul or mind—that guarantees a quality of reality and permanence behind the changing conditions of the body. The human being, as such, straddles the "two worlds" with the soul belonging to the higher, originative, and enduring world, and the body belonging to the realm of appearance. The soul, being the same in kind as the permanent principles that order the cosmos, has access to them through reason and revelation, and thus has a claim to knowledge. It is through the discovery of the underlying order that the universe becomes intelligible and predictable for the human being.

SOME CLASSICAL CHINESE ASSUMPTIONS: A "THIS-WORLD" VIEW

Turning to the dominant world view of classical China, we begin not from a "two-world" theory, but from the assumption that there is only the one continuous concrete world that is the source and locus of all of our experience. Order within the classical Chinese world view is "immanental"—indwelling in things themselves—like the grain in wood, like striations in stone, like the cadence of the surf, like the veins in a leaf. The classical Chinese believed that the power of creativity resides in the world itself, and that the order and regularity this world evidences is not derived from or imposed upon it by some independent, activating power, but inheres in the world. Change and continuity are equally "real."

The world, then, is the efficient cause of itself. It is resolutely dynamic, autogenerative, self-organizing, and in a real sense, alive. This one world is constituted as a sea of *ch'i*—psychophysical energy that disposes itself in various concentrations, configurations, and perturbations. The intelligible pattern that can be discerned and mapped from each different perspective within the world is *tao*—a "pathway" that can, in varying degrees, be traced out to make one's place and one's context coherent. *Tao* is, at any given time, both *what* the world is, and *how* it is. In this tradition, there is no final distinction between some independent source of order, and what it orders. There is no determinative beginning or teleological end. The world and its order at any particular time is self-causing, "so-of-itself" (*tzu-jan*). It is for this reason Confucius would say that "It is the person who extends order in the world (*tao*), not order that extends the person."[38] Truth, beauty, and goodness as standards of order are not "givens"—they are historically emergent, something done, a cultural product.

The "two-world" order of classical Greece has given our tradition a theoretical basis for *objectivity*—the possibility of standing outside and taking a wholly external view of things. Objectivity allows us to decontextualize things as "objects" in our world. By contrast, in the "this world" of classical China, instead of starting abstractly from some underlying, unifying, and originating principle, we begin from our own specific place within the world. Without objectivity, "objects" dissolve into the flux and flow, and existence becomes a continuous, uninterrupted process. Each of us is invariably experiencing the world as one perspective within the context of many. Since there is only this world, we cannot get outside of it. From the always unique place one occupies within the continuum of classical China, one interprets the order of the world around one as contrastive "thises" and "thats"—"this person" and "that person"—more or less proximate to oneself. Since each and every person or thing or event in the field of existence is perceived from some position or other, and hence is continuous with the position that entertains it, each thing is related to and a condition of every other. All human relationships are continuous from ruler and subject to friend and friend, relating everyone as an extended "family." Similarly, all "things," like all members of a family, are correlated and interdependent. Every thing is what it is at the pleasure of everything else. Whatever can be predicated of one thing or one person is a function of a network of relationships, all of which conspire to give it its role and to constitute its place and its definition. A father is "this" good father by virtue of the quality of the relationships that locate him in this role and the deference of "these" children and "that" mother, who all sustain him in it.

Because all things are unique, there is no strict notion of identity in the sense of some self-same identical characteristic that makes all members of a class or category or species the same. For example, there is no essential defining feature—no divinely endowed soul, rational capacity, or natural locus of rights—that makes all human beings equal. In the absence of such equality that would make us essentially the same, the various relationships that define one thing in relation to another tend to be hierarchical and contrastive: bigger or smaller, more noble or more base, harder or softer, stronger or weaker, more senior or more junior. Change in the quality of relationships between things always occurs on a continuum as movement between such polar oppositions. The general and most basic language for articulating such correlations among things is metaphorical: In some particular aspect at some specific point in time, one person or thing is "overshadowed" by another; that is, made *yin* to another's *yang*. Literally, *yin* means "shady" and *yang* means "sunny," defining in the most general terms those contrasting and hierarchical relationships that constitute indwelling order and regularity.

It is important to recognize the *interdependence* and correlative character of the *yin/yang* kind of polar opposites, and to distinguish this contrastive tension from the dualistic opposition implicit in the vocabulary of the classical Greek world we explored above, where one primary member of a set such as Creator stands *independent* of and is more "real" than the world He creates. The implications of this difference between dualism and polar contrast are fundamental and pervasive.

One such implication is the way in which things are categorized. In what came to be the dominant Western world view, categories were constituted analytically by an assumed formal and essential identity—all human beings who qualify for the category "human beings" are defined as having an essential *psyche* or soul. All just or pious actions share some essential element in common. The many diverse things or actions can be reduced to one essential identical feature or defining function.

In the dominant Chinese world view, "categories" (*lei*)

are constituted not by "essences," but by analogy. One thing is associated with another by virtue of the contrastive and hierarchical relations that sets it off from other things. This particular human being evokes an association with other similar creatures in contrast with other less similar things, and hence gathers around itself a collection of analogous particulars as a general category. "This" evokes "that"; one evokes many. Coherence in this world, then, is not so much analytic or formally abstract. Rather it tends to be synthetic and constitutive—the pattern of continuities that lead from one particular phenomenon to some association with others. It is a "concrete" coherence that begins from the full consequence of the particular itself, and carries on through the category that it evokes.

If we were going to compare these two senses of "categorization," instead of "hammer, chisel, screwdriver, saw" being defined as "tool" by the assumption of some identical formal and abstract function, we are more likely to have a Chinese category that includes "hammer, nail, board, pound, blister, bandage, house, whitewash"—a category of "building a house" constituted by a perceived interdependence of factors in the process of *successfully* completing a given project. Where the former sense of category, defined by abstract essences, tends to be descriptive—what something "is"—the latter Chinese "category" is usually prescriptive and normative—what something "should be" in order to be successful.

The relative absence in the Chinese tradition of Western-style teleology that assumes a given "end" has encouraged the perception among Western historians that the Chinese, with libraries of carefully recorded yet seemingly random detail, are inadequate chroniclers of their own past. There seems to be little concern to recover an intelligible pattern from what seriously threatens to remain formless and meaningless. Jorge Luis Borges captures this Western perception in his well-known citation of "a certain Chinese encyclopedia" in which the category "animals" is divided into: 1) belonging to the Emperor, 2) embalmed, 3) tame, 4) suckling pigs, 5) sirens, 6) fabulous, 7) stray dogs, 8) included in the present classification, 9) frenzied, 10) innumerable, 11) drawn with a very fine camel-hair brush, 12) et cetera, 13) having just broken the water pitcher, and 14) that from a long way off look like flies.[39] From the perspective of the more rationalistic Western world view, the penalty the Chinese must pay for the absence of that underlying metaphysical infrastructure necessary to guarantee a single-ordered universe is what we take to be intelligibility and predictability. The compensation for this absence in the Chinese world is perhaps a heightened awareness of the immediacy and wonder of change, and one's complicity in it—the motive for revering the *Book of Changes* as the ultimate defining statement of the tradition, and as an apparatus for shaping a propitious world.

For the classical Greek philosophers, knowledge entailed the discovery and "grasping" of the defining "essence" or "form" or "function" behind elusively changing appearances. Hence the language of knowing includes "concept," "conceive," "comprehend." Reality is what is permanent, and hence its natural state is inertia. The paradigm for knowledge, then, is mathematics, and more specifically, geometry. Over the door of Plato's Academy was written: "Let none who have not studied geometry enter here." Visual and spatial language tends to predominate in the philosophical vocabulary, and knowledge tends to be understood in representational terms that are isomorphic and unambiguous—a true copy impressed on one's mind of that which exists externally and objectively.

In the classical Chinese model, knowledge is conceived somewhat differently. Form is not some permanent structure to be discovered behind a changing process, but a perceived intelligibility and continuity that can be mapped within the dynamic process itself. Spatial forms—or "things"—are temporal flows. "Things" and "events" are mutually shaping and being shaped, and exist as a dynamic calculus of contrasting foci emerging in tension with each other. Changing at varying degrees of speed and intensity, the tensions constitutive of things reveal a site-specific regularity and pattern, like currents in the water, sound waves in the air, or weather systems in the sky. Etymologically, the character *ch'i*—"the stuff of existence"—is probably acoustic, making "resonance" and "tensions" a particularly appropriate way of describing the relations that obtain among things. In contrast with the more static visual language of classical Greek thought typified by geometry, classical Chinese tends to favor a dynamic aural vocabulary, where wisdom is closely linked with communication—that keenness of hearing and those powers of oral persuasion that will enable one to encourage the most productive harmony out of relevant circumstances. Much of the key philosophic vocabulary suggests etymologically that the sage orchestrates communal harmony as a virtuoso in communicative action.

"Reason" is not a human faculty independent of experience that can discover the essences of things, but the palpable determinacy that pervades both the human experience and the world experienced. Reason is coherence—the pattern of things and functions. Rational explanation does not lie in the discovery of some antecedent agency or the isolation and disclosure of relevant causes, but in mapping out the local conditions that collaborate to sponsor any particular event or phenomenon. And these same conditions, once understood, can be manipulated to anticipate the next moment.

An important factor in classical Chinese "knowing" is comprehensiveness. Without an assumed separation between the source of order in the world and the world itself, causal agency is not so immediately construed in terms of relevant cause and effect. All conditions interrelate and collaborate in greater or lesser degree to constitute a particular event as a confluence of experiences. "Knowing" is thus being able to trace out and manipulate those conditions far or near that will come to affect the shifting configuration of one's own place. There is a direct and immediate affinity between the human being and the natural world so that no firm distinction is made between natural and man-made conditions—they are all open to cultivation and manipulation. In fact, it is because of the fundamental continuity between the human pattern and the natural pattern that all of the conditions, human and otherwise, that define a situation such as battle can be brought into sharp focus. In the absence of a severe animate/inanimate dualism, the battlefield with its complex of conditions is very much alive.

The inventory of philosophical vocabulary used in

classical China to define this kind of "knowing" tends to be one of tracing out, unraveling, penetrating, and getting through. Knowing entails "undoing" something, not in an analytic sense to discover what it essentially "is," but to trace out the connections among its joints and sinews, to discern the patterns in things, and, on becoming fully aware of the changing shapes and conditions of things, to anticipate what will ensue from them. The underlying metaphor of "tracing a pattern" is implicit in the basic epistemic vocabulary of the tradition such as "to tread a pathway, a way" (*tao*), "to trace out, coherence" (*li*), "to figure, image, model" (*hsiang*), "to unravel, to undo" (*chieh*), "to penetrate" (*t'ung*), "to break through" (*ta*), "to name, to make a name, to inscribe" (*ming*), "to ritualize" (*li*), "to inscribe, markings, culture" (*wen*), and so on. In contrast with its classical Greek counterpart where "knowing" assumes a mirroring correspondence between an idea and an objective world, this Chinese "knowing" is resolutely participatory and creative—"tracing" in both the sense of etching a pattern and of following it. To know is "to realize," to "make real." The path is not a "given," but is made in the treading of it. Thus, one's own actions are always a significant factor in the shaping of one's world.

Because this emergent pattern invariably arises from within the process itself, the tension that establishes the line between one's own focus and one's field gives one a physical, psychological, social, and cosmological "skin"—a shape, a continuing, insistently particular identity. This dynamic pattern is reflexive in the sense that one's own dispositions are implicate in and affect the shaping of one's environment. One's own "shape" is constantly being reconstrued in tension with what is most immediately pressing in upon one and vice versa.

To continue the "person" example from our discussion of the classical Greek world view, generally in classical Chinese philosophy a particular person is not a discrete individual defined in terms of some inherent nature familiar in recent liberal democratic theory, but is a configuration of constitutive roles and relationships: Yang Ta-wei's father, An Lo-che's teacher, Kao Ta-jen's neighbor, a resident of Yung-ho village, and so on. These roles and relationships are dynamic, constantly being enacted, reinforced, and ideally deepened through the multiple levels of communal discourse: embodying (*t'i*), ritualizing (*li*), speaking (*yen*), playing music (*yüeh*), and so on. Each of these levels of discourse is implicit in every other, so there is a sense in which a person can be fairly described as a nexus of specific patterns of discourse. By virtue of these specific roles and relationships, a person comes to occupy a place and posture in the context of family and community. The human being is not shaped by some given design that underlies natural and moral order in the cosmos and that stands as the ultimate objective of human growth and experience. Rather, the "purpose" of the human experience, if it can be so described, is more immediate: to coordinate the various ingredients that constitute one's particular world here and now, and to negotiate the most productive harmony out of them. Simply put, it is to get the most out of what you've got here and now.

Creativity also has a different place in the classical Chinese world. Again, in gross terms, the preassigned design and ultimate purpose assumed in classical Western cosmology means that there is a large investment of creativity "up front" in the "birth" of a phenomenon—a condition reflected rather clearly in the preestablished "Ideas" of Plato, the "potentiality/actuality" distinction of Aristotle, or the Creator/creature dualism of the Judaeo-Christian tradition. For the classical Chinese world view, in the absence of an initial creative act that establishes a given design and a purpose governing change in the cosmos, the order and regularity of the world emerges from the productive juxtapositions of different things over the full compass of their existence. No two patterns are the same, and some dispositions are more fruitfully creative than others. For this reason, human knowledge is fundamentally performative—one "knows" a world not only passively in the sense of recognizing it, but also in the active shaping and "realizing" of it. It is the capacity to anticipate the patterned flow of circumstance, to encourage those dispositions most conducive to a productive harmony, and ultimately to participate in negotiating a world order that makes best advantage of its creative possibilities. Harmony is attained through the art of contextualizing.

A major theme in Confucius and in Confucianism alluded to earlier is captured in the phrase, "the exemplary person pursues harmony (ho), not sameness."[40] This Confucian conception of "harmony" is explained in the classical commentaries by appeal to the culinary arts. In the classical period, a common food staple was keng—a kind of a millet gruel in which various locally available and seasonal ingredients were brought into relationship with one another. The goal was for each ingredient—the cabbage, the squash, the bit of pork—to retain its own color, texture, and flavor, but at the same time to be enhanced by its relationship with the other ingredients. The key to this sense of harmony is that it begins from the unique conditions of a specific geographical site and the full contribution of those particular ingredients readily at hand—*this* piece of cabbage, *this* fresh young squash, *this* tender bit of pork—and relies upon artistry rather than recipe for its success. In the *Spring and Autumn Annals of Master Lü*, cooking as the art of contextualizing is described in the following terms:

> In combining your ingredients to achieve a harmony (*ho*), you have to use the sweet, sour, bitter, acrid and the salty, and you have to mix them in an appropriate sequence and proportion. Bringing the various ingredients together is an extremely subtle art in which each of them has its own expression. The variations within the cooking pot are so delicate and subtle that they cannot be captured in words or fairly conceptualized.[41]

The Confucian distinction between an inclusive harmony and an exclusive sameness has an obvious social and political application. There is a passage in the *Discourses of the States (Kuo-yü)*, a collection of historical narratives probably compiled around the fourth century B.C., which underscores the fertility of the kind of harmony that maximizes difference:

> Where harmony (*ho*) is fecund, sameness is barren. Things accommodating each other on equal

terms is called blending in harmony, and in so doing they are able to flourish and grow, and other things are drawn to them. But when same is added to same, once it is used up, there is no more. Hence, the Former Kings blended earth with metal, wood, fire, and water to make their products. They thereby harmonized the five flavors to satisfy their palate, strengthened the four limbs to protect the body, attuned the six notes to please the ear, integrated their various senses to nourish their hearts and minds, coordinated the various sectors of the body to complete their persons, established the nine main visceral meridians to situate their pure potency, instituted the ten official ranks to organize and evaluate the bureaucracy ... and harmony and pleasure prevailed to make them as one. To be like this is to attain the utmost in harmony. In all of this, the Former Kings took their consorts from other clans, required as tribute those products which distinguished each region, and selected ministers and counsellors who would express a variety of opinions on issues, and made every effort to bring things into harmony. . . . There is no music in a single note, no decoration in a single item, no relish in a single taste.[42]

A contemporary poet, Wing Tek Lum, reflects on the importation of this enduring Chinese sensibility to the new ways of immigrant life in his "Chinese Hot Pot":

My dream of America
is like *dá bìn lòuh*
with people of all persuasions and tastes
sitting down around a common pot
chopsticks and basket scoops here and there
some cooking squid and others beef
some tofu or watercress
all in one broth
like a stew that really isn't
as each one chooses what he wishes to eat
only that the pot and fire are shared
along with the good company
and the sweet soup
spooned out at the end of the meal.[43]

This "harmony" is not a given in some preassigned cosmic design, but it is the quality of the combination at any one moment created by effectively correlating and contextualizing the available ingredients, whether they be foodstuffs, farmers, or infantry. It is not a quest of discovery, grasping an unchanging reality behind the shadows of appearance, but a profoundly creative journey where the quality of the journey is itself the end. It is making the most of any situation.

In summary, at the core of the classical Chinese world view is the cultivation of harmony—a specifically "center-seeking" or "centripetal" harmony. This harmony begins from what is most concrete and immediate—that is, from the perspective of any particular human being—and draws from the outside in toward its center. Hence there is the almost pervasive emphasis on personal cultivation and refinement as the starting point for familial, social, political, and as we shall see, military order. A preoccupation in classical Chinese philosophy, then, is the cultivation of this centripetal harmony as it begins with oneself, and radiates outward. The cultivation of this radial harmony is fundamentally aesthetic. Just as Leonardo arranged those specific bits of paint to constitute the one and only Mona Lisa, so one coordinates those particular details that constitute one's own self and context, and in so doing seeks a harmony that maximizes their creative possibilities.

The Chinese world view is thus dominated by this "bottom-up" and emergent sense of order that begins from the coordination of concrete detail. It can be described as an "aestheticism," exhibiting concern for the artful way in which particular things can be correlated efficaciously to thereby constitute the ethos or character of concrete historical events and cultural achievements. Order, like a work of art, begins with always-unique details, from "this bit" and "that," and emerges out of the way in which these details are juxtaposed and harmonized. As such, the order is embedded and concrete—the coloration that differentiates the various layers of earth, the symphony of the morning garden, the striations in a wall of stone, the veins in the leaf of a plant, the wind piping through the orifices of the earth, the rituals and roles that constitute a communal grammar to give community meaning. Such an achieved harmony is always particular and specific—resistant to notions of formula and replication.

CENTRIPETAL HARMONY AND
AUTHORITY

We begin from the premise in classical Chinese culture that human beings are irreducibly communal. The human being is a center of a radial pattern of roles and relationships. The question that emerges, then, is how do these overlapping yet disparate human "centers," having defined themselves as persons, families, and communities, come to be interrelated? And how is authority among them established and continued?

The answer: Authority is constituted as other centers are drawn up into one encompassing center and suspended within it through patterns of deference. This calculus of centers through their interplay produces a balancing centripetal center that tends to distribute the forces of its field symmetrically around its own axis. Authority has several parts. It resides in a role ("father," "commander," "ruler"), in the scope and quality of the extended pattern of relationships this role entails ("family members," "soldiers," "subjects"), and in the cultural tradition as it is conveyed within these relationships. Effective application of the cultural wealth of the tradition to prevailing circumstances through one's roles and relationships inspires deference and extends one's influence.

The analog to the hierarchical complex of relationships that make up a family or community can be found and illustrated in the political world by appeal to any number of concrete historical examples. Within the subcontinent that was Warring States China, the full spectrum of peoples—some paying their allegiance to traditional hereditary houses, some ruled by locally powerful warlords, others organized around religious doctrines, yet others governed by clan or tribal regulation—was suspended in the Han harmony, with each of them contributing in greater or lesser degree to the definition of Han culture. This political order was one in which all of the diversity and difference characteristic of the multiple, competing centers of the Warring States period was drawn up and suspended in the harmony of the Han dynasty. Moving from the radial extremes toward the center, the very disparate "zones" contributed to the imperial order in increasing degree to influence the authority at the center, shaping and bringing into focus the character of the social and political entity—its standards and values. Whatever constitutes the authority at the center is holographic. In this political example, the ruler derives his authority from having his field of influence implicate within him. He is the empire. The attraction of the center is such that, with varying degrees of success, it draws into its field and suspends within its web the disparate and diverse centers that constitute its world. It is the quality of these suspended centers in relationship to one another that defines the harmony of the field.

This same dynamic that defines Han culture politically can be discerned in its intellectual character. During the Warring States period, philosophical diversity flourished and schools of thought proliferated to become what the *Chuang-tzu* describes as "the doctrines of the Hundred Schools."[44] As the Han dynasty became established, the intellectual contest of the Hundred Schools gave way to a syncretic Confucianism-centered doctrine. This state ideology absorbed into itself (and in important degree concealed) the richness of what were competing elements, and out of this diversity articulated the philosophical and religious character of the period. The syncretism of Han dynasty Confucianism is harmony teased out of difference. This transition from diversity in the late Chou to coherent order in the Han is better expressed in the language of incorporation and accommodation than of suppression.

As the centripetal center of the Han court weakened in the second century A.D., and as the political order gradually dissolved into a period of disunity, disparate foci reasserted themselves, and what had been their contribution to a harmonious diversity became the energy of contest among them. What was a tightening centripetal spire in the early Han dynasty became a centrifugal gyre, disgorging itself of its now disassociated contents. It is not surprising that during this same period, there was a resurgence and interplay of competing philosophical schools and religious movements that reflected a contemporaneous disintegration of the centrally driven intellectual order. This is the familiar pattern of dynasty and interregnum repeated throughout the career of imperial China.[45]

Given the commitment to a centripetal sense of order pervasive at every level in the classical Confucian world view, a father or a magistrate or a commander or a ruler would derive his authority from being at the center, and having implicate within him the order of the whole. It is for this reason that "the exemplary person's errors are like an eclipse: When he errs, everyone sees him; when he rights himself, everyone looks up to him."[46]

John Fairbank's essay, "The Grip of History on China's Leadership," makes a convincing argument that the social and political order of China under Mao Tse-tung was fully consistent with the tradition, from "the Chinese readiness to accept a supreme personality" to the phenomenon of a population continuing to struggle for proximity to the center.[47] It is by virtue of the supreme personality's embodiment of his world, as in the case of Mao Tse-tung, that he is able to lay claim to impartiality—his actions are not self-interested (*li*) but always appropriate (*yi*), accommodating the interests of all. Just as the traditional conception of Heaven (*t'ien*), encompassing within itself the world order, is credited with total impartiality, so the "Son of Heaven" (*t'ien-tzu*) with similar compass is devoid of a divisive egoism. As long as the center is strong enough to draw the deference and tribute of its surrounding spheres of influence, it retains its authoritativeness—that is, not only do these spheres willingly acknowledge this order, but actively participate in reinforcing it. Standing at the center, the ruler acts imperceptibly, a pole star that serves as a bearing for the ongoing negotiation of the human order while appearing to be unmoved and unmoving himself.[48]

WARFARE AS THE ART OF CONTEXTUALIZING

To return to the central contention, then, I want to suggest that the achieved harmony that we have identified as the goal of personal, social, and political cultivation in classical Confucianism is not limited to this school of thought or historical period, but is a signatory feature of the Chinese tradition more broadly construed. Centripetal harmony as the model of order operating in the classical Chinese world view is pervasive. To illustrate this, I want to juxtapose what for us might seem to be only marginally related concerns of personal cultivation and of effectiveness in battle in order to attempt to understand why concepts central to philosophy and to military affairs cannot be separated and, in fact, can only be fully explicated by appeal to one another. How then does this conception of achieved centripetal harmony figure into the military experience?

Beginning from the most general attitudes toward warfare in early China, John Fairbank makes the following observation:

> Since the ideal of proper conduct was built into the Chinese concept of the cosmos, a rupture of this ideal threatened to break down the whole cosmic system. Consequently, the Chinese "right of rebellion" could not be asserted simply in the name of individual or corporate freedom against ruling class tyranny. It had to be asserted in the name of the system, alleging that the ruler had forfeited Heaven's mandate by not maintaining the social order adequately and correctly. . . . Rebels usually rose in the name of the social order, which was the great legitimizing myth of the state and the underlying moral sanction for all resort to warfare.[49]

Stated in another way, what makes any military action "appropriate" and "proper" (yi) as opposed to "self-seeking" (li) is the claim that it serves the quality of the sociopolitical order as a whole rather than any particular interest group within it. Those persons promoting military engagement must make their argument on the necessity of such action to revive and reshape the shared world order.

A note of explanation is needed to avoid a possible equivocation. The notion of sociopolitical order here is not justified as service to some universally applicable standard *independent* of oneself that sanctions conduct within its jurisdiction, as is the case where such service is devotion to the One True God, commitment to some doctrine of natural law, or respect for a universal Bill of Rights. Rather, it is a notion of sociopolitical order in which all orders are *interdependent* and mutually entailing, so that realization for oneself, one's family, one's community, and for one's state are codetermining and coextensive. The "legitimizing myth" is symbiosis, where service to oneself and to one's community is the same. There is no "means/end" distinction that subordinates one's personal achievement to the social or political end, or vice versa. Hence, any assertion on behalf of any part is always an assertion on behalf of the whole. And by the same token, any protest is ultimately self-referential—a criticism of an order in which one's self is a constitutive factor.

Perhaps an analogy that might be illustrative here is the relationship that exists between any particular note in a symphonic performance and the symphony as a whole. There is a sense in which the value and meaning of each note can only be understood within the context of the entire symphony. In these terms, then, each note has the entire symphony implicate within it. At the same time, the symphony is only available through one note at a time as particular perspectives on the symphony, and the only sense of "objective" vantage point from which the entire symphony can be entertained lies in the presumption that each note appropriately executed serves the interests of the symphony as a whole.

The qualification on "order" that needs to be introduced here, then, is that even righteous war in service to the social order as a whole is invariably pursued from some particular perspective within the whole—some claim to authority that occupies or seeks to occupy the center. At the same time, it is impartial and "objective" in that it claims as one perspective to represent all interests. Military action, then, is generally seen as an attunement on the existing order from within—ideally it is always responsive, always punitive, always pro-social.

There is a deep and abiding association in the Chinese world between the execution of punishments and of warfare. In both instances, the central authority is acting in the interests of the whole to define the sociopolitical order at its boundaries. The character used for "punishment" (*hsing*) is homophonous and often used interchangeably with the character meaning "to shape," and carries with it a strong sense of drawing a line and configuring a defined order by excluding those who are antisocial, usually by amputating something or disfiguring them, and thus, quite literally, reshaping them. Similarly, warfare frequently occurs on the borders as a final effort to define what belongs within one's circle and what lies beyond it. There is an obvious cognate relationship between the characters "to order" (*cheng*), "to govern" (*cheng*), and "to dispatch a punitive expedition" (*cheng*). Warfare is an attempt to redefine sociopolitical order.

STRATEGIC ADVANTAGE (*SHIH*)

The key and defining idea in the *Sun-tzu: The Art of Warfare* is *shih* (pronounced like the affirmative, "sure").[50] Although I have translated *shih* consistently as "strategic advantage," it is a complex idea peculiar to the Chinese tradition, and resists easy formulaic translation.[51] In fact, an understanding of *shih* entails not only the collation of an inventory of seemingly alternative meanings, but also a familiarity with those presuppositions outlined above that make the classical Chinese world view so very different from our own. *Shih*, like ritual practices and role playing (*li*), speaking (*yen*), playing music (*yüeh*), and embodying (*t'i*), is a level of discourse through which one actively determines and cultivates the leverage and influence of one's particular place.

In studying the Chinese corpus, one consults dictionaries that encourage us to believe that many if not most of the characters such as *shih* have "multiple" alternative meanings from which the translator, informed by the context, is required to select the most appropriate one. This approach to the language, so familiar to the translator, signals precisely the problem that I have worried over in the introductory comments about alternative world views. The irony is that we serve clarity in highlighting what makes sense in our own conceptual vocabulary only to bury the unfamiliar implications that, in themselves, are the most important justification for the translation.

I would suggest that with the appearance of any given character in the text, with varying degree of emphasis, the full seamless range of its meaning is introduced. And our project as interpreters and translators is to negotiate an understanding and rendering that is sensitive to this full undifferentiated range of meaning. In fact, it is this effort to reconstitute the several meanings as an integrated whole and to fathom how the character in question can carry what for us might well be a curious, often unexpected, and sometimes even incongruous combination of meanings that leads us most directly to a recognition of difference.

For example, the character *shen* does not *sometimes* mean "human spirituality" and *sometimes* "divinity." It always means both and, moreover, it is our business to try and understand philosophically how it *can* mean both. Given the prominence of transcendent Deity in our tradition, human beings do not generally get to be gods. Reflection on the range of meaning represented by *shen* reveals that gods in the Chinese world are by and large dead people—they are ancestors who have embodied, enriched, and transmitted the cultural tradition. They are cultural heroes, as in the case of Confucius, who do the work of our transcendent Deity by establishing the enduring standards of truth, beauty, and goodness. Culturally productive ancestors such as Confucius are not *like* gods—they are precisely what the word "gods" conveys in this alternative tradition. Gods are historical, geographical, and cultural. They grow out of the ground, and when neglected, fade and die. Such gods have little to do with the notion of a transcendent Creator Deity that has dominated the Western religious experience, and unless we are sensitive to the "this-world" presuppositions that ground the classical Chinese world view, we stand the risk of willy-nilly translating Chinese religiousness into our own.

The key militarist idea, *shih*, is as complex as *shen*, "spirituality/divinity," and, fortunately for our grasp of the tradition, as revealing of the underlying sense of order. We must struggle to understand how *shih* can combine in one idea the following cluster of meanings:

1. "aspect," "situation," "circumstances," "conditions"
2. "disposition," "configuration," "outward shape"
3. "force," "influence," "momentum," "authority"
4. "strategic advantage," "purchase"

In defining *shih* or any of the other key ideas, the military texts such as the *Sun-tzu* and *Sun Pin* do not rely solely or even primarily upon the currency of abstract concepts and theoretical programs. Rather, these texts, emerging as they do out of concrete historical experience, tend to communicate through the mediums of image, historical allusion, and analogy. What constitutes evidence and makes things clear in the text is often an effectively focused image, not a theory; an inexpressible and inimitable experience, not an argument; an evocative metaphor, not a logically demonstrated truth. The style, then, respects the priority of the unique particular—a defining characteristic of emergent harmony. It resists the abstractness of universalizing principles in favor of the concrete image. The aphoristic statements seek, with the assistance of a sympathetic reading, to make points rather than lay down categorical imperatives. The readers, on their part, are required to generate a specific set of circumstances that make the assertions meaningful and important.

This claim that image has an important role is illustrated in the putative origins of the term *shih* itself. The *Sun Pin* states:

> Thus, animals not equipped with natural "weapons" have to fashion them for themselves. Such were the contributions of the sages. . . . Yi created the bow and crossbow and derived the notion of strategic advantage (*shih*) from them. . . . How do we know that the notion of strategic advantage is derived from the bow and crossbow? An archer shoots from between shoulder and chest and kills a soldier over a hundred paces away who does not even know where the bolt came from. Hence it can be said: the bow and crossbow exemplify strategic advantage (*shih*).[52]

The images used to express *shih* in these texts are many, each of them focused in such a way as to suggest some specific area in its range of meaning. Round boulders and logs avalanching down a precipitous ravine and cascading water sending boulders bobbing about underscore the sense of fluidity and momentum.[53] The taut trigger on the drawn crossbow emphasizes timing and precision.[54] The bird of prey swooping down to knock its victim out of the air stresses the agility that gives one full control over one's own movement, the coordination of this movement and that of one's target, and the resolutely aggressive posture one assumes throughout. The drawn crossbow locates one well beyond the range of the enemy. The scales tilting in one's favor highlights the logistical advantage of one's po-

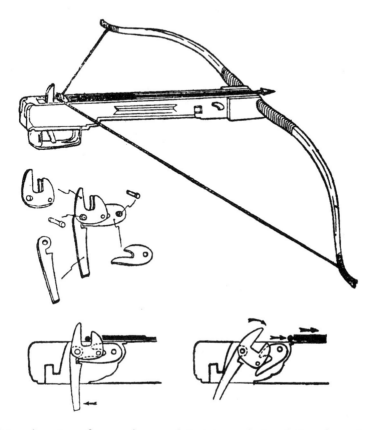

Line drawing of a crossbow and its trigger device dating from the Warring States period (403–221 B.C.) unearthed in a 1952 excavation at Ch'ang-hsia Tomb #138

sition relative to one's enemy.[55] The "sudden striker" snake suggests the flexibility and the total preparedness that turns defense into offense.[56]

Lifting the discussion from the metaphorical to a more theoretical level, the first point that can be made is *shih* (like immanental order generally) begins from the concrete detail. It begins from a recognition that the business of war does not occur as some independent and isolated event, but unfolds within a broad field of unique natural, social, and political conditions. These conditions and the relations that exist among them are ever changing. Further, although the changes that occur within any local field of conditions are always unique to it, they proceed according to a general pattern that can not only be anticipated, but can be manipulated to one's advantage. It is the changing configuration of these specific conditions that determines one's place at any point in time, and gives one a defining disposition and "shape."

The constantly shifting "disposition" of any thing or event is constituted in tension with environing others, where their dispositions condition one's own. The enemy is always implicated in one's own shifting position. The "skin" that defines one's "inner/outer" circle and separates one from the enemy also conjoins one to him, making any change mutual and pervasive. If he moves, one is thereby moved. And more importantly, if one moves, he is moved. This presumption of continuity between self and other means that each focus is holographic in the sense that the entire field is implicate in every one. Each position brings the whole into focus from its own unique perspective.

One of the "supplemental chapters" to the *Sun Pin: The Art of Warfare* provides us with a cosmological explanation for how *shih* functions. This treatise on the complementarity of "straightforward and surprise operations" begins from a description of how, in an immanental cosmos, change is always movement between polar opposites on a continuum. This explanation of change is fundamental to the classical Chinese world view, and although probably most familiar to us from the Taoist sources, is pervasive in the culture.[57]

> In the pattern of the heavens and the earth: when something has reached its extreme, it then returns; when something has waxed full, it then wanes. This is exemplified by [*the sun and the moon*]. Flourishing and fading succeed each other. This is exemplified in the succession of the four seasons. Something prevails only to then be prevailed over. This is exemplified in the succession of the five phases (*wu hsing*). Life and death succeed one another. This is exemplified in the life cycle of the myriad things. Capacity and incapacity succeed each other. This is exemplified in the maturation process of the myriad life-forms. And that while some things are had in surplus, there is a deficiency in others—this is exemplified in the dynamics of shapes or dispositions (*hsing*), and strategic advantages (*shih*).[58]

It is because change is always movement between polar opposites that the fluid dispositions that obtain among phenomena can be described in the language of *yin-yang* "sunny/shady" contrasts. Since these contrasts can only be explained by reference to each other, they are correlative (as opposed to dualistic) opposites. The vocabulary used to express military insights in these treatises depends heavily upon a cluster of just such correlations: us/enemy (*wo/ti*); aggressor/defender (*chu/k'o*); attack/defend (*kung/shou*); many/few (*chung/kua*); strong/weak (*ch'iang/jo*); courage/timidity (*yung/ch'ieh*), intimate/distant (*chi/shu*); full/empty (*ying/hsü*); slow/fast (*hsü/chi*); movement/stillness (*tung/ching*); rested/exhausted (*yi/lao*); order/disorder (*chih/luan*); viable/fatal (*sheng/ssu*); victory/defeat (*sheng/pai*); surprise/straight-forward (*ch'i/cheng*); advance/retreat (*chin/t'ui*); and so on. This correlative vocabulary reflects the assumption that any situation definable on a continuum can be manipulated into its polar opposite: Order can be teased out of disorder, courage can be stoked out of timidity, largeness can be conjured out of smallness, victory can be lifted out of defeat. As the *Sun-tzu* observes:

> Disorder is born from order; cowardice from courage; weakness from strength. The line between disorder and order lies in logistics (*shu*); between cowardice and courage, in strategic advantage (*shih*); and between weakness and strength, in strategic positioning (*hsing*).[59]

All determinate situations can be turned to advantage. The able commander is able to create differentials and thus opportunities by manipulating his position and the position of the enemy. By developing a full understanding of those factors that define one's relationship with the enemy, and by actively controlling and shaping the situation so that the weaknesses of the enemy are exposed to one's acquired strength, one is able to ride the force of circumstances to victory.

All things and events that have a distinguishing shape or disposition can be named, and all things that can be named can be prevailed over. Thus, because the sages would use that characteristic in which any one thing excels to prevail over all other things, they were always successful in whatever they did.[60]

This general observation, of course, has an immediate military application:

Battle then is simply one disposition trying to prevail over another. All distinguishable dispositions can be prevailed over. The problem lies in knowing which disposition will enable one to prevail. The changing calculus of dispositions that can lead one thing to prevail over another is as inexhaustible as all that happens between the heavens and earth. These dispositions that can lead one thing to prevail over another could not be fully described if you were to write on all of the bamboo that could be cut from the states of Ch'u and Yüeh. Such dispositions are, in all cases, using that characteristic in which a particular thing excels to prevail over other things.[61]

While the military strategist can articulate general principles concerning the nature of change and how to manipulate it to one's own advantage, a real limitation on what can be said arises from the fact that each situation is site-specific; it is local and unique, and must be dealt with on its own terms.

> But you will never find a winning characteristic of one particular disposition that will enable you to prevail in all situations. The need to figure out a disposition is in principle the same, but what disposition will actually prevail is always different.[62]

A central theme of both the *Sun-tzu* and the *Sun Pin* is the need for flexibility and negotiation in dealing with the specific conditions that make each situation particular.

> In the business of war, there is no invariable strategic advantage (*shih*) which can be relied upon at all times.[63]

In fact, a fundamental insight into nature that one must accord with in prosecuting military affairs is the irrepressibility of change itself. One must find security by revising and redefining one's own strength by immediate yet unannounced responsiveness to the enemy's shifting position.

> Thus an army does not have fixed strategic advantages (*shih*) or an invariable position (*hsing*). To be able to take the victory by varying one's position according to the enemy's is called being inscrutable (*shen*). Thus of the five phases (*wu hsing*), none is the constant victor; of the four sea-

sons, none occupies a constant position; the days are both short and long; the moon waxes and wanes.[64]

The able commander does not resist the rhythm of change, but, finding its pulse, translates defining conditions into correlative terms as a means of controlling the situation, anticipating the enemy's movements, and making his victory inevitable.

> Thus, the expert at warfare can infer the enemy's weaknesses from observing his strengths, and can infer his surpluses from observing his deficiencies. He can see the victory as clearly as the sun or moon, and can grasp it as certainly as water douses fire.[65]

If we allow that there are several different ways in which we can look at *shih*, it enables us to bring its cluster of meanings together. When looked at spatially from outside of one's own "skin," *shih* is that set of conditions that is defining of one's situation. It is one's context in relationship to oneself. When looked at from an internal perspective, *shih* is one's own place and posture relative to one's context. When looked at temporally, taking into account the full calculus of dispositions, *shih* is the tension of forces and the momentum that brings one position in immediate contact with another. And, of course, what brings these various dimensions of meaning together is the acknowledgment that, in this classical Chinese world view, the spatial (*yü*) and the temporal (*chou*) are themselves correlatives that require reference to each other for explanation. In fact, the combination of these two terms as "space-time" means "cosmos" (*yü-chou*) in the classical language.

STRATEGIC ADVANTAGE (*SHIH*) AND STRATEGIC POSITIONING (*HSING*)

What is the difference, then, between strategic advantage (*shih*) and strategic positioning (*hsing*)? As D. C. Lau has indicated, in the *Sun-tzu* there are passages in which these two terms are used as near-synonyms.[66] This is because *shih* overlaps with *hsing* in having the connotation of physical position—not position as specific location, but rather as a fluid disposition ever responsive to context. Where *hsing* is limited to the tangible and determinate shape of physical strength, *shih* includes intangibles such as morale, opportunity, timing, psychology, and logistics. Effective strategic positioning (*hsing*) creates a situation where we can use "the undivided whole to attack his one,"[67] "weigh in a full hundredweight against a few ounces,"[68] and "use many to strike a few"[69]—that is, to win the war before joining battle.[70] Strategic advantage (*shih*), by contrast, is the full concentrated release of that latent energy inherent in one's position, physical and otherwise.

The military treatise in the Han dynasty work, the *Master of Huai Nan*, describes in some detail those several factors implied by *shih* that go beyond one's physical position:

82

When the commander is full of courage and regards the enemy with contempt, when his troops are steeled in their resolve and delight in the prospect of battle, when the determination of his troops, countless in number, outstrips the skies, when their fury is like a tempest and their battle cries ring out like thunder, when utterly committed they thoroughly intimidate the enemy—this is called a morale advantage (*ch'i shih*).

A narrow crossing in the mountain gorges, a well-known obstruction in high and mountainous terrain, a snaking and coiling pathway, the summit of a rise, a road that spirals like a ram's horn, a bottleneck through which there is entry but no retreat, a point at which one man holds a thousand enemy at bay—this is called a terrain advantage (*ti shih*).

Capitalizing fully on the enemy's fatigue, his ill-preparedness and disorder, his hunger and thirst, and his exposure to the elements, to press in upon him where he has lost his footing, and to give him no quarter where he is most vulnerable—this is called an opportunity advantage (*yin shih*).[71]

ACCORDING WITH THE ENEMY (*YIN*)

Another elusive notion essential to an understanding of classical Chinese philosophy in general, and militarist thought specifically, is *yin*, conventionally translated "to avail oneself of," "to make the best of," "to rely upon." Every situation has its "give and take," and, as such, can be parlayed into an opportunity. The basic meaning of *yin* is responsiveness to one's context: to adapt oneself to a situation in such a manner as to take full advantage of the defining circumstances, and to avail oneself of the possibilities of the situation in achieving one's own purposes.

Yin requires sensitivity and adaptability. Sensitivity is necessary to register the full range of forces that define one's situation, and, on the basis of this awareness, to anticipate the various possibilities that can ensue. Adaptability refers to the conscious fluidity of one's own disposition. One can only turn prevailing circumstances to account if one maintains an attitude of readiness and flexibility. One must adapt oneself to the enemy's changing posture as naturally and as effortlessly as flowing water winding down a hillside:

> As water varies its flow according to (*yin*) the fall
> of the land, so an army varies its method of gain-
> ing victory according to (*yin*) the enemy.[72]

Yin means feeding your army from the enemy's fields;[73] *yin* means taking advantage of inflammable materials in the vicinity of the enemy's camp;[74] *yin* means shifting your posture so adroitly and imperceptibly that, from the enemy's perspective, you are inscrutable.[75]

When this notion of *yin* is applied to espionage, it designates a "local" spy—the enemy's own countrymen in our employ. It means using the enemy against himself.

84

Both the *Sun-tzu* and its literary descendant, the *Sun Pin*,
are military treatises that share a fundamental distaste for
warfare. Warfare always constitutes a loss. As the *Sun-tzu*
observes, "If one is not fully cognizant of the evils of waging war, he cannot be fully cognizant either of how to turn
it to best account."[76] It is on this principle that the *Sun Pin*
claims that "a distaste for war is the most basic principle
of the True King."[77] This being the case, "you must go to
war only when there is no alternative."[78] At times, however, virtuous government is not enough to maintain social
and political order, and it can become necessary to resort
to arms.[79] This unfortunate reality is tempered by the assertion that even military victory is "defeat" in the sense
that it requires an expenditure of a state's manpower and
resources. As the *Sun-tzu* states, "To win a hundred victories in a hundred battles is not the highest excellence; the
highest excellence is to subdue the enemy's army without
fighting at all."[80] Similarly, the *Sun Pin* insists that "even
ten victories out of ten, while evidencing an able commander, is still a source of national misfortune."[81] For this
reason, war is justifiable only when all possible alternatives
have been exhausted, and must be entertained with the utmost seriousness. The first line of the *Sun-tzu* declares:
"War is a vital matter of state."[82] The first priority is the
avoidance of warfare if at all possible. Once, however, a
commitment has been made to a military course of action,
the project becomes to achieve victory at the minimum
cost. The able commander's first concern is to guarantee the integrity of his own forces: "He must use the

principle of keeping himself intact to compete in the world."[83] After all, "invincibility depends on oneself."[84] The ruler commissions the able commander as a means of achieving victory with minimum loss. From the perspective of his cultivated humanity, he, like his ruler, regards warfare as a losing proposition that must be approached with the utmost caution and gravity, and with absolute control.

A second characteristic of the able commander is that he is active rather than reactive—he takes the offense and controls the situation: The expert in battle moves the enemy, and is not moved by him.[85] Such control is evident where defense itself is always offense:

> Do not depend on the enemy not coming; depend rather on being ready for him. Do not depend on the enemy not attacking; depend rather on having a position that cannot be attacked.[86]

Always maintaining the offense requires precision: "War is such that the supreme consideration is speed."[87] Speed is certainly defined in terms of timing:

> In advancing he cannot be resisted because he bursts through the enemy's weak points; in withdrawing he cannot be pursued because, being so quick, he cannot be caught.[88]

Moreover, speed in the sense of a short duration of battle is also desirable:

In joining battle, seek the quick victory. . . . I have
heard tell of a foolish haste, but I have yet to see
a case of cleverly dragging on the hostilities.
There never has been a state that has benefited
from an extended war.[89]

Any deviation from this attitude represents military adven-
turism, and is outrightly condemned: ". . . one who takes
pleasure in military affairs shall ultimately perish, while one
who seeks to profit from victory shall incur disgrace."[90]

The fundamental question the *Sun-tzu* seeks to respond to is how does the enlightened ruler achieve victory
at the minimum cost? The answer, then, is the ruler must
give free rein to the consummate military commander.

THE EXEMPLARY COMMANDER

The emphasis in the *Sun-tzu* placed on the effective selection of military personnel reflects a fundamental assumption in the tradition. The first and foremost defining feature
of the consummate military commander is that he must be
an exemplary person (*chün tzu*), and must ply his military
skills from a foundation of superior character. In this respect,
the military commander is like any other officer in the service
of the state. His ability to achieve great things within the
parameters of his office—his efficacy—is a function of his cultivated humanity rather than any specific set of skills:

A commander who advances without any thought
of winning personal fame and withdraws in spite

87

of certain punishment, whose only concern is to protect his people and promote the interests of his ruler, is the nation's treasure.[91]

What it means to be a person of exemplary character is defined in the text in the standard Confucian "virtue" vocabulary of "wisdom, integrity, humanity, courage, and discipline."[92] A commander defined in such holistic terms "is the side-guard on the carriage of state. Where this guard is in place, the state will certainly be strong. . . ."[93] It is by virtue of his status as an exemplary person, and the consonance this gives him with the tradition as embodied in his ruler, that the commander has sufficient authority on the battlefield to place him at the center of the centripetal field. It is from this particular perspective in the hierarchy, then, that he sets about the configuring of an optimal harmony.

The exemplary commander in the context of warfare stands as the self-organizing center, where the chaos of battle, far from interfering with order, feeds into and stimulates it. For the *Sun-tzu*, "the commander who understands war is the final arbiter of people's lives, and lord over the security of the state."[94] The first condition of effective command is that this commander must have complete control of the campaign, unchallenged even by the authority of the ruler at home: "The side on which the commander is able and the ruler does not interfere will take the victory."[95] The *Sun-tzu* is both explicit and emphatic on this point: "There are . . . commands from the ruler not to be obeyed."[96]

The reason why, in this model, the commander must have sole control over his localized area is because an effective harmony must be pursued through the coordination of the immediate constituent elements, unmediated by some distant and undoubtedly less informed perspective:

> Thus, if the way (tao) of battle guarantees you victory, it is right for you to insist on fighting even if the ruler has said not to; where the way (tao) of battle does not allow victory, it is right for you to refuse to fight even if the ruler has said you must.[97]

If the military command has to take its orders from a source that cannot possibly be apprised of the full circumstances, the situation is tantamount to making decisions without a comprehensive understanding of the battlefield.

FOREKNOWLEDGE (CHIH)

The nature and effectiveness of the commander's "wisdom" requires comment. The commander must understand that any set of circumstances is the consequence of a dynamic process of organically related, mutually determining conditions. All of the characteristics of the able military commander follow from this insight into the interdependent nature of circumstances. He is aware that conditions constituting a situation are correlative and interdependent, and that what affects any one situation in this process to some greater or lesser degree has an effect on the whole field of conditions.

The complex of forces that define a battle situation are

organically related, and hence, in spite of analogies that might be made with other seemingly similar engagements, each event must be respected for its particularity. Familiar patterns can be unpredictable because slight variations, when magnified through this organic relationship, can have massive consequences; minute fluctuations can amplify into dramatic changes. The uniqueness of each and any situation makes globalization precarious, and forces the commander to take each engagement on its own terms.

Complex systems such as battle conditions are rich in information—information that must be acquired immediately. The commander's wisdom must be funded by direct access to persons who serve him as eyes on the site-specific conditions, and who enable him to anticipate the outcome. To be reliable, information must be firsthand. The commander in defining the configuration of his forces treats his spatial form as a temporal flow. There is thus an important relationship between intelligence and timing. Once the specific time has past, information loses its strategic function and importance, and at best retains only historical value.

The effective gathering and dissemination of information can constitute an additional, albeit intangible, battle line:

Intelligence is of the essence in warfare—it is what the armies depend upon in their every move.[98]

Ideally, effective intelligence provides clear discernment of the enemy's situation and a full concealment of one's own:

If we can make the enemy show his position (*hsing*) while concealing ours from him, we will be at full force where he is divided.[99]

Such intelligence is by its immediacy distinguished from other apparent sources of information, such as the application of historical precedents, or revelatory knowledge gained from divination practices:

Thus the reason the farsighted ruler and his superior commander conquer the enemy at every move, and achieve successes far beyond the reach of the common crowd, is foreknowledge. Such foreknowledge cannot be had from ghosts and spirits, educed by comparison with past events, or verified by astrological calculations. It must come from people—people who know the enemy's situation.[100]

Even though *Sun-tzu* advocates seeking victory from strategic advantage rather than from one's men, he also makes it clear that it is only by selecting the right person that one is able to exploit the strategic advantage.[101] The commander must spare no cost in finding the right person and in acquiring reliable intelligence:

If, begrudging the outlay of ranks, emoluments, and a hundred pieces of gold, a commander does not know the enemy's situation, his is the height of inhumanity. Such a person is no man's commander, no ruler's counsellor, and no master of victory.[102]

Front-line reconnaissance must be fortified by covert operations. Of particular importance is the selection of operatives and saboteurs for espionage.

> Thus only those farsighted rulers and their superior commanders who can get the most intelligent people as their spies are destined to accomplish great things.[103]

It is because the commander's wisdom is resolutely performative that it is foreknowledge—it creates the victory. This wisdom entails a cognitive understanding of those circumstances that bear on the local situation, an awareness of possible futures, the deliberate selection of one of these futures, and the capacity to manipulate the prevailing circumstances and to dispose of them in such a way as to realize the desired future. The emphasis here is on the commander's access to intelligence acquired directly from the specific situation, and his capacity to thus control events.

Given that warfare is always defeat, the commander in pursuing the best possible outcome seeks to disarm the enemy without ever joining him on the battlefield:

> . . . the expert in using the military subdues the enemy's forces without going to battle, takes the enemy's walled cities without launching an attack, and crushes the enemy's state without a protracted war.[104]

The *Sun-tzu* defines military wisdom in terms of sober and methodical deliberation and planning. Where at all possible, the commander attempts to defeat the enemy with this careful planning rather than military might:

> . . . the best military policy is to attack strategies; the next to attack alliances; the next to attack soldiers; and the worst to assault walled cities.[105]

In any case, the commander never enters a battle where there is any question of defeat. Victory must be a predetermined certainty:

> . . . the victorious army only enters battle after having first won the victory, while the defeated army only seeks victory after having first entered the fray.[106]

As a consequence, the able commander is not the one who is celebrated for daring and courage, for his victory requires neither:

> He whom the ancients called an expert in battle gained victory where victory was easily gained. Thus the battle of the expert is never an exceptional victory, nor does it win him reputation for wisdom or credit for courage. His victories in battle are unerring. Unerring means that he acts where victory is certain, and conquers an enemy that has already lost.[107]

The foreknowledge required to be in complete control of events is gained by acquiring complete information, by anticipating the ensuing situations, and by going over and scoring the battle strategy in a formal exercise:

> It is by scoring many points that one wins the war beforehand in the temple rehearsal of the battle. . . .[108]

This is a somewhat obscure passage, which seems to describe "mock battles" acted out in advance. But it likely refers to the practice of assessing relative battlefield strengths by identifying a set of relevant categories, and then using counting rods or some similar device to indicate an advantage on one side or the other, enabling one to thus predict the outcome.[109]

Since all *yin*-like correlations can only be fully fathomed by reference to *yang*, understanding the local situation completely entails understanding both sides of all correlative pairs:

> . . . the deliberations of the wise commander are sure to assess jointly both advantages and disadvantages. In taking full account of what is advantageous, he can fulfill his responsibilities; in taking full account of what is disadvantageous, his difficulties become resolvable.[110]

It is as important to keep information from the enemy as it is to acquire information about him. In the absence of information, the enemy has only unconcentrated force that is dissipated across the lines of attack:

94

If our army is united as one and the enemy's is fragmented, in using the undivided whole to attack his one, we are many to his few.[111]

The integrity of one's position conceals the details of his battle configuration from the enemy's view, and makes one impenetrable:

The ultimate skill in taking up a strategic position (*hsing*) is to have no form (*hsing*). If your position is formless (*hsing*), the most carefully concealed spies will not be able to get a look at it, and the wisest counsellors will not be able to lay plans against it.[112]

Another way to achieve this desired "formlessness" is through deceit. Deceit is used to become "one" by reconciling correlations. If one is close but seems far to the enemy, his distance is indeterminate. If one is slow but seems fast to the enemy, his speed is indeterminate.

Warfare is the art (*tao*) of deceit. Therefore, when able, seem to be unable; when ready, seem unready; when nearby, seem far away; and when far away, seem near. If the enemy seeks some advantage, entice him with it. If he is in disorder, attack him and take him. If he is formidable, prepare against him. If he is strong, evade him. If he is incensed, provoke him. If he is humble, encourage his arrogance. If he is rested, wear him down. If he is internally harmonious, sow divisiveness in his ranks. Attack where he is not prepared; go by way of places where it would never occur to him you would go.[113]

The consummate commander is able to achieve and retain control of a military situation in a way analogous to an able ruler's control of the civil situation and a farmer's control over his crops: by a thorough understanding of the conditions determining the situation and the manipulation of these circumstances to his chosen end:

He who knows the enemy and himself
Will never in a hundred battles be at risk.[114]

INTRODUCTION TO THE
TRANSLATIONS

In translating the core thirteen chapters of the *Sun-tzu: The Art of Warfare* that comprise Part I of this volume, I have relied upon the *Sun-tzu chiao-shih* edited by Wu Chiu-lung et al. and published in 1990. It reflects the judgment of a group of China's most prominent scholars presently working on the reconstruction of the military texts and is informed by a detailed knowledge of the recent archaeological finds. I have followed this work for the Chinese text with a few typographical corrections.

In translasting the five additional chapters recovered in the Yin-ch'üeh-shan dig that comprise Part II, I have followed the authoritative *Yin-ch'üeh-shan Han-mu chu-chien* (Bamboo strips recovered from the Han tombs at Silver Sparrow mountain) Collection, Vol. I prepared by the Yin-ch'üeh-shan Han-mu chu-chien cheng-li hsiao-tsu (Committee for the Reconstruction of the Yin-ch'üeh-shan Han strips) and published by Wen-wu Publishing House in 1985.

For the encyclopedic materials I have translated in Part III, I worked from the appendixes of Yang Ping-an's *Sun-*

tzu hui-chien (1986) and Huang K'uei's *Sun-tzu tao-tu* (1989) which are based on the Ch'ing dynasty collections of Pi I-hsün, *Sun-tzu hsü-lu (Citations from Sun-tzu)*, and Wang Jen-chün, *Sun-tzu i-wen* (unpublished text preserved in the archives of the Shanghai Library). I have then checked these citations against authoritative editions of the encyclopedias and corrected them accordingly (see Bibliography). These Ch'ing dynasty collections have been augmented from the cache of strips dating from the late Western Han dynasty discovered in 1978 in Tomb #115 of the Sun family compound in Ta-t'ung county, Ch'ing-hai province. Of the sixty-odd fragments reported in the *Wen-wu (Cultural Relics* 1981:2) description of this find, six strips had "Master Sun" on them, suggesting some relationship with the *Sun-tzu*. The contemporary scholar Li Ling (1983) rejects any suggestion that these strips are lost text of the *Sun-tzu* or some related military treatise, as was suggested in first reports of this find in *Wen-wu*. He argues that these strips are works on military regulations that cite the *Sun-tzu*.

The disorderly and corrupt condition of the bamboo strips and the fact that there has not always been an extant text that can be used for comparison has made the project of arranging these strips and reconstructing an intelligible text from them a task fraught with difficulties. Given the necessary amount of speculation involved in reassembling the strips, conclusions can often be no more than tentative. There is a good possibility, for example, that material from texts other than the original *Sun-tzu* has crept into the reconstructed text.

Even where it is clear that certain strips belong together in a given chapter, the position of the chapter relative to the other chapters cannot always be determined with any confidence. Further, there are some strips that for one reason or another seem to belong to a given chapter, but are devoid of any further context. Where these fragments make sense and add to our understanding of the chapter, they have been translated and appended separately at the end of the chapter. Otherwise, they have been omitted.

Chapter titles that have been added at the discretion of the Yin-ch'üeh-shan Committee are provided in square brackets. Where it is apparent that the bamboo strips contained in any one chapter, in spite of missing characters or strips, constitute a continuous passage, they are translated accordingly. Where there is a break in a passage, the translation is also broken at this point. If the text is interrupted with lacunae, this is indicated by ellipses. Where what is missing can be restored from context with some degree of confidence, a translation is provided in italics within square brackets.

SUN-TZU: PART I

THE THIRTEEN-CHAPTER TEXT

孫子曰：兵者，國之大事也。死生之地，存亡之道，不可不察也。故經之以五，效（校）之以計而索其請（情）：一曰道，二曰天，三曰地，四曰將，五曰法。道者，令民與上同意也，故可與之死，可與之生而不詭也。天者，陰陽、寒暑、時制也。地者，高下、遠近、險易、廣狹、死生也。將者，知（智）、信、仁、勇、嚴也。法者，曲制、官道、主用也。凡此五者，將莫不聞，知之者勝，不知者不勝。故校之以計，而索其情。曰：主孰有道？將孰有能？天地孰得？法令孰行？兵衆孰強？士卒孰練？賞罰（罰）孰明？吾以此知勝負矣。

將聽吾計，用之必勝，留之；將不聽吾計，用之必敗，去之。計利以聽，乃爲之勢，以佐其外。勢者，因利而制權也。兵者，詭道也。故能而示之不能，用而示之不用，近而視（示）之遠，遠而視（示）之近。利而誘之，亂而取之，實而備之，強而避之，怒而撓（撓）之，卑而驕之，佚而勞之，親而離之。攻其無備，出其不意。此兵家之勝，不可先傳也。

夫未戰而廟筭勝者，得筭多也；未戰而廟筭不勝者，得筭少也。多筭勝，少筭不勝，而況於无筭乎！吾以此觀之，勝負見矣。

102

CHAPTER 1: ON ASSESSMENTS

Master Sun said:

War[115] is a vital matter of state. It is the field on which life or death is determined and the road that leads to either survival or ruin, and must be examined with the greatest care.

Therefore, to gauge the outcome of war we must appraise the situation on the basis of the following five criteria, and compare the two sides by assessing their relative strengths. The first of the five criteria is the way (tao), the second is climate, the third is terrain, the fourth is command, and the fifth is regulation.

The way (tao) is what brings the thinking of the people in line with their superiors. Hence, you can send them to their deaths or let them live, and they will have no misgivings one way or the other.

Climate is light and shadow, heat and cold, and the rotation of the seasons.[116]

Terrain refers to the fall of the land,[117] proximate distances, difficulty of passage, the degree of openness, and the viability of the land for deploying troops.

Command is a matter of wisdom, integrity, humanity, courage, and discipline.

And regulation entails organizational effectiveness, a chain of command, and a structure for logistical support.

All commanders are familiar with these five criteria, yet it is he who masters them who takes the victory, while he who does not will not prevail.

Therefore, to gauge the outcome of war we must compare the two sides by assessing their relative strengths. This is to ask the following questions:

Which ruler has the way (tao)?
Which commander has the greater ability?
Which side has the advantages of climate and terrain?
Which army follows regulations and obeys orders more strictly?
Which army has superior strength?
Whose officers and men are better trained?
Which side is more strict and impartial in meting out rewards and punishments?

On the basis of this comparison I know who will win and who will lose.

If you heed my assessments, dispatching troops into battle would mean certain victory, and I will stay. If you do not heed them, dispatching troops would mean certain defeat, and I will leave.[118]

Having heard what can be gained from my assessments, shape a strategic advantage (shih) from them to strengthen our position. By "strategic advantage" I mean making the most of favorable conditions (yin) and tilting the scales in our favor.

Warfare is the art (tao) of deceit. Therefore, when able, seem to be unable; when ready, seem unready; when nearby, seem far away; and when far away, seem near. If the enemy seeks some advantage, entice him with it. If he is in disorder, attack him and take him. If he is formidable, prepare against him. If he is strong, evade him. If he is in-

104

censed, provoke him. If he is humble, encourage his arrogance. If he is rested, wear him down. If he is internally harmonious, sow divisiveness in his ranks. Attack where he is not prepared; go by way of places where it would never occur to him you would go. These are the military strategist's calculations for victory—they cannot be settled in advance.

It is by scoring many points that one wins the war beforehand in the temple rehearsal of the battle; it is by scoring few points that one loses the war beforehand in the temple rehearsal of the battle. The side that scores many points will win; the side that scores few points will not win, let alone the side that scores no points at all. When I examine it in this way, the outcome of the war becomes apparent.[119]

孫子曰：凡用兵之法，馳車千駟，革車千乘，帶甲十萬，千里饋糧（糧），則內外之費，賓客之用，膠漆之材，車甲之奉，日費千金，然後十萬之師舉矣。其用戰也貴勝，久則頓（鈍）兵挫銳，攻城則力屈，久暴師則國用不足。夫鈍兵挫銳，屈力殫貨，則諸侯乘其弊而起，雖有知（智）者，不能善其後矣。故兵聞拙速，未覩巧之久也。夫兵久而國利者，未之有也。故不盡知用兵之害者，則不能盡知用兵之利也。善用兵者，役不再籍，糧不三載，取用於國，因糧（糧）於敵，故軍食可足也。國之貧於師者：遠師者遠輸，遠輸則百姓貧。近市（師）者貴賣，貴賣則財竭，財竭則急於丘役。屈力中原，內虛於家，百姓之費十去其七。公家之費，破車罷馬，甲冑矢弩，戟楯矛櫓，丘牛大車，十去其六。故智將務食於敵，食敵一鍾，當吾二十鍾；萁稈一石，當吾二十石。故殺適（敵）者，怒也；取敵之利者，貨也。故車戰，得車十乘已上，賞其先得者，而更其旌旗，車雜而乘之，卒善而養之，是胃（謂）勝敵而益強。故兵貴勝，不貴久。故知兵之將，民之司命，國家安危之主也。

106

CHAPTER 2: ON WAGING BATTLE

Master Sun said:

The art of warfare is this:[120]

For an army of one thousand fast four-horse chariots, one thousand four-horse leather-covered wagons, and one hundred thousand armor-clad troops, and for the provisioning of this army over a distance of a thousand *li*,[121] what with expenses at home and on the field, including foreign envoys and advisors, materials such as glue and lacquer, and the maintenance of chariots and armor, only when you have in hand one thousand pieces of gold for each day can the hundred thousand troops be mobilized.

In joining battle, seek the quick victory. If battle is protracted, your weapons will be blunted and your troops demoralized. If you lay siege to a walled city, you exhaust your strength. If your armies are kept in the field for a long time, your national reserves will not suffice. Where you have blunted your weapons, demoralized your troops, exhausted your strength and depleted all available resources, the neighboring rulers will take advantage of your adversity to strike. And even with the wisest of counsel, you will not be able to turn the ensuing consequences to the good.

Thus in war, I have heard tell of a foolish haste, but I have yet to see a case of cleverly dragging on the hostilities. There has never been a state that has benefited from an extended war. Hence, if one is not fully cognizant of the evils of waging war, he cannot be fully cognizant either of how to turn it to best account.

The expert in using the military does not conscript soldiers more than once or transport his provisions repeatedly from home. He carries his military equipment with him, and commandeers (*yin*) his provisions from the enemy. Thus he has what he needs to feed his army.

A state is impoverished by its armies when it has to supply them at a great distance. To supply an army at a great distance is to impoverish one's people. On the other hand, in the vicinity of the armies, the price of goods goes up. Where goods are expensive, you exhaust your resources, and once you have exhausted your resources, you will be forced to increase district exactions for the military. All your strength is spent on the battlefield, and the families on the home front are left destitute. The toll to the people will have been some 70 percent of their property; the toll to the public coffers in terms of broken-down chariots and worn-out horses, body armor and helmets, crossbows and bolts, halberds and bucklers, lances and shields, draft oxen and heavy supply wagons will be some 60 percent of its reserves.

Therefore, the wise commander does his best to feed his army from enemy soil. To consume one measure of the enemy's provisions is equal to twenty of our own; to use up one bale of the enemy's fodder is equal to twenty of our own.

Killing the enemy is a matter of arousing the anger of our men; snatching the enemy's wealth is a matter of dispensing the spoils.[122] Thus, in a chariot battle where more than ten war chariots have been captured, reward those who captured the first one and replace the enemy's flags and standards with our own. Mix the chariots in with our ranks and send them back into battle; provide for the captured soldiers and treat them well. This is called increasing our own strength in the process of defeating the army.

Hence, in war prize the quick victory, not the protracted engagement. Thus, the commander who understands war is the final arbiter of people's lives, and lord over the security of the state.

謀攻篇

孫子曰：凡用兵之法，全國爲上，破國次之；全軍爲上，破軍次之；全旅爲上，破旅次之；全卒爲上，破卒次之；全伍爲上，破伍次之。是故百戰百勝，非善之善者也；不戰而屈人之兵，善之善者也。 故上兵伐謀，其次伐交，其次伐兵，其下攻城。攻城之法，爲不得已，脩（修）櫓轒輼，具器械，三月而後成，距闉，有（又）三月而後已。將不勝其忿而蟻附之，殺士三分之一，而城不拔者，此攻之災（災）也。故善用兵者，詘（屈）人之兵而非戰也，拔人之城而非攻也，毀人之國而非久也，必以全爭於天下，故兵不頓而利可全，此謀攻之法也。

故用兵之法：十則圍之，五則攻之，倍則戰之，敵則能分之，少則能守之，不若則能避之。故小敵之堅，大敵之擒也。

夫將者，國之輔也，輔周則國必強，輔隙則國必弱。故君之所以患於軍者三：不知軍之不可以進而謂之進，不知軍之不可以退而謂之退，是謂縻軍。不知三軍之事，而同三軍之政，則軍士惑矣；不知三軍之權，而同三軍之任，則軍士疑矣。三軍澰（既）惑且疑，則諸侯之難至矣，是謂亂軍引勝。

故知勝有五：知可以戰與不可以戰者勝，識衆寡之用者勝，上下同欲者勝，以虞侍（待）不虞者勝，將能而君不御者勝。此五者，知勝之道也。 故曰：知皮（彼）知己，百戰不殆；不知彼而知己，一勝一負；不知彼，不知己，每戰必殆。

110

CHAPTER 3: PLANNING THE ATTACK

Master Sun said:

The art of warfare is this:

It is best to keep one's own state intact; to crush the enemy's state is only a second best. It is best to keep one's own army, battalion, company, or five-man squad intact; to crush the enemy's army, battalion, company, or five-man squad is only a second best.[123] So to win a hundred victories in a hundred battles is not the highest excellence; the highest excellence is to subdue the enemy's army without fighting at all.

Therefore, the best military policy is to attack strategies; the next to attack alliances; the next to attack soldiers; and the worst to assault walled cities.

Resort to assaulting walled cities only when there is no other choice. To construct siege screens and armored personnel vehicles and to assemble all of the military equipment and weaponry necessary will take three months, and to amass earthen mounds against the walls will take another three months. And if your commander, unable to control his temper, sends your troops swarming at the walls, your casualties will be one in three and still you will not have taken the city. This is the kind of calamity that befalls you in laying siege.

Therefore, the expert in using the military subdues the enemy's forces without going to battle, takes the enemy's walled cities without launching an attack, and crushes the enemy's state without a protracted war. He must use the

111

principle of keeping himself intact to compete in the world. Thus, his weapons will not be blunted and he can keep his edge intact. This then is the art of planning the attack.[124]

Therefore the art of using troops is this:

When ten times the enemy strength, surround him; when five times, attack him; when double, engage him; when you and the enemy are equally matched, be able to divide him;[125] when you are inferior in numbers, be able to take the defensive; and when you are no match for the enemy, be able to avoid him. Thus what serves as secure defense against a small army will only be captured by a large one.[126]

The commander is the side-guard on the carriage of state.[127] Where this guard is in place, the state will certainly be strong; where it is defective, the state will certainly be weak.

There are three ways in which the ruler can bring grief to his army:[128]

To order an advance, not realizing the army is in no position to do so, or to order a retreat, not realizing the army is in no position to withdraw—this is called "hobbling the army."

To interfere in the administration of the army while being ignorant of its internal affairs will confuse officers and soldiers alike.

To interfere in military assignments while being ignorant of exigencies will lose him the confidence of his men.

Once his army has become confused and he has lost the confidence of his men, aggression from his neighboring rulers will be upon him. This is called sowing disorder in your own ranks and throwing away the victory.

Therefore there are five factors in anticipating which side will win:

The side that knows when to fight and when not to will take the victory.

The side that understands how to deal with numerical superiority and inferiority in the deployment of troops will take the victory.

The side that has superiors and subordinates united in purpose will take the victory.

The side that fields a fully prepared army against one that is not will take the victory.

The side on which the commander is able and the ruler does not interfere will take the victory.

These five factors are the way (*tao*) of anticipating victory.

Thus it is said:

He who knows the enemy and himself
Will never in a hundred battles be at risk;
He who does not know the enemy but knows himself
Will sometimes win and sometimes lose;
He who knows neither the enemy nor himself
Will be at risk in every battle.[129]

形　篇

孫子曰：昔之善戰者，先爲不可勝，以侍（待）適（敵）之可勝。不可勝在己，可勝在適（敵）。故善戰者，能爲不可勝，不能使適（敵）必可勝。故曰：勝可智（知），而不可爲。不可勝者，守也；可勝者，攻也。守則有餘，攻則不足。善守者，臧（藏）於九地之下；善攻者，動於九天之上，故能自葆（保）而全勝也。見勝不過衆人之所知，非善之善者也；戰勝而天下曰善，非善之善者也。故舉秋毫不爲多力，見日月不爲明目，聞雷霆不爲蔥（聰）耳。古之所胃（謂）善戰者，勝於易勝者也。故善戰者之勝也，無奇〔勝〕，無智名，無勇功。故其戰勝不貸（忒）；不貸（忒）者，其所錯（措）必勝，勝已敗者也。故善戰者，立於不敗之地，而不失敵之敗也。是故，勝兵先勝而後求戰，敗兵先戰而後求勝。善用兵者，脩（修）道而保法，故能爲勝敗正。法：一曰度，二曰量，三曰數，四曰稱，五曰勝。地生度，度生量，量生數，數生稱，稱生勝。故勝兵若以溢（鎰）稱朱（銖），敗兵若以朱（銖）稱溢（鎰）。稱勝者之戰民也，若決積水於千邪（仞）之谿者，形也。

114

Master Sun said:

Of old the expert in battle would first make himself invincible and then wait for the enemy to expose his vulnerability. Invincibility depends on oneself; vulnerability lies with the enemy.[131] Therefore the expert in battle can make himself invincible, but cannot guarantee for certain the vulnerability of the enemy. Hence it is said:

Victory can be anticipated,
But it cannot be forced.

Being invincible lies with defense; the vulnerability of the enemy comes with the attack.[132] If one assumes a defensive posture, it is because the enemy's strength is overwhelming; if one launches the attack, it is because the enemy's strength is deficient.[133] The expert at defense conceals himself in the deepest recesses of the earth; the expert on the attack strikes from out of the highest reaches of the heavens. Thus he is able to both protect himself and to take the complete victory.

To anticipate the victory is not going beyond the understanding of the common run; it is not the highest excellence. To win in battle so that the whole world says "Excellent!" is not the highest excellence. Hence, to lift an autumn hair is no mark of strength; to see the sun and moon is no mark of clear-sightedness; to hear a thunder clap is no mark of keen hearing. He whom the ancients called an expert in battle gained victory where victory was easily gained. Thus the battle of the expert is never an exceptional victory, nor does it win him reputation for wisdom or credit for courage.[134] His victories in battle are unerring.[135] Unerring means that he acts where victory is certain, and conquers an enemy that has already lost.

Therefore, the expert in battle takes his stand on ground that is unassailable, and does not miss his chance to defeat the enemy. For this reason, the victorious army only enters battle after having first won the victory, while the defeated army only seeks victory after having first entered the fray.[136]

The expert in using the military builds upon the way (tao) and holds fast to military regulations,[137] and thus is able to be the arbiter of victory and defeat.[138]

Factors in the art of warfare are: First, calculations; second, quantities; third, logistics; fourth, the balance of power; and fifth, the possibility of victory. Calculations are based on the terrain, estimates of available quantities of goods are based on these calculations, logistical strength is based on estimates of available quantities of goods, the balance of power is based on logistical strength, and the possibility of victory is based on the balance of power.

Thus a victorious army is like weighing in a full hundredweight against a few ounces, and a defeated army is like pitting a few ounces against a hundredweight.[139] It is a matter of strategic positioning (hsing) that the army that has this weight of victory on its side, in launching its men into battle, can be likened to the cascading of pent-up waters thundering through a steep gorge.[140]

孫子曰：凡治衆如治寡，分數是也；鬭衆如鬭寡，形名是也；三軍之衆，可使畢受適（敵）而无敗者，奇正是也。兵之所加，如以段（碫）投卵者，虛實是也。凡戰者，以正合，以奇勝。故善出奇者，無窮如天地，不謁（竭）如江河。冬（終）而復始，日月是也；死而復生，四時是也。聲不過五，五聲之變不可勝聽也；色不過五，五色之變不可勝觀也；味不過五，五味之變不可勝嘗也。戰勢不過奇正，奇正之變不可勝窮也。奇正環（還）相生，如環之毋（無）端，孰能窮之？激水之疾，至於漂石者，勢也；鷙鳥之擊，至於毀折者，節也。是故善戰者，其勢險，其節短。勢如彍弩，節如發機。紛紛紜紜，鬭亂而不可亂也；渾渾沌沌，形圓而不可敗也。亂生於治，脅（怯）生於惠（勇），弱生於強。治亂，數也；惠（勇）脅（怯），埶（勢）也；強弱，形也。故善動適（敵）者，刑（形）之，適（敵）必從之；予之，敵必取之。以此動之，以卒侍（待）之。故善戰者，求之於埶（勢），不責於人，故能擇人而任勢。任勢者，其戰人也，如轉木石；木石之生（性）：安則静，危則動，方則止，圓則行。故善戰人之勢，如轉圓石於千仞之山者，勢也。

CHAPTER 5: STRATEGIC ADVANTAGE
(*SHIH*)

Master Sun said:

In general, it is organization[141] that makes managing many soldiers the same as managing a few. It is communication with flags and pennants[142] that makes fighting with many soldiers the same as fighting with a few. It is "surprise" (*ch'i*) and "straightforward" (*cheng*) operations that enable one's army to withstand the full assault of the enemy force[143] and remain undefeated.[144] It is the distinction between "weak points" and "strong points" that makes one's army falling upon the enemy a whetstone being hurled at eggs.

Generally in battle use the "straightforward" to engage the enemy and the "surprise" to win the victory. Thus the expert at delivering the surprise assault is as boundless as the heavens and earth, and as inexhaustible as the rivers and seas.[145] Like the sun and moon, he sets only to rise again; like the four seasons, he passes only to return again.

There are no more than five cardinal notes, yet in combination, they produce more sounds than could possibly be heard; there are no more than five cardinal colors, yet in combination, they produce more shades and hues than could possibly be seen; there are no more than five cardinal tastes, yet in combination, they produce more flavors than could possibly be tasted. For gaining strategic advantage (*shih*) in battle, there are no more than "surprise" and "straightforward" operations, yet in combination, they produce inexhaustible possibilities. "Surprise" and "straight-forward" operations give rise to each other endlessly just as a ring is without a beginning or an end.[146] And who can exhaust their possibilities?

That the velocity of cascading water can send boulders bobbing about is due to its strategic advantage (*shih*). That a bird of prey when it strikes[147] can smash its victim to pieces is due to its timing. So it is with the expert at battle that his strategic advantage (*shih*) is channeled and his timing is precise. His strategic advantage (*shih*) is like a drawn crossbow and his timing is like releasing the trigger. Even amidst the tumult and the clamor of battle, in all its confusion, he cannot be confused. Even amidst the melee and the brawl of battle, with positions shifting every which way, he cannot be defeated.

Disorder is born from order; cowardice from courage; weakness from strength. The line between disorder and order lies in logistics (*shu*); between cowardice and courage, in strategic advantage (*shih*); and between weakness and strength, in strategic positioning (*hsing*). Thus the expert at getting the enemy to make his move shows himself (*hsing*), and the enemy is certain to follow. He baits the enemy, and the enemy is certain to take it. In so doing,[148] he moves the enemy, and lies in wait for him with his full force.

The expert at battle seeks his victory from strategic advantage (*shih*) and does not demand it from his men. He is thus able to select the right men and exploit the strategic advantage (*shih*).[149] He who exploits the strategic advantage (*shih*) sends his men into battle like rolling logs and boulders. It is the nature of logs and boulders that on flat ground, they are stationary, but on steep ground, they roll;

the square in shape tends to stop but the round tends to roll. Thus, that the strategic advantage (*shih*) of the expert commander in exploiting his men in battle can be likened to rolling round boulders down a steep ravine thousands of feet high says something about his strategic advantage (*shih*).[150]

虛 實 篇

孫子曰：凡先處戰地而恃（待）敵者失（佚），後處戰地而趨戰者勞。故善戰者，致人而不致於人。能使適（敵）人自至者，利之也；能使適（敵）人不得至者，害之也。故敵佚能勞之、飽能飢之、安能動之者，出其所不趨也。行於无人之地也；攻而必取者，攻其所不守也；守而必固者，守其所必攻也。故善攻者，適（敵）不知其所守；善守者，適（敵）不知其所攻。微乎微乎，至於無形；神乎神乎，至於無聲，故能爲適（敵）之司命。進而不可御者，衝其虛也；退而不可追者，速而不可及也。故我欲戰，適（敵）雖高壘深溝，不得不與我戰者，攻其所必救也；我不欲戰，畫地而守之，適（敵）不得與我戰者，乖其所之也。故刑（形）人而我无刑（形），則我專（專）而適（敵）分；我專（專）爲壹，適（敵）分而爲十，是以十攻其壹也。則我衆而適（敵）寡，能以衆擊寡者，則吾之所與戰者約矣。吾所與戰之地不可知，不可知，則適（敵）所備者多；敵所備者多，則吾所與戰者寡矣。故備

CHAPTER 6: WEAK POINTS AND
STRONG POINTS

Master Sun said:

Generally he who first occupies the field of battle to await the enemy will be rested; he who comes later and hastens into battle will be weary. Thus the expert in battle moves the enemy, and is not moved by him. Getting the enemy to come of his own accord is a matter of making things easy for him; stopping him from coming is a matter of obstructing him. Thus being able to wear down a well-rested enemy, to starve one that is well-provisioned, and to move one that is settled, lies in going by way of places where the enemy must hasten in defense.[151]

To march a thousand *li* without becoming weary is because one marches through territory where there is no enemy presence. To attack with the confidence of taking one's objective is because one attacks what the enemy does not defend. To defend with the confidence of keeping one's charge secure is because one defends where the enemy will not attack.[152] Thus against the expert in the attack, the enemy does not know where to defend, and against the expert in defense, the enemy does not know where to strike.

So veiled and subtle,
To the point of having no form (*hsing*);
So mysterious and miraculous,
To the point of making no sound.
Therefore he can be arbiter of the enemy's fate.

前則後寡，備後則前寡；備左則右寡，備右則左寡；無所不備，則無所不寡。寡者，備人者也；衆者，使人備己者也。故知戰之地，知戰之日，則可千里而戰；不知戰地，不知戰日，則左不能救右，右不能救左，前不能救後，後不能救前，而（況）遠者數十里，近者數里乎！以吾度之，越人之兵雖多，亦奚益於勝戈（哉）？故曰：勝可爲也。

適（敵）唯（雖）衆，可使無鬭（鬬）。故策之而知得失之計，作之而知動静之理，形之而知死生之地，角之而知有餘不足之處。故刑（形）兵之極，至於无刑（形）；无刑（形），則深間不能規（窺），知（智）者不能謀。因刑（形）而錯勝於衆，衆不能知；人皆知我所勝之形，而莫知吾所以制勝之形。故其戰勝不復，而應刑（形）於無窮。夫兵刑（形）象水，水之行，辟（避）高而趨下；兵之勝，辟（避）實而擊虚。水因地而制行，兵因敵而制勝。故兵无成埶（勢），无恒刑（形）。能因敵變化而取勝者，謂之神。故五行无常勝，四時無常立（位）；日有短長，月有死生。

In advancing he cannot be resisted because he bursts through the enemy's weak points; in withdrawing he cannot be pursued because, being so quick, he cannot be caught.

Thus, if we want to fight, the enemy has no choice but to engage us, even though safe behind his high walls and deep moats, because we strike at what he must rescue. If we do not want to fight, the enemy cannot engage us, even though we have no more around us than a drawn line, because we divert him to a different objective.

If we can make the enemy show his position (*hsing*) while concealing ours from him, we will be at full force where he is divided.[153] If our army is united as one and the enemy's is fragmented, in using the undivided whole to attack his one, we are many to his few. If we are able to use many to strike few, anyone we take the battle to will be in desperate circumstances.[154]

The place we have chosen to give the enemy battle must be kept from him. If he cannot anticipate us, the positions the enemy must prepare to defend will be many. And if the positions he must prepare to defend are many, then any unit we engage in battle will be few in number.

Thus if the enemy makes preparations by reinforcing his numbers at the front, his rear is weakened; if he makes preparations at the rear, his front is weakened; if he makes them on his left flank, his right is weakened; if he makes them on his right flank, his left is weakened. To be prepared everywhere is to be weak everywhere.

One is weak because he makes preparations against others; he has strength because he makes others prepare against him.

Thus if one can anticipate the place and the day of battle, he can march a thousand *li* to join the battle. But if one cannot anticipate either the place or the day of battle, his left flank cannot even rescue his right, or his right his left; his front cannot even rescue his rear, or his rear his front. How much more is this so when your reinforcements are separated by at least a few *li*, or even tens of *li*.

The way I estimate it, even though the troops of Yüeh are many, what good is this to them in respect to victory?[155] Thus it is said: Victory can be created. For even though the enemy has the strength of numbers, we can prevent him from fighting us.

Therefore, analyze the enemy's battle plan to understand its merits and its weaknesses; provoke him to find out the pattern of his movements; make him show himself (*hsing*) to discover the viability of his battle position; skirmish with him to find out where he is strong and where he is vulnerable.

The ultimate skill in taking up a strategic position (*hsing*) is to have no form (*hsing*).[156] If your position is formless (*hsing*), the most carefully concealed spies will not be able to get a look at it, and the wisest counsellors will not be able to lay plans against it. I present the rank and file with victories gained through (*yin*) strategic positioning (*hsing*), yet they are not able to understand them. Everyone knows the position (*hsing*) that has won me victory, yet none fathom how I came to settle on this winning position (*hsing*). Thus one's victories in battle cannot be repeated—they take their form (*hsing*) in response to inexhaustibly changing circumstances.

The positioning (*hsing*) of troops can be likened to wa-

126

ter: Just as the flow of water avoids high ground and rushes to the lowest point, so on the path to victory avoid the enemy's strong points and strike where he is weak.[157] As water varies its flow according to (*yin*) the fall of the land, so an army varies its method of gaining victory according to (*yin*) the enemy.

Thus an army does not have fixed strategic advantages (*shih*) or an invariable position (*hsing*).[158] To be able to take the victory by varying one's position according to (*yin*) the enemy's is called being inscrutable (*shen*).[159]

Thus, of the five phases (*wu hsing*), none is the constant victor; of the four seasons, none occupies a constant position; the days are both short and long; the moon waxes and wanes.[160]

孫子曰：凡用兵之法，將受命於君，合軍聚衆，交和而舍，莫難於軍争。軍争之難者，以迂爲直，以患爲利。故迂其途而誘之以利，後人發，先人至，此知迂直之計者也。故軍争爲利，軍争爲危。舉軍而争利則不及，委軍而争利則輜重捐。是故絭（卷）甲而趨，日夜不處倍道兼行，百里而争利，則擒三軍將；勁者先，罷者後，其法十一而至。五十里而争利，則厥（蹶）上軍將，其法半至。三十里而争利，則三分之二至。是故軍毋（無）輜重則亡，無糧食則亡，无委責（積）則亡。故不知諸侯之謀者，不能豫交；不知山林、險阻、沮澤之刑（形）者，不能行軍；不用鄉（向）道（導）者，不能得地利。故兵以詐立，以利動，以分合爲變者也。故其疾如風，其徐如林，侵掠如火，不動如山，難知如陰，動如雷震。掠鄉分衆，廓地分利，縣（懸）權而動。先知迂（迂）直之計者勝，此軍争之法也。軍政曰：言不相聞，故爲金鼓；視不相見，故爲旌旗。故夜戰多金鼓，晝戰多旌旗。夫金鼓旌旗者，所以一民之耳目也，民蹕（既）摶（專）壹，則勇者不得獨進，怯者不得獨退。此用衆之法也。故三軍可奪氣，將軍可奪心。是故朝氣銳，晝氣惰，暮氣歸。故善用兵者，辟（避）其兌（銳）氣，擊其惰歸，此治氣者也。以治待亂，以静待譁，此治心者也。以近待遠，以失（佚）待勞，以飽侍（待）飢，此治力者也。無邀正正之旗，勿擊堂堂之陳（陣），此治變者也。故用兵之法：高陵勿向，背丘勿逆，佯北勿從，銳卒勿攻，餌兵勿食，歸師勿遏，圍師必闕，窮寇勿迫，此用兵之法也。

128

CHAPTER 7: ARMED CONTEST

Master Sun said:

The art of using troops is this: In the process of the commander's receiving his orders from the ruler, assembling his armies, mobilizing the population for war, and setting up his camp facing the enemy, there is nothing of comparable difficulty to the armed contest itself. What is difficult in the armed contest is to turn the long and tortuous route into the direct, and to turn adversity into advantage. Thus, making the enemy's road long and tortuous, lure him along it by baiting him with easy gains. Set out after he does, yet arrive before him. This is to understand the tactic of converting the tortuous and the direct.

Armed contest can be both a source of advantage and of danger.[161] If you mobilize your entire force to contend for some advantage, you arrive too late; if you abandon your base camp to contend for advantage, your equipment and stores will be lost. For this reason, if an army were to stow its armor and set off in haste, and stopping neither day nor night, force-march at double time for a hundred *li* to contend for some advantage, its commanders would all be taken, its strongest men would be out in front, the exhausted ones would lag behind, and as a rule only one tenth of its strength would reach the target.

Were it to travel fifty *li* at such a pace to contend for some advantage, the commander of the advance force would be lost, and as a rule only half of its strength would reach the target. Were it to travel thirty *li* at such a pace to contend for some advantage, only two thirds of its strength would reach the target. For this reason, if an army is without its equipment and stores, it will perish; if it is without provisions, it will perish; if it is without its material support, it will perish.

[*Therefore, unless you know the intentions of the rulers of the neighboring states, you cannot enter into preparatory alliances with them; unless you know the lay of the land—its mountains and forests, its passes and natural hazards, its wetlands and swamps— you cannot deploy the army on it; unless you can employ local scouts, you cannot turn the terrain to your advantage.*][162]

Therefore, in warfare rely on deceptive maneuvers to establish your ground, calculate advantages in deciding your movements, and divide up and consolidate your forces to make your strategic changes.

Thus, advancing at a pace, such an army is like the wind; slow and majestic, it is like a forest; invading and plundering, it is like fire; sedentary, it is like a mountain; unpredictable, it is like a shadow; moving, it is like lightning and thunder.

In plundering the countryside, divide up your numbers;[163] in extending your territory, divide up and hold the strategic positions; weigh the pros and cons before moving into action.

He who first understands the tactic of converting the tortuous and the direct will take the victory. This is the art of armed contest.[164]

The Book of Military Policies[165] states: It is because commands cannot be heard in the din of battle that drums and gongs are used; it is because units cannot identify each other in battle that flags and pennants are used. Thus, in night battle make extensive use of torches and drums, and in battle during the day make extensive use of flags and pennants.[166] Drums, gongs, flags, and pennants are the way to coordinate the ears and eyes of the men.[167] Once the men have been consolidated as one body, the courageous will not have to advance alone, and the cowardly will not get to retreat alone.[168] This is the art of employing large numbers of troops.

An entire enemy army can be demoralized, and its commander can be made to lose heart.[169] Now, in the morning of the war, the enemy's morale is high; by noon, it begins to flag; by evening, it has drained away.[170] Thus the expert in using the military avoids the enemy when his morale is high, and strikes when his morale has flagged and has drained away. This is the way to manage morale.

Use your proper order to await the enemy's disorder; use your calmness to await his clamor. This is the way to manage the heart-and-mind.

Use your closeness to the battlefield to await the far-off enemy; use your well-rested troops to await his fatigued; use your well-fed troops to await his hungry. This is the way to manage strength.

Do not intercept an enemy that is perfectly uniform in its array of banners; do not launch the attack on an enemy that is full and disciplined in its formations. This is the way to manage changing conditions.

Therefore, the art of using troops is this:

Do not attack an enemy who has the high ground; do not go against an enemy that has his back to a hill; do not follow an enemy that feigns retreat; do not attack the enemy's finest; do not swallow the enemy's bait; do not obstruct an enemy returning home; in surrounding the enemy, leave him a way out; do not press an enemy that is cornered. This is the art of using troops. (465 characters)[171]

九變篇

孫子曰：凡用兵之法：將受命於君，合軍聚衆，圮地無舍，衢（衢）地合交，絕地無留，圍地則謀。死地則戰。途有所不由，軍有所不擊，城有所不攻，地有所不爭，君命有所不受。故將通於九變之利者，知用兵矣。將不通於九變之利者，雖知地形，不能得地之利矣。治兵不知九變之術，雖知五利，不能得人之用矣。是故，智者之慮，必雜於利害。雜於利，而務可信也；雜於害，而患可解也。是故，屈諸侯者以害，役諸侯者以業，趨諸侯者以利。故用兵之法：無恃其不來，恃吾有以待也；無恃其不攻，恃吾有所不可攻也。故將有五危：必死，可殺也；必生，可虜也；忿速，可侮也；潔廉，可辱也；愛民，可煩也。凡此五者，將之過也，用兵之災也。覆軍殺將，必以五危，不可不察也。

CHAPTER 8: ADAPTING TO THE NINE CONTINGENCIES (*PIEN*)[172]

Master Sun said:

The art of using troops is this: When the commander receives his orders from the ruler, assembles his armies, and mobilizes the population for war,[173] he should not make camp on difficult terrain;[174] he should join with his allies on strategically vital intersections;[175] he should not linger on cutoff terrain; [176] he should have contingency plans on terrain vulnerable to ambush;[177] and he should take the fight to the enemy on terrain from which there is no way out.[178] There are roadways not to be traveled,[179] armies not to be attacked,[180] walled cities not to be assaulted,[181] territory not to be contested,[182] and commands from the ruler not to be obeyed.[183]

Thus, a commander fully conversant with the advantages to be gained in adapting to these nine contingencies will know how to employ troops; a commander who is not, even if he knows the lay of the land, will not be able to use it to his advantage. One who commands troops without knowing the art of adapting to these nine contingencies, even if he knows the five advantages,[184] will not be able to get the most from his men.

For this reason, the deliberations of the wise commander are sure to assess jointly both advantages and disadvantages. In taking full account of what is advantageous, he can fulfill his responsibilities; in taking full account of what is disadvantageous, his difficulties become resolvable.

135

For this reason, to subjugate neighboring states, use the threat of injury; to keep them in service, drive them on; to lure them out, use the prospect of gain.

The art of using troops is this:[185]

Do not depend on the enemy not coming; depend rather on being ready for him. Do not depend on the enemy not attacking; depend rather on having a position that cannot be attacked.

There are five traits that are dangerous in a commander:[186] If he has a reckless disregard for life, he can be killed; if he is determined to live at all costs, he can be captured; if he has a volatile temper, he can be provoked; if he is a man of uncompromising honor, he is open to insult; if he loves his people, he can be easily troubled and upset. These five traits are generally faults in a commander, and can prove disastrous in the conduct of war. Since an army's being routed and its commander slain is invariably the consequence of these five dangerous traits, they must be given careful consideration.

行軍篇

孫子曰：凡處軍、相敵，絕山依谷，視生處高，戰隆無登，此處山之軍也。絕水必遠水；客絕水而來，勿迎之於水內，令半濟而擊之，利；欲戰者，無附於水而迎客；視生處高，無迎水流，此處水上之軍也。絕斥澤，惟亟去無留，若交軍於斥澤之中，必依水草而背衆樹，此處斥澤之軍也。平陸處易，而右背高，前死後生，此處平陸之軍也。凡此四軍之利，黃帝之所以勝四帝也。

凡軍好高而惡下，貴陽而賤陰，養生而處實，軍无百疾，是謂必勝。陵丘隄防，必處其陽而右倍（背）之。此兵之利，地之助也。上雨，水沫至，待其定也。絕天澗、天井、天牢、天羅、天陷、天隙，必亟去之，勿近也。吾遠之，敵近之；吾迎之，敵背之。軍**旁**有險阻、潢井、葭葦（葦）、山林、蘙薈（薈）者，必謹覆索之，此伏姦之所處也。敵近而靜者，恃其險也；遠而挑戰者，欲人之進也。其所居易者，利也。衆樹動者，來也；衆草多障者，疑也。鳥起者，伏也；獸駭者，覆也。塵高而銳者，車來也；卑而廣者，徒來也；散

138

CHAPTER 9: DEPLOYING THE ARMY

Master Sun said:

In positioning your armies and assessing the enemy:

Pass through the mountains keeping to the valleys; pitch camp on high ground facing the sunny side; and joining battle in the hills, do not ascend to engage the enemy.[187] This is positioning an army when in the mountains.

Crossing water, you must move to distance yourself from it. When the invading army crosses water in his advance, do not meet him in the water. It is to your advantage to let him get halfway across and then attack him. Wanting to join the enemy in battle, do not meet his invading force near water. Take up a position on high ground facing the sunny side that is not downstream from the enemy. This is positioning an army when near water.

Crossing salt marshes, simply get through them in all haste and without delay. If you engage the enemy's force on the salt marshes, you must take your position near grass and water and with your back to the woods. This is positioning an army when on salt marshes.

On the flatlands, position yourself on open ground, with your right flank backing on high ground, and with dangerous ground in front and safe ground behind.[188] This is positioning an army when on flatlands.

Gaining the advantageous position for his army in these four different situations was the way the Yellow Emperor defeated the emperors of the four quarters.[189]

Generally speaking, an army prefers high ground and

而條達者,薪來也;少而往來者,營軍也;辭庫(卑)而益備者,進也;辭強而進驅(驅)者,退也。輕車先出,居其側者,陳也;無約而請和者,謀也;奔走而陳兵者,期也;半進半退者,誘也。杖而立者,飢也;汲役先飲者,渴也;見利而不進者,勞也;鳥集者,虛也;夜嘑(呼)者,恐也;軍獲(擾)者,將不重也;旌旗動者,亂也;吏怒者,倦也;粟馬肉食,軍無懸瓿(甀)不反(返)其舍者,窮寇也;諄諄翕翕,徐言入人者,失衆也;數賞者,窘也;數罰者,困也;先暴而後畏其衆者,不精之至也;來委謝者,欲休息也;兵怒而相迎,久而不合,又不相去,必謹察之。

夫唯無慮而易敵者,必擒於人。卒未親附而罰之,則不服,不服則難用也;卒已親附而罰不行,則不可用也。故合之以文,濟(齊)之以武,是謂必取。令素行以教其民,則民服;令素不行以教其民,則民不服。令素行者,與衆相得也。

140

dislikes the low, prizes the sunny side and shuns the shady side, seeks a place in which food and water are readily available and ample to supply its needs, and wants to be free of the numerous diseases. These conditions mean certain victory. Encountering rises, hills, embankments, and dikes, you must position yourself on the sunny side and on your right flank have your back to the slope. This is an advantage for the troops, and is exploiting whatever help the terrain affords.

When it is raining upstream and churning waters descend, do not try to cross, but wait for the waters to subside.[190]

Encountering steep river gorges, natural wells, box canyons, dense ground cover, quagmires, or natural defiles,[191] quit such places with haste. Do not approach them. In keeping our distance from them, we can maneuver the enemy near to them; in keeping them to our front, we can maneuver the enemy to have them at his back.

If the army is flanked by precipitous ravines, stagnant ponds, reeds and rushes, mountain forests, and tangled undergrowth, these places must be searched carefully and repeatedly, for they are where ambushes are laid and spies are hidden.

If the enemy is close and yet quiet,
He occupies a strategic position;
If he is at a distance and yet acts provocatively,
He wants us to advance.
Where he has positioned himself on level ground,
He is harboring some advantage;
If there is movement in the trees,

He is coming;
If there are many blinds in the bushes,
He is looking to confuse us;
If birds take to flight,
He is lying in ambush;
If animals stampede in fear,
He is mounting a surprise attack;
If the dust peaks up high,
His chariots are coming;
If the dust spreads out low to the ground,
His infantry is coming;
If the dust reaches out in scattered ribbons,
His firewood details have been dispatched;
If a few clouds of dust come and go,
He is making camp.
If his envoys are modest of word yet he continues to
     increase his readiness for war,
He will advance;
If his language is belligerent and he advances
     aggressively,
He will withdraw;
If his light chariots move out first
And take up position on the flanks,
He is moving into formation;
If he has suffered no setback and yet sues for
     peace,[192]
He is plotting;
If he moves rapidly with his troops in formation,[193]
He is setting the time for battle;
If some of his troops advance and some retreat,
He is seeking to lure us forward.

If the enemy soldiers lean on their weapons,
They are hungry;
If those sent for water first drink themselves,
They are thirsty;
If there is an advantage to be had yet they do not
    advance to secure it,
They are weary;
Where birds gather,
The enemy position is unoccupied;
Where there are shouts in the night,
The enemy is frightened;
Where there are disturbances in the ranks,
The enemy commander is not respected;
Where their flags and pennants are shifted about,
The enemy is in disorder;
Where his officers are easily angered,
The enemy is exhausted.
Where the enemy feeds his horses grain and his men
    meat,
And where his men no longer bother to hang up
    their water vessels,
Or return to camp,
The now-desperate enemy is ready to fight to the
    death.
Where, hemming and hawing,
The enemy commander speaks to his subordinates in
    a meek and halting voice,
He has lost his men.
Meting out too many rewards
Means the enemy is in trouble,
And meting out too many punishments

143

Means he is in dire straits.
The commander who erupts violently at his
subordinates,
Only then to fear them,
Is totally inept.
When the enemy's emissary comes with conciliatory
words
He wants to end hostilities.

When an angry enemy confronts you for an extended time, without either joining you in battle or quitting his position, you must watch him with the utmost care.

In war it is not numbers that give the advantage. If you do not advance recklessly, and are able to consolidate your own strength, get a clear picture of the enemy's situation, and secure the full support of your men, it is enough. It is only the one who has no plan and takes his enemy lightly who is certain to be captured by him. If you punish troops who are not yet devoted to you, they will not obey, and if they do not obey, they are difficult to use. But once you have their devotion, if discipline is not enforced, you cannot use them either. Therefore, bring them together by treating them humanely and keep them in line with strict military discipline. This will assure their allegiance.

If commands are consistently enforced in the training of the men, they will obey; if commands are not enforced in their training, they will not obey. The consistent enforcement of commands promotes a complementary relationship between the commander and his men.

孫子曰：地形有通者，有挂者，有支者，有隘者，有險者，有遠者。我可以往，彼可以來，曰通。通形者，先居高陽，利糧道，以戰則利。可以往，難以返，曰挂。挂形者，敵無備，出而勝之；敵有備，出而不勝，難以返，不利。我出而不利，彼出而不利，曰支。支形者，敵雖利我，我無出也；引而去之，令敵半出而擊之，利。隘形者，我先居之，必盈之以待敵；若敵先居之，盈而勿從，不盈而從之。險形者，我先居之，必居高陽以待敵；若敵先居之，引而去之，勿從也。遠形者，勢均，難以挑戰，戰而不利。凡此六者，地之道也，將之至任，不可不察也。故兵有走者，有弛者，有陷者，有崩者，有亂者，有北者。凡此六者，非天地之災，將之過也。夫勢均，以一擊十，曰走。卒強吏弱，曰弛。吏強卒弱，曰陷。大吏怒而不服，遇敵懟

CHAPTER 10: THE TERRAIN

Master Sun said:

Kinds of terrain include the accessible, that which entangles, that which leads to a stand-off, the narrow pass, the precipitous defile and the distant.

Terrain that both armies can approach freely is called accessible. On accessible terrain, the army that enters the battle having been first to occupy high ground on the sunny side and to establish convenient supply lines, fights with the advantage.

Terrain that allows your advance but hampers your return is entangling. On entangling ground, if you go out and engage the enemy when he is not prepared, you might defeat him. But when the enemy is prepared, if you go out and engage him and fail to defeat him, you will be hard-pressed to get out, and will be in trouble.

Terrain that when entered disadvantages both our side and the enemy is ground that will lead to a stand-off. On this kind of terrain, even if the enemy tempts us out, we must not take the bait, but should quit the position and withdraw. Having lured the enemy halfway out, we can then strike to our advantage.

With the narrow pass, if we can occupy it first, we must fully garrison it and await the enemy. Where the enemy has occupied it first, if he garrisons it completely, do not follow him, but if he fails to, we can go after him.

With the precipitous defile, if we can occupy it first, we must take the high ground on the sunny side and await

而自戰，將不知其能，曰崩。將弱不嚴，教道不明，吏卒無常，陳兵縱橫，曰亂。將不能料敵，以少合衆，以弱擊強，兵無選鋒，曰北。凡此六者，敗之道也；將之至任，不可不察也。夫地形者，兵之助也。料敵制勝，計險易遠近，上將之道也，知此而用戰者必勝，不知此而用戰者必敗。故戰道必勝，主曰無戰，必戰可也；戰道不勝，主曰必戰，無戰可也。故進不求名，退不避罪，惟民是保，而利合於主，國之寶也。視卒如嬰兒，故可與之赴深谿；視卒如愛子，故可與之俱死。厚而不能使，愛而不能令，亂而不能治，譬如驕子，不可用也。知吾卒之可以擊，而不知敵之不可擊，勝之半也。知敵之可擊，而不知吾卒之不可以擊，勝之半也。知敵之可擊，知吾卒之可以擊，而不知地形之不可以戰，勝之半也。故知兵者，動而不迷，舉而不窮。故曰：知彼知己，勝乃不殆；知地知天，勝乃可全。

148

the enemy. Where the enemy has occupied it first, quit the position and withdraw, and do not follow him.

When the enemy is at some distance, if the strategic advantages of both sides are about the same, it is not easy to provoke him to fight, and taking the battle to him is not to our advantage.

Now these are the six guidelines (tao) governing the use of terrain. They are the commander's utmost responsibility, and must be thoroughly investigated.

In warfare there is flight, insubordination, deterioration, ruin, chaos, and rout.[194] These six situations are not natural catastrophes but the fault of the commander.

Where the strategic advantages of both sides are about the same, for an army to attack an enemy ten times its size will result in flight.

If the troops are strong but the officers weak, the result will be insubordination.

If the officers are strong but the troops weak, the result will be deterioration.

If your ranking officers are angry and insubordinate and, on encountering the enemy, allow their rancor to spur them into unauthorized engagements so that their commander does not know the strength of his own forces, the result will be ruin.

If the commander is weak and lax, his instructions and leadership unenlightened, his officers and troops undisciplined, and his military formations in disarray, the result will be chaos.

If the commander, unable to assess his enemy, sends a small force to engage a large one, sends his weak troops to attack the enemy's best, and operates without a vanguard of crack troops, the result will be rout.

These are six ways (*tao*) to certain defeat. They are the commander's utmost responsibility, and must be thoroughly investigated.

Strategic position (*hsing*) is an ally in battle. To assess the enemy's situation and create conditions that lead to victory, to analyze natural hazards and proximate distances—this is the way (*tao*) of the superior commander.[195] He who fights with full knowledge of these factors is certain to win; he who fights without it is certain to lose.

Thus, if the way (*tao*) of battle guarantees you victory, it is right for you to insist on fighting even if the ruler has said not to; where the way (*tao*) of battle does not allow victory, it is right for you to refuse to fight even if the ruler has said you must.

Hence a commander who advances without any thought of winning personal fame and withdraws in spite of certain punishment, whose only concern is to protect his people and promote the interests of his ruler, is the nation's treasure. Because he fusses over his men as if they were infants, they will accompany him into the deepest valleys; because he fusses over his men as if they were his own beloved sons, they will die by his side. If he is generous with them and yet they do not do as he tells them, if he loves them and yet they do not obey his commands, if he is so undisciplined with them that he cannot bring them into proper order, they will be like spoiled children who can be put to no good use at all.

To know our troops can attack and yet be unaware

that the enemy is not open to attack, reduces our chances of victory to half; to know the enemy is open to attack and yet be unaware that our own troops cannot attack, reduces our chances of victory again to half; to know the enemy is open to attack and our troops can attack, and yet be unaware that the terrain does not favor us in battle, reduces the chances of victory once again to half.

Thus when one who understands war moves, he does not go the wrong way, and when he takes action, he does not reach a dead end.

Hence it is said:

Know the other, know yourself,
And the victory will not be at risk;
Know the ground, know the natural conditions,
And the victory can be total.[196]

孫子曰：用兵之法，有散地，有輕地，有爭地，有交地，有瞿（衢）地，有重地，有圯地，有圍地，有死地。諸侯自戰其地者，爲散地。入人之地而不深者，爲輕地。我得則利，彼得亦利者，爲爭地。我可以往，彼可以來者，爲交地。諸侯之地三屬，先至而得天下之衆者，爲瞿（衢）地。入人之地深，倍（背）城邑多者，爲重地。山林、險阻、沮澤，凡難行之道者，爲圯地。所由入者隘，所從歸者迂，彼寡可以擊吾之衆者，爲圍地。疾戰則存，不疾戰則亡者，爲死地。是故散地則無戰，輕地則無止，爭地則無攻，交地則無絕，瞿（衢）地則合交，重地則掠，圯地則行，圍地則謀，死地則戰。所謂古之善用兵者，能使敵人前後不相及，衆寡不相恃，貴賤不相救，上下不相收，卒離而不集，兵合而不齊。合於利而動，不合於利而止。敢問：適（敵）衆以正（整）將來，侍（待）之若何？曰：先奪其所愛，則聽矣。兵之情主速，乘人之不及，由不虞之道，攻其所不戒也。凡爲客之道：深入則專，主人不克，掠於饒野，三軍足食；謹養而勿勞，併氣積力；運兵計謀，爲不可測。投之無所往，死且不北，死，焉不得士人盡力。兵士甚陷則不懼，無所往則固，入深則

CHAPTER 11: THE NINE KINDS OF
TERRAIN

Master Sun said:

In the art of employing troops, the kinds of terrain include scattering terrain, marginal terrain, contested terrain, intermediate terrain, the strategically vital intersection, critical terrain, difficult terrain, terrain vulnerable to ambush, and terrain from which there is no way out.

Where a feudal ruler does battle within his own territory, it is a terrain that permits the scattering of his troops.

Where one has penetrated only barely into enemy territory, it is marginal terrain.

Ground that gives us or the enemy the advantage in occupying it is contested terrain.

Ground accessible to both sides is intermediate terrain.

The territory of several neighboring states at which their borders meet is a strategically vital intersection. The first to reach it will gain the allegiance of the other states of the empire.

When an army has penetrated deep into enemy territory, and has many of the enemy's walled cities and towns at its back, it is on critical terrain.

Mountains and forests, passes and natural hazards, wetlands and swamps, and any such roads difficult to traverse constitute difficult terrain.

Ground that gives access through a narrow defile, and where exit is tortuous, allowing an enemy in small num-

拘，不得已則鬪。是故不修而戒，不求而得，不約而親，不令而信，禁祥去疑，至

死無所之。吾士無餘財，非惡貨也；無餘命，非惡壽也。令發之日，士坐者涕

襟，臥者涕交頤。投之無所往者，諸劌（劌）之勇也。故善用兵者，譬如率

然者，恒山之蛇也，擊其首則尾至，擊其尾則首至，擊其中則首尾俱至。敢問：兵

可使如率然乎？曰：可。夫吳人與越人相惡也，當其同周（舟）而濟，其相救也，

如左右手。是故方馬埋輪，未足恃也；齊勇若一，政之道也；剛柔皆得，地之理也。

故善用兵者，攜手若使一人，不得已也。將軍之事，靜以幽，正以治。能愚士卒之

耳目，使民無知。易其事，革其謀，使民無識；易其居，迂其途，使民不得慮。帥與

之期，如登高而去其梯，帥與之深入諸侯之地，而發其機；若驅羣羊，驅而往，驅

而來，莫知所之。聚三軍之衆，投之於險，此謂將軍之事也。九地之變，屈伸之

利，人情之理，不可不察也。凡爲客之道，深則專，淺則散。去國越境而師者，絕

地也；四徹者，衢地也；入深者，重地也；入淺者，輕地也；背固前隘者，圍地也；

無所往者，死地也。是故散地，吾將壹其志；輕地，吾將使之屬；爭地，吾將趨其

bers to attack our main force, is terrain vulnerable to ambush.

Ground on which you will survive only if you fight with all your might, but will perish if you fail to do so, is terrain with no way out.

This being the case, do not fight on scattering terrain; do not stay on marginal terrain; do not attack the enemy on contested terrain; do not get cut off on intermediate terrain; form alliances with the neighboring states at strategically vital intersections; plunder the enemy's resources on critical terrain; press ahead on difficult terrain; devise contingency plans on terrain vulnerable to ambush; and on terrain from which there is no way out, take the battle to the enemy.

The commanders of old said to be expert at the use of the military were able to ensure that with the enemy:

> His vanguard and rearguard could not relieve each
>   other,
> The main body of his army and its special detach-
>   ments could not support each other,
> Officers and men could not come to each other's aid,
> And superiors and subordinates could not maintain
>   their lines of communication.
> The enemy forces when scattered could not regroup,
> And when their army assembled, it could not form
>   ranks.

If it was to the advantage of these expert commanders, they would move into action; if not, they would remain in place. Suppose I am asked: If the enemy, in great numbers and

後；交地，吾將謹其守；衢地，吾將固其結；重地，吾將繼其食；圮地，吾將進其途；圍地，吾將塞其闕；死地，吾將示之以不活。故兵之情，圍則禦，不得已則鬬，過則從。是故，不知諸侯之謀者，不能豫交；不知山林、險阻、沮澤之形者，不能行軍。不用鄉（向）道（導）者，不能得地利。四五者，一不智（知），非王霸之兵也。

夫王霸之兵，伐大國，則其衆不得聚；威加於敵，則其交不得合。是故，不爭天下之交，不養天下之權，信己之私，威加於敵。故其城可拔，其國可隳（隳）。施无法之賞，懸无正（政）之令，犯三軍之衆，若使一人。犯之以事，勿告以言；犯之以害，勿告以利。

投之亡地然後存，陷之死地然後生。夫衆陷於害，然後能爲勝敗。故爲兵之事，在於順詳敵之意，并敵一向，千里殺將，此謂巧能成事者也。是故，正（政）舉之日，夷關折符，無通其使，厲於郎（廊）廟之上，以誅其事。敵人開闔，必亟入之。先其所愛，微與之期。踐墨隨敵，以決戰事。是故始如處女，敵人開戶，後如脫兔，敵不及拒。

156

with strict discipline in the ranks, is about to advance on us, how do we deal with him? I would reply: If you get ahead of him to seize something he cannot afford to lose, he will do your bidding.

War is such that the supreme consideration is speed. This is to take advantage of what is beyond the reach of the enemy, to go by way of routes where he least expects you, and to attack where he has made no preparations.[197]

The general methods of operation (*tao*) for an invading army are:

The deeper you penetrate into enemy territory, the greater the cohesion of your troops, and the less likely the host army will prevail over you.

Plunder the enemy's most fertile fields, and your army will have ample provisions.

Attend to the nourishment of your troops and do not let them get worn down; lift their morale and build up their strength.

Deploy your troops and plan out your strategies in such a way that the enemy cannot fathom your movements.

Throw your troops into situations from which there is no way out, and they will choose death over desertion. Once they are ready to die, how could you get less than maximum exertion from your officers and men?

Even where your troops are in the most desperate
    straits,
They will have no fear,
And with nowhere else to turn,
They will stand firm;

157

Having penetrated deep into enemy territory,
They are linked together,
And if need be,
They will fight.
For this reason, with no need of admonishment, they
   are vigilant;[198]
Without compulsion, they carry out their duties;
Without tying them down, they are devoted;
With no need for orders, they follow army
   discipline.
Proscribe talk of omens and get rid of rumors,
And even to the death they will not retreat.

Our soldiers do not have an abundance of wealth, but it is not because they despise worldly goods; their life expectancy is not long, but it is not because they despise longevity. On the day these men are ordered into battle, those sitting have tears soaking their collars, and those lying on their backs have tears crossing on their cheeks. But throw them into a situation where there is no way out and they will show the courage of any Chuan Chu or Ts'ao Kuei.[199]

Therefore, those who are expert at employing the military are like the "sudden striker." The "sudden striker" is a snake indigenous to Mount Heng.[200] If you strike its head, its tail comes to its aid; if you strike its tail, its head comes to its aid; if you strike its middle, both head and tail come to its aid.[201]

Suppose I am asked: Can troops be trained to be like this "sudden striker" snake? I would reply: They can. The men of Wu and Yüeh hate each other. Yet if they were crossing the river in the same boat and were caught by gale winds, they would go to each other's aid like the right hand helping the left.

For this reason, it has never been enough to depend on tethered horses and buried chariot wheels.[202] The object (*tao*) of military management is to effect a unified standard of courage. The principle of exploiting terrain is to get value from the soft as well as the hard.[203] Thus the expert in using the military leads his legions as though he were leading one person by the hand. The person cannot but follow.

As for the urgent business of the commander:

He is calm and remote, correct and disciplined. He is able to blinker the ears and eyes of his officers and men, and to keep people ignorant. He makes changes in his arrangements and alters his plans, keeping people in the dark.[204] He changes his camp, and takes circuitous routes, keeping people from anticipating him. On the day he leads his troops into battle, it is like climbing up high and throwing away the ladder. He leads his troops deep into the territory of the neighboring states and releases the trigger.[205] Like herding a flock of sheep, he drives them this way and that, so no one knows where they are going. He assembles the rank and file of his armies, and throws them into danger.

This then is the urgent business of the commander.

The measures needed to cope with the nine kinds of terrain, the advantages that can be gained by flexibility in maneuvering the army, and the basic patterns of the human character must all be thoroughly investigated.

The general methods of operation (*tao*) for an invading force are:

The deeper you penetrate into enemy territory, the

greater the cohesion of your troops; the more shallow the penetration, the more easily you are scattered. When you quit your own territory and lead your troops across the border, you have entered cut-off terrain. When you are vulnerable on all four sides, you are at a strategically vital intersection. When you have penetrated deep into enemy territory, you are on critical terrain; when you have penetrated only a short distance, you are on marginal terrain. When your back is to heavily secured ground, and you face a narrow defile, you are on terrain vulnerable to ambush. When you have nowhere to turn, you are on terrain with no way out.

Therefore, on terrain where the troops are easily scattered, I would work to make them one of purpose; on marginal terrain, I would keep the troops together; on contested terrain, I would pick up the pace of our rear divisions;[206] on intermediate terrain, I would pay particular attention to defense; [207] at a strategically vital intersection, I would make sure of my alliances;[208] on critical terrain, I would maintain a continuous line of provisions;[209] on difficult terrain, I would continue the advance along the road; on terrain vulnerable to ambush, I would block off the paths of access and retreat; on terrain from which there is no way out, I would show our troops my resolve to fight to the death.

Thus the psychology of the soldier[210] is:

Resist when surrounded,
Fight when you have to,
And obey orders explicitly when in danger.

160

Unless you know the intentions of the rulers of the neighboring states, you cannot enter into preparatory alliances with them;[211] unless you know the lay of the land (*hsing*)— its mountains and forests, its passes and natural hazards, its wetlands and swamps—you cannot deploy the army on it; unless you can employ local scouts, you cannot turn the terrain to your advantage.[212] If an army is ignorant of even one of these several points, it is not the army of a king or a hegemon.[213]

When the army of a king or hegemon attacks a large state, it does not allow the enemy to assemble his forces; when it brings its prestige and influence to bear on the enemy, it prevents his allies from joining with him. For this reason, one need not contend for alliances with the other states in the empire or try to promote one's own place vis-à-vis these states. If you pursue your own program, and bring your prestige and influence to bear on the enemy, you can take his walled cities and lay waste to his state.

Confer extraordinary rewards and post extraordinary orders, and you can command the entire army as if it were but one man. Give the troops their charges, but do not reveal your plans; get them to face the dangers, but do not reveal the advantages.[214] Only if you throw them into life-and-death situations will they survive; only if you plunge them into places where there is no way out will they stay alive. Only if the rank and file have plunged into danger can they turn defeat into victory.

Therefore, the business of waging war lies in carefully studying the designs of the enemy.[215]

> Focus your strength on the enemy
> And you can slay his commander at a thousand *li*.

This is called realizing your objective by your wits and your skill.

For this reason, on the day a declaration of war is made, close off the passes, destroy all instruments of agreement, and forbid any further contact with enemy emissaries. Rehearse your plans thoroughly in the ancestral temple and finalize your strategy. When the enemy gives you the opening, you must rush in on him. Go first for something that he cannot afford to lose, and do not let him know the timing of your attack. Revise your strategy according to the changing posture of the enemy to determine the course and outcome of the battle.[216] For this reason,

> At first be like a modest maiden,
> And the enemy will open his door;
> Afterward be as swift as a scurrying rabbit,
> And the enemy will be too late to resist you.

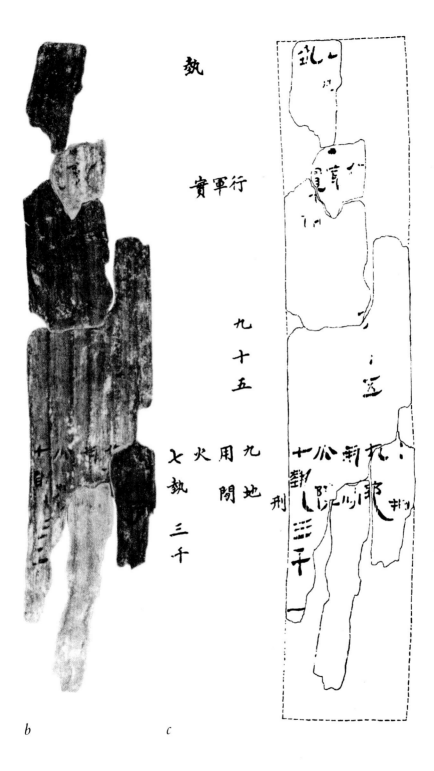

執

行軍實

九十五

九地　用閒　火　七
　　　　　　　　熱　三千

b　　　　　　c

7. *A bronze drum of the Han period.*

8. *Rear and front views of an iron-scale armor helmet of the Late Warring States period.*

9. *Details of the armor from the life-size pottery army from the Lin-t'ung excavation near the tomb of Ch'in Shih-huang. Late third century* B.C.

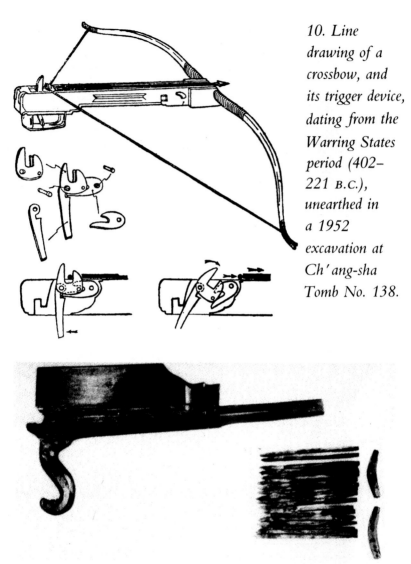

10. Line drawing of a crossbow, and its trigger device, dating from the Warring States period (402–221 B.C.), unearthed in a 1952 excavation at Ch'ang-sha Tomb No. 138.

11. A Late Warring States era magazine-loading crossbow which fired two bolts at a time. The small crescent-shaped objects are the bow. This short-range weapon carried nearly twenty bolts and was probably intended for close-in defense, i.e., it was the equivalent of a sawed-off shotgun. The grip on the left is at the front of the weapon and the short bows were mounted above it.

火攻篇

孫子曰：凡火攻有五：一曰火人，二曰火積（積），三曰火輜，四曰火庫，五曰火隊。行火必有因，因必素具。發火有時，起火有日。時者，天之燥也；日者，月在箕、壁、翼、軫也。凡此四宿者，風起之日也。凡火攻，必因五火之變而應之。火發於內，則早應之於外。火發其兵靜而勿攻，極其火央，可從而從之，不可從而止之。火可發於外，無寺（待）於內，以時發之。火發上風，無攻下風。晝風久，夜風止。凡軍必知有五火之變，以數守之。故以火佐攻者明，以水佐攻者強。水可以絕，不可以奪。夫戰勝攻取，而不修其功者，凶，命曰費留。故曰：明主慮之，良將修之，非利不動，非得不用，非危不戰。主不可以怒而興軍，將不可以溫（慍）而戰。合乎利而動，不合於利而止。怒可復喜，溫（慍）可復悅，亡國不可以復存，死者不可以復生。故明主慎之，良將警之，此安國全軍之道也。

164

CHAPTER 12: INCENDIARY ATTACK

Master Sun said:

There are five kinds of incendiary attack: The first is called setting fire to personnel; the second, to stores; the third, to transport vehicles and equipment; the fourth, to munitions; the fifth, to supply installations.

In order to use fire there must be some inflammable fuel (*yin*), and such fuel must always be kept in readiness.[217] There are appropriate seasons for using fire, and appropriate days that will help fan the flames. The appropriate season is when the weather is hot and dry; the appropriate days are those when the moon passes through the constellations of the Winnowing Basket, the Wall, the Wings, and the Chariot Platform.[218] Generally these four constellations mark days when the winds rise.

With the incendiary attack, you must vary your response to the enemy according to (*yin*) the different changes in his situation induced by each of the five kinds of attack. When the fire is set within the enemy's camp, respond from without at the earliest possible moment. If in spite of the outbreak of fire, the enemy's troops remain calm, bide your time and do not attack. Let the fire reach its height, and if you can follow through, do so. If you cannot, stay where you are. If you are able to raise a fire from outside, do not wait to get inside, but set it when the time is right. If the fire is set from upwind, do not attack from downwind. If the wind blows persistently during the day, it will die down at night.[219] In all cases an army must understand the changes induced by the five kinds of incendiary attack, and make use of logistical calculations to address them.

> He who uses fire to aid the attack is powerful;
> He who uses water to aid the attack is forceful.[220]
> Water can be used to cut the enemy off,
> But cannot be used to deprive him of his supplies.[221]

To be victorious in battle and win the spoils, and yet fail to exploit your achievement, is disastrous. The name for it is wasting resources.

Thus it is said:

> The farsighted ruler thinks the situation through
>   carefully;
> The good commander exploits it fully.
> If there is no advantage, do not move into action;
> If there is no gain, do not deploy the troops;
> If it is not critical, do not send them into battle.

A ruler cannot mobilize his armies in a rage; a commander cannot incite a battle in the heat of the moment.[222] Move if it is to your advantage; bide your time if it is not. A person in a fit of rage can be restored to good humor and a person in the heat of passion can be restored to good cheer, but a state that has perished cannot be revived, and the dead cannot be brought back to life. Thus the farsighted ruler approaches battle with prudence, and the good commander moves with caution. This is the way (*tao*) to keep the state secure and to preserve the army intact.

用間篇

孫子曰：凡興師十萬，出征千里，百生（姓）之費，公家之奉，日費千金，內外騷動，怠於道路，不得操事者，七十萬家。相守數年，以爭一日之勝，而愛爵祿百金，不知適（敵）之請（情）者，不仁之至也，非民之將也，非主之佐也，非勝之注（主）也。故明君賢將，所以動而勝人，成功出於衆者，先知也。先知者，不可取於鬼神，不可象於事，不可驗於度，必取於人，知敵之情者也。故用間有五：有鄉間、有內間、有反間、有死間、有生間。五間俱起，莫知其道，是謂神紀，人君之葆（寶）也。鄉間者，因其鄉人而用之。內間者，因其官人而用之。反間者，因其敵間而用之。死間者，爲誑事於外，令吾間知之，而傳於敵間也。生間者，反報也。故三軍之親，莫親於間，賞莫厚於間，事莫密於間。非聖不能用間，非仁不能使間，非微妙不能得間之實。微戈（哉）微戈（哉），毋（無）所不用間也。間事未發，而先聞者，間與所告者皆死。凡軍之所欲擊，城之所欲攻，人之所欲殺，必先知其守將、左右、謁者、門者、舍人之姓名，令吾間必索知之。必索敵人之間來間我者，因而利之，導而舍之，故反間可得而用也。因是而知之，故鄉間、內間可得而使也；因是而知之，故死間爲誑事，可使告敵；因是而知之，故生間可使如期。五間之事，主必知之，知之必在於反間，故反間不可不厚也。昔殷之興也，伊摯在夏；周之興也，呂牙在殷。故唯明君賢將，能以上智爲間者，必成大功，此兵之要，三軍之所恃而動也。

CHAPTER 13: USING SPIES

Master Sun said:

In general, the cost to the people and to the public coffers to mobilize an army of 100,000 and dispatch it on a punitory expedition of a thousand *li* is a thousand pieces of gold per day. There will be upheaval at home and abroad, with people trekking exhausted on the roadways and some 700,000 households kept from their work in the fields. Two sides will quarrel with each other for several years in order to fight a decisive battle on a single day. If, begrudging the outlay of ranks, emoluments, and a hundred pieces of gold, a commander does not know the enemy's situation, his is the height of inhumanity. Such a person is no man's commander, no ruler's counsellor, and no master of victory.

Thus the reason the farsighted ruler and his superior commander conquer the enemy at every move, and achieve successes far beyond the reach of the common crowd, is foreknowledge. Such foreknowledge cannot be had from ghosts and spirits, educed by comparison with past events, or verified by astrological calculations. It must come from people—people who know the enemy's situation.

There are five kinds of spies that can be employed:[223] local (*yin*) spies, inside agents, double agents, expendable spies, and unexpendable spies. When the five kinds of spies are all active, and no one knows their methods of operation (*tao*), this is called the imperceptible web,[224] and is the ruler's treasure.

169

Local spies are the enemy's own countrymen in our employ.

Inside agents are enemy officials we employ.

Double agents are enemy spies who report to our side.

Expendable spies are our own agents who obtain false information we have deliberately leaked to them, and who then pass it on to the enemy spies.

Unexpendable spies are those who return from the enemy camp to report.

Thus, of those close to the army command, no one should have more direct access than spies,[225] no one should be more liberally rewarded than spies, and no matters should be held in greater secrecy than those concerning spies.

Only the most sagacious ruler is able to employ spies; only the most humane and just commander is able to put them into service; only the most sensitive and alert person can get the truth out of spies.

So delicate! So secretive! There is nowhere that you cannot put spies to good use. Where a matter of espionage has been divulged prematurely, both the spy and all those he told should be put to death.

In general terms, whether it is armies we want to attack, walled cities we want to besiege, or persons we want to assassinate, it is necessary to first know the identities of the defending commander, his retainers, counsellors, gate officers, and sentries. We must direct our agents to find a way to secure this information for us.

It is necessary to find out who the enemy has sent as agents to spy on us. If we take care of them (*yin*) with generous bribes, win them over and send them back,[226] they can thus be brought into our employ as double agents. On the basis of what we learn from (*yin*) these double agents, we can recruit and employ local and inside spies. Also, from (*yin*) this information we will know what false information to feed our expendable spies to pass on to the enemy. Moreover, on what we know from (*yin*) this same source, our unexpendable spies can complete their assignments according to schedule. The ruler must have full knowledge of the covert operations of these five kinds of spies. And since the key to all intelligence is the double agent, this operative must be treated with the utmost generosity.

Of old the rise of the Yin (Shang) dynasty was because of Yi Yin who served the house of Hsia; the rise of the Chou dynasty was because of Lü Ya who served in the house of Shang.[227] Thus only those farsighted rulers and their superior commanders who can get the most intelligent people as their spies are destined to accomplish great things. Intelligence is of the essence in warfare—it is what the armies depend upon in their every move.

SUN-TZU:
PART II

TEXT RECOVERED FROM
THE YIN-CH'ÜEH-SHAN
HAN DYNASTY
STRIPS[228]

吴 問

吴問

吴王問孫子曰：六將軍分守晉國之地，孰先亡？孰固成？孫子曰：范、中行是（氏）先亡。孰爲之次？智是（氏）爲次。韓、巍（魏）爲次。趙毋失其故法，晉國歸焉。吴王曰：其説可得聞乎？孫子曰：可。范、中行是（氏）制田，以八十步爲婉（畹），以百六十步爲畛，而伍税之。其□田陝（狹），置士多，伍税之，公家富。公家富，置士多，主喬（驕）臣奢，冀功數戰，故曰先【亡】……公家富，置士多，主喬（驕）臣奢，冀功數戰，故爲范、中行是（氏）次。韓、巍（魏）制田，以百步爲婉（畹），以二百步爲畛，而伍税【之】。其□田陝（狹），其置士多，伍税之，公家富。公家富，置士多，主喬（驕）臣奢，冀功數戰，故爲智是（氏）次。趙是（氏）制田，以百廿步爲婉（畹），以二百卌步爲畛，公无税焉。公家貧，其置士少，主僉臣收，以御富民，故曰固國。晉國歸焉。吴王曰：善。王者之道，□□厚愛其民者也。二百八十四

1: THE QUESTIONS OF WU

The King of Wu asked Master Sun: "Which of the six commanders[229] who divided up the territory of the state of Chin were the first to perish? And which succeeded in holding on to their lands?"

Master Sun replied: "Fan and Chung-hang were the first to perish."

"Who was next?"

"Chih was next."

"And who was next?"

"Han and Wei were next. It was because Chao did not abandon the traditional laws that the state of Chin turned to him."

The King of Wu said: "Could you explain this to me?" Master Sun replied: "Indeed. In regulating the measurement of land area, Fan and Chung-hang took eighty square paces as a *yüan*, and took one hundred and sixty square paces as a *chen*, and then made five households their basic tax unit.[230] The land area was small and the officials in office were many. With five households as the basic tax unit, the public coffers prospered. With the public coffers prospering and the officials in office many, the ruler became arrogant and his ministers wasteful. And in pursuit of great exploits they embarked on frequent wars. Thus I say they were the first to perish.

"*[In regulating the measurement of land area, Chih took ninety square paces as a* yüan *and took one hundred and eighty square paces as a* chen, *and then made five households his basic tax unit. The land area was also small and the officials in office were also many. With five households as the basic tax unit, the public coffers prospered.*] With the public coffers prospering and the officials in office many, the ruler became arrogant and his ministers wasteful. And in pursuit of great exploits they embarked on frequent wars. Thus I say he was the next to perish after Fan and Chung-hang.

"In regulating the measurement of land area, Han and Wei took one hundred square paces as a *yüan*, and took two hundred square paces as a *chen*, and then made five households their basic tax unit. The land area was again small and the officials in office were again many. With five households as the basic tax unit, the public coffers prospered. With the public coffers prospering and the officials in office many, the ruler became arrogant and his ministers wasteful. And in pursuit of great exploits they embarked on frequent wars. Thus I say they were the next to perish after Chih.

"In regulating the measurement of land area, Chao took one hundred and twenty square paces as a *yüan*, and took two hundred and forty square paces as a *chen*, and so there were no new taxes forthcoming for the public coffers. With the public coffers empty and the officials in office few, the ruler was frugal and his ministers humble in their management of what was a prosperous people. Thus I say that he held on to his lands, and the whole state of Chin turned to him."

The King of Wu said: "Excellent! The way (*tao*) of the True King is [*that he should*] love the people generously."
(284 characters)

四 變

徐（途）有所不由，軍有所不擊，城有所不攻，地有所不爭，君令有所不行，徐（途）之所不由者，曰：淺入則前事不信，深入則後利不棲（接）。動則不利，立則囚。如此者，弗由也。軍之所不毄（擊）者，曰：兩軍交和而舍，計吾力足以破其軍，獵其將。遠計之，有奇埶（勢）巧權於它，而軍……□將。如此者，軍唯（雖）可毄（擊），弗毄（擊）也。 城之所不攻者，曰：計吾力足以拔之，拔之而不及利於前，得之而後弗能守。若力〔不〕足，城必不取。及於前，利得而城自降，利不得而不爲害於後。若此者，城唯（雖）可攻，弗攻也。地之所不爭者，曰：山谷水□无能生者，□□……虛。如此者，弗爭也。 君令有所不行者，君令有反此四變者，則□而□□……變者，則智（知）用兵矣。□□□□□□□□行也。事……弗行也。

2: [THE FOUR CONTINGENCIES][231]

[*There are roadways not to be traveled, armies not to be attacked,*] walled cities not to be assaulted, territory not to be contested, and commands from the ruler [*not to be obeyed*].

That there are roadways not to be traveled refers to a roadway where if we penetrate only a short distance we cannot bring the operations of our vanguard into full play, and if we penetrate too deeply we cannot link up effectively with our rearguard. If we move, it is not to our advantage, and if we stop, we will be captured. Given these conditions, we do not travel it.

That there are armies not to be attacked refers to a situation in which the two armies make camp and face off. We estimate we have enough strength to crush the opposing army and to capture its commander. Taking the long view, however, there is some surprise advantage (*shih*) and clever dodge he has, so his army . . . its commander. Given these conditions, even though we can attack, we do not do so.

That there are walled cities not to be assaulted refers to a situation in which we estimate we have enough strength to take the city. If we take it, it gives us no immediate advantage, and having gotten it, we would not be able to garrison it. If we are [*lacking*] in strength,[232] the walled city must by no means be taken. If in the first instance we gain advantage, the city will surrender of its own accord; and if we do not gain advantage, it will not be a

179

source of harm afterward. Given these conditions, even though we can launch an assault, we do not do so.

That there is territory not to be contested refers to mountains and gorges ... that are not able to sustain life ... vacant. Given these conditions, do not contest it.

That there are commands from the ruler not to be obeyed means that if the commands of the ruler are contrary to these four contingencies, do not obey them ... obey them. Where affairs ... contingencies, one understands how to use troops.

黃帝伐赤帝

孫子曰：【黃帝南伐】赤帝，【至於□□】，戰於反山之原，右陰，順術，倍（背）衝，大威（滅）有之。【□年】休民，埶（熟）穀，赦罪。東伐□帝，至於襄平，戰於平□，【右】陰，順術，倍（背）衝，大威（滅）【有之】。□年休民，埶（熟）穀，赦罪。

北伐黑帝，至於武隧，戰於□□，右陰，順術，倍衝，大威有之。□年休民，埶（熟）穀，赦罪。　西伐白帝，至於武剛，戰於□□，右陰，順術，倍衝，大威有之。已勝四帝，大有天下，暴者……以利天下，天下四面歸之。湯之伐桀也，【至於□□】，戰於薄田，右陰，順術，倍（背）衝，大威（滅）有之。武王之伐紂，至於鏿遂，戰牧之野，右陰，順術，倍（背）衝，大威有之。一帝二王皆得天之道、□之□、民之請（情），

故……

3: THE YELLOW EMPEROR
ATTACKS THE RED EMPEROR[233]

Master Sun said: [*The Yellow Emperor to the south attacked the Red Emperor, penetrated as far as . . .*] and did battle on the steppes of Mount Pan.[234] Advancing with the *yin* conditions on his right, following the roadway, and keeping his back to strategic ground[235] he exterminated the enemy and annexed his territory. For [. . . *years*] he gave his people respite, allowed the grains to ripen, and gave amnesty to the criminals.

Then to the east he attacked the [*Green*] Emperor, penetrated as far as Hsiang-p'ing, and did battle at P'ing. . . . Advancing with the *yin* conditions [*on his right*], following the roadway, and keeping his back to strategic ground, he exterminated the enemy [*and annexed his territory. For . . .*] years he gave his people respite, allowed the grains to ripen, and gave amnesty to the criminals.

Then to the north he attacked the Black Emperor, penetrated as far as Wu-sui, and did battle at . . . Advancing with the *yin* conditions on his right, following the roadway, [*and keeping his back to strategic ground, he exterminated the enemy and annexed his territory. For . . . years he gave his people respite, allowed the grains to ripen, and gave amnesty to the criminals*].

Then to the west he attacked the White Emperor, penetrated as far as Wu-kang, and did battle at [. . . *Advancing with the* yin *conditions on his right, following the roadway, and keeping his back to strategic ground, he exterminated the enemy*

183

and annexed] his territory. Having defeated the four emperors he ruled over all under heaven. The violent . . . for the advantage of the empire, and the people under heaven from all four directions turned to him.

When King T'ang of Shang attacked King Chieh of Hsia, [*he penetrated as far as* . . .], and did battle at Po-t'ien. Advancing with the *yin* conditions on his right, following the roadway, and keeping his back to strategic ground, he exterminated the enemy and annexed his territory.

When King Wu of Chou attacked King Chou of Shang, he penetrated as far as Shu-sui, and did battle on the fields of Mu. Advancing with the *yin* conditions on his right, following the roadway, [*and keeping his back to strategic ground, he exterminated the enemy*] and annexed his territory.

This one emperor and these two kings all realized the way (*tao*) of heaven, . . . the basic nature of the people. Thus . . .

地形 二

【□】地刑（形）東方爲左，西方爲【右

□】……

首，地平用左，軍……

地也。交□水□……

者，死地也。産草者□……

地剛者，毋□□□也……

【天】離、天井、天宛□……

是胃（謂）重利。前之，是胃（謂）獻守。右之，是胃（謂）天固。左之，是胃

（謂）……

所居高曰建堂，□曰□□【□】□遂左水曰利，右水曰積……

□五月度□地，七月□……

三軍出陳（陣），不問朝夕，右負丘陵，左前水澤，順者……

九地之法，人請（情）之里（理），不可不□……

186

4: THE DISPOSITION
[OF THE TERRAIN] II[236]

. . . in the disposition of terrain, east is left and west is [*right*] . . .

. . . head, on terrain that is flat, use the left, and the army . . .

. . . is terrain from which there is no way out. Places that produce grasses . . .

. . . the ground is hard, do not . . .

. . . [*natural*] net, natural well, and natural prison . . .[237]

. . . This is called an important advantage. If it is in front, this is called a concealed guard; if it is on the right, it is called a natural fortification; if it is on the left, it is called . . .

. . . what dwells on high is said to be the Constant Hall, . . . is said to be . . .

. . . follow, water on the left is said to be advantageous, and water on the right is said to be pent up . . .

. . . when the army enters into formation, regardless of the time of day, on the right flank to its back should be rises and hills, and on its left flank to its front should be waters and marshes. Those who follow . . .

. . . the measures needed to cope with the nine kinds of terrain, and the basic patterns of the human character must all be [*thoroughly investigated*.][238]

【見吳王】

……□於孫子之館，曰：不穀好……

乎？不穀之好兵□□□□□兵者與（歟）？孫……

也。兵，□〔也〕，非戲也。□□□之□□□□也，適之好之也。孫……

聞道也，不敢趣之利與……君王以好與戲問之，外臣不敢對。蓋（盍）曰：兵，利也，非好

婦人可也。試男於右，□□□孫子曰：唯君王之所欲，以貴者可也，賤者可也，

曰：婦人多所不忍，臣請代……畏，有何悔乎？孫子曰：不穀願（願）以婦人。孫子

之國左後璽圉之中，以爲二陳□□……□曰：陳（陣）未成，不足見也。及

已成，□□不辟（辭）其難。君曰：若（諾）。孫子以其御爲……參乘爲輿司

空，告其御、參乘曰：□□□□□婦人而告之曰：知女（汝）右手？……之。知女

（汝）心？曰：知之。知女（汝）北（背）？曰：知之。……左手。□胃（謂）女（汝）前，

從女（汝）心？……□不從令者也。七周而澤（釋）之，鼓而前

之……【三告而】五申之，鼓而前之，婦人亂而□□□金而坐之，有（又）三告而五

申之，鼓而前之，婦人亂而笑。三告而五申之者三矣，而令猶不行。孫子乃召其

司馬與輿司空而告之曰：兵法曰：弗令弗聞，君將之罪也；已令已申，卒長之罪

也。兵法曰：賞善始賤，罰……□請謝之。孫子曰：君□……引而員（圓）之，

190

5: [AN INTERVIEW WITH THE KING OF WU][239]

[EDITOR'S NOTE: This passage is similar in content to the story recorded in the *Historical Records* biography of Sun Wu, where he has an interview with King Ho-lu of Wu and where he applies his military arts to discipline the court beauties. See the section entitled "Sun Wu as a Historical Person" in the Introduction above.

In comparing these two accounts, to the extent that they overlap, the language in the *Historical Records* biography is more summary, and also more polished. The account preserved in the archaeological dig is more didactic, portraying Sun Wu as a serious-minded teacher addressing King Ho-lu of Wu in a way reminiscent of Mencius's lecturing King Hui of Liang in the opening chapter of the *Mencius*. The surface difference between Sun Wu and Mencius is that Sun Wu espouses a positive position on "advantage" where Mencius condemns it. Sun Wu makes a distinction between pursuing "advantage" in warfare that redounds to the national good, and treating the brutality of warfare as a kind of royal blood sport. Mencius, on the other hand, rejects "advantage" as an unworthy consideration for a ruler when morality should be his first and major concern. Both Sun Wu and Mencius at a more fundamental level would agree that warfare, taking its toll in lives and property, is invariably a national sacrifice, and must be pursued only as a last and unavoidable resort.

We can speculate that the *Historical Records* might be a

191

員（圓）中規，引而方之，方中巨（矩）。……蓋（闔）廬六日不自□□□□□……

□□□孫子再拜而起曰：道得矣。……□□□長遠近習此教也，以爲恒命。

素教也，將之道也。民……□莫貴於威。　威行於眾，嚴行於吏，三軍信其將畏

（威）者，乘其適（敵）。

而用之，□□□得矣。　若□十三扁（篇）所……

【十】三扁（篇）所明道言功也，誠將聞□……

【孫】子曰：「古（姑）試之，得而用之，無不□……

□而試之□得□……

□□□之孫子曰：「外內貴賤得矣。」孫

【孫】子曰：「唯……

也，君王居臺上而侍（待）之，」臣……

□至日中請令……

人主也。　若夫發令而從，不聽者誅□□……

□也。　請合之於□□之於……

陳（陣）已成矣，教□□聽……

□不穀請學之。」爲終食而□……

將軍□不穀不敢不□……

192

revised version of an earlier and more primitive account similar to the one preserved here.

The references to the "thirteen chapters" and *The Art of Warfare* indicate that both versions of this story are later than the core text.]

. . . to Master Sun's guest house, the King of Wu asked: "I am fond of . . . the use of the military?" Again he inquired: "Sun . . . ? My fondness for using the military . . . is using them properly and being fond of them."

Master Sun replied: "Using the military is to gain the advantage; it is not a matter of being fond of it. Using the military is to . . . ; it is not a matter of sport. If Your Majesty wants to ask about war in terms of fondness and sport, I dare not reply."

King Ho-lu said: "I have never been told about the way of warfare; I dare not go after advantage and . . ."

Master Sun responded: "It is only important that it be what Your Majesty wants to do. We can use noble persons, we can use common folk, we can use your court ladies. We will train the men on the right and the ladies on the left. . . ."

[*King Ho-lu*] said: "I want to use my court ladies."

Master Sun replied: "Many of the court ladies lack the stamina. I would rather use . . ."

[*King Ho-lu replied*:] ". . . awe, what is there to regret?"

Master Sun said: "In that case, then from your palace please let me have . . . , to go to the outer hunting park to the east side of the capital . . . , and get them to form two lines. . . ."

[*Master Sun*] said: "When they have not yet been drilled in their formations, they are not ready for parade. Once

193

they have been drilled, . . . cannot excuse their difficulties. [*Could Your Majesty please go to the high balcony and wait there for us? . . . at midday I will ask for Your orders. Once they have been drilled in their formations, following commands . . . not . . . not difficult.*]"240

The ruler replied: "I consent."

Master Sun used his chariot driver as [*his major*] and his arms bearer as field officer, and instructed the driver and the arms bearer, saying: ". . ."

[*Master Sun then turned to*] the court ladies and instructed them, saying: "Do you know which is your right hand?"

"[*We know*] it, [*they replied*]."

"Do you know your heart?"

"We know it," they replied.

"Do you know your back?"

"We know it," they replied.

[*"Do you know which is your left hand?"*

"We know it," they replied.]

. . . "[*When I tell you 'Left,' follow the direction of*] your left hand. When I tell you 'Front,' follow the direction of your heart. When I tell you [*'Back,' follow the direction of your back. When I tell you 'Right,' follow the direction of your right hand.*] . . . it is your life. [*But my commands are to be obeyed. Those who do not obey will be executed . . .*]241 . . . those who do not obey commands. Having circled seven times, fall out. On hearing the drums, advance . . ."

Going through and explaining his commands several times, he then drummed for them to advance, but the court ladies being all out of place, [*they broke into laughter*] . . . Striking the gong, he had them kneel. Again going through and explaining his commands several times, he drummed

194

for them to advance, but the court ladies were all out of place, and broke into laughter. Three times he went through and explained his commands, but still his orders were not carried out. Master Sun then summoned his major and his field commander, and told them: "It says in *The Art of Warfare*: If one does not order them, or if one's orders are not understood, it is the fault of the commander. If one has already issued orders and has explained them, it is the fault of the field officers. *The Art of Warfare* also says: In rewarding the good, begin from the lowliest; in punishing . . ."

[*King Ho-lu said:*] ". . . please excuse them."

Master Sun replied: "The ruler . . ."

. . . [*Master Sun said:*] "Now if you direct them to assume a circular formation, their circle will satisfy the compass; if you direct them to assume a square formation, their square will satisfy the set square."

. . . for six days King Ho-lu did not . . .

. . . Master Sun, bowing several times, arose and said: "You now know the way of warfare . . . far and near practice this doctrine, and take it as their constant rule. This unadorned doctrine is the way of the commander. For the masses . . . nothing is more exalted than authority. If the commander acts with authority over his men and enforces discipline among his officers, the entire army will have faith in his authority, and will conquer the enemy."

. . . and use it, . . . will get. As the thirteen chapters . . .

. . . the way elucidated and the attainments spoken of in the thirteen chapters is really what the commander told . . .

———

... Master Sun said: "In the meantime we will try them, and if they get it we will use them. There is nothing that is not ...

... and try them ... getting ...

... to Master Sun, and said: "We have those within and without and the noble and the base." Master Sun ...

"... I, your ruler, would like to practice it." For the duration of the meal ...

"... the commander, I would not dare to not ...

SUN-TZU: PART III

TEXT RECOVERED FROM LATER WORKS

[EDITOR'S NOTE: The textual materials that comprise Part III are passages recovered from later encyclopedic works and commentaries. I have grouped these passages into "chapters," sometimes on the basis of a shared theme, and sometimes because they come from the same source or archaeological site. The specific reference for each passage is indicated in the endnotes.]

(i)★

吳王問孫武曰：散地，士卒顧家，不可與戰，則必固守不出。敵攻我小城，掠吾田野，禁吾樵採，塞吾要道，待吾空虛而急來攻，則如之何？武曰：敵人深入吾都，多背城邑，士卒以軍爲家，專志輕鬪。吾兵在國，安土懷生，以陣則不堅，以鬪則不勝，當集人衆，聚穀蓄帛，保城備險，遣輕兵絶其糧道。彼挑戰不得，轉輸不至，野無所掠，三軍困餒，因而誘之，可以有功。若與戰，必因勢。勢者，依險設伏，無險則隱於天陰暗昏霧，出其不意，襲擊懈怠。

★The topic of this passage, "scattering terrain," is defined in Chapter 11 above: "Where a feudal ruler does battle within his own territory, it is a terrain that permits the scattering of his troops." Master Sun is explicit in his warning, "On scattering terrain do not fight."

The King of Wu enquired of Sun Wu, saying: "If on 'scattering terrain' my officers and men are thinking of their homes, and cannot engage the enemy in battle, we must consolidate our defenses, and not go out against him. If the enemy then attacks our smaller walled cities, plunders our fields and meadowlands, prevents us from gathering our crops, blocks off our main thoroughfares, and, waiting until we have nothing left, attacks us in earnest, then what are we to do?"

Sun Wu replied: "If the enemy has penetrated deep into our territory, many of our walled cities and towns will be to his back. His officers and men will take the army as family, and with a united resolve, will think nothing of going to battle. But our troops are fighting on the home front, are comfortable on their native soil and have a great love of life. If you deploy them in a defensive position, they are not solid; if you send them into battle, they will not win.

"You should assemble a large number of troops, lay in ample provisions, stockpile cloth, fortify your walled cities, and guard the strategic passes. Dispatch light infantry to cut off the enemy's supply lines. If he tries to provoke an engagement do not give it to him. His supply wagons will not get through, and the countryside will have nothing left for him to pillage. With his whole army in the grips of hunger, you can succeed in drawing him into a blind. If you engage him in battle, you must make the most of strategic advantage (*shih*). Making the most of strategic advantage (*shih*) means occupying the key passes and lying in ambush. Where there is no such terrain, hide in the shadows and the mist, go by way of places where it would never occur to him you would go, and attack him when he is off his guard."

吳王問孫武曰：吾至輕地，始入敵境，士卒思還，難進易退；未背險阻，
三軍恐懼；大將欲進，士卒欲退，上下異心。而敵盛守，修其城壘，整其
車騎，或當吾前，或擊吾後，則如之何？孫武曰：軍入敵境，敵人固壘
不戰，士卒思歸，欲退且難，謂之輕地。當選驍騎伏要路，我退敵追，
來則擊之。軍在輕地，士卒未專以入爲務，無以戰爲。故無近其名城，無
由其通路，設疑佯惑，示若將去。乃選驍騎，銜枚先入，掠其牛馬六畜。三
軍見得進，乃不懼。分吾良卒，密有所伏，敵人若來，擊之勿疑；若其不
至，捨之而去。

"The King of Wu enquired of Sun Wu, saying: "We have reached marginal terrain, and have begun to press into enemy territory. Officers and men alike are thinking of the

★The topic of this passage, "marginal terrain," is defined in Chapter 11 above: "Where one has penetrated only barely into enemy territory, it is marginal terrain." Master Sun is explicit in his warning, "Do not stay on marginal terrain."

return home; it is hard to advance, and so easy to withdraw. With no passes or natural hazards to their backs, the armies are fearful. The commanders want to advance, and their officers and men want to withdraw; superiors and subordinates are of two minds. Moreover, the enemy is amply defended. He has reinforced his walled cities and fortifications, and strengthened his chariot and mounted detachments. With some of his forces blocking our front and others attacking us from the rear, what are we to do?"

Sun Wu replied: "[*A situation in which our troops have entered enemy territory, the enemy is secure behind his walls and does not bring the battle to us, our officers and men are thinking of the return home, and for us to withdraw would be difficult indeed is called occupying marginal terrain. We should select our elite mounted troops and place them in ambush on the main thoroughfare. As we withdraw, the enemy will give us chase, and when they reach us, we attack them.*]²⁴³ When an army is on marginal terrain, the officers and men are not one in spirit, they are doing what they must only because they are on enemy ground, and are going into battle without the heart for it. Therefore, do not approach the enemy's major walled cities, and do not advance on his main thoroughfares. Set up decoys and feign confusion, and give the enemy the impression we are about to quit our position. Then select our elite mounted troops, and send them on ahead into enemy territory under a cloak of silence to seize cattle, horses, and livestock. When our armies see the spoils, they will be ready to advance without fear. Separate off our best troops and lay them secretly in ambush. If the enemy comes, attack him in full fury; if he does not, break camp and quit the position."

又問曰：爭地，敵先至，據要保利，簡兵練卒，或出或守，以備我奇，則如之何？武曰：爭地之法，讓之者得，求之者失。敵得其處，慎勿攻之。引而佯走，建旗鳴鼓，趣其所愛，曳柴揚塵，惑其耳目；分吾良卒，密有所伏，敵必出救，人欲我與，人棄吾取，此爭先之道。若我先至而敵用此術，則選吾銳卒，固守其所，輕兵追之，分伏險阻，敵人還鬥，伏兵旁起，此全勝之道也。

The King of Wu enquired of Sun Wu, saying: "The enemy has been first to reach contested terrain, has taken up key strategic positions and has secured the advantageous

*The topic of this passage, "contested terrain," is defined in Chapter 11 above: "Ground that gives us or the enemy the advantage in occupying it is contested terrain." Master Sun is explicit in his warning, "Do not attack the enemy on contested terrain."

ground. In an effort to check our mounted detachments, he then dispatches some of his select troops and crack officers to attack us while others are kept defending their position. What are we to do?"

Sun Wu replied: "The principle governing contested terrain is that if you let the enemy have it, you can get it, but if you try to get it, you will lose it. If the enemy has occupied the contested terrain, move carefully and do not attack him. Feign retreat and withdraw. Set up the flags and sound the drums, and hasten to the enemy's most vital points. Drag brush behind the troops and raise the dust to confuse the ears and eyes of the enemy. Separate off our best troops and lay them secretly in ambush. The enemy must come out to the rescue. What he wants we give him, and what he abandons we take. This is the way of contested terrain.

"If we are first to arrive, and the enemy tries to use this strategy on us, select out our finest troops and reinforce the defenses of our position, and send our light infantry in pursuit. Deploy a detachment to lay in ambush in some difficult stretch of terrain, and when the enemy comes out to meet our pursuing force, our concealed troops launch an attack from both sides. This is the way to take the complete victory."

(iv)*

又問曰：武曰：交地，吾將絕敵，令不得來，必全吾邊城，修其所備，深絕通道，固其阨塞。若不先圖，敵人已備，彼可得來，而吾不可往，衆寡又均，則如之何？武曰：既吾不可以往，彼可以來，吾分卒匿之，守而易怠，示其不能。敵人且至，設伏隱廬，出其不意也。

The King of Wu enquired of Sun Wu, saying: "On intermediate terrain, we want to cut off the enemy line and prevent him from advancing. We must preserve our border

*The topic of this passage, "intermediate terrain," is defined in Chapter 11 above: "Ground accessible to both sides is intermediate terrain." Master Sun is explicit in his warning, "Do not get cut off on intermediate terrain."

walled cities intact and fortify their defenses, make a deep cut in the main road and reinforce our hazards and block-ades. What if we have not planned in advance and the enemy is already prepared, so he can advance at will and yet we cannot get away? Where the numerical strength of our armies is about the same, what are we to do?"

Sun Wu replied: "Since we cannot leave and yet the enemy can come at will, we deploy a detachment and secrete the men in ambush. We are vigilant in our defenses, but give the enemy the impression we are not up to battle. Then when the enemy arrives, our troops in ambush will appear from hiding places where it would never occur to the enemy they would."

(v)*

又問曰：衢地必先，吾道遠，發後，雖馳車驟馬，至不能先，則如之何？　武曰：諸侯參屬，其道四通，我與敵相當，而傍有國。所謂先者，必重幣輕使，約和傍國，交親結恩，兵雖後至，衆以屬矣。　簡兵練卒，阻利而處，親吾軍事，實吾資糧，令吾軍騎出入瞻候。我有衆助，彼失其黨，諸國犄角，震鼓齊攻，敵人驚恐，莫知所當。

*The topic of this passage, the "strategically vital intersection," is defined in Chapter 11 above: "The territory of several neighboring states at which their borders meet is a strategically vital intersection. The first to reach it will gain the allegiance of the other states of the empire." Master Sun is explicit in his injunction, "Form alliances with the neighboring states at strategically vital intersections."

The King of Wu enquired of Sun Wu, saying: "The strategically vital intersection must be reached before the enemy forces, but our road is long and we have gotten under way after the enemy. If, even with racing our chariots and galloping our horses, we cannot possibly reach the intersection before the enemy, what are we to do?"

Sun Wu replied: "The territories of our neighboring rulers border on three sides and our thoroughfares go in all four directions. Our military strength is about the same as the enemy's, but there are other neighboring states involved. What is meant by arriving first is we must send lavish gifts by swift envoys and effect alliances with our neighboring states, so that relationships are intimate and there is mutual good will. Even if our armies arrive after the enemy, we are more numerous by virtue of these alliances. Dispatch our select troops and crack officers to check enemy operations and get the upper hand. People sympathetic to our troops will provide us with the full complement of supplies and provisions, and will act as lookouts for our chariots and mounted troops in their comings and goings. While we have abundant support, the enemy will have lost all those who might have sided with him. The neighboring states will be one flank in our united front, the sound of our drums will rock the heavens, and we will attack as one. The enemy will be alarmed, and will not know how to respond."

又問曰：吾引兵深入重地，多所踰越，糧道絕塞，設欲歸還，勢不可過。欲食於敵，持兵不失，則如之何？　武曰：凡居重地，士卒輕勇，轉輸不通，則掠以繼食。下得粟帛，皆貢於上，多者有賞，士無歸意。若欲還出，切爲戒備，深溝高壘，示敵且久，敵疑通途，私除要害之道，乃令輕車銜枚而行，塵埃氣揚，以牛馬爲餌。敵人若出，鳴鼓隨之，陰伏吾士，與之中期。内外相應，其敗可知。

The King of Wu enquired of Sun Wu, saying: "Our forces have pushed deep into critical terrain and have passed

★The topic of this passage, "critical terrain," is defined in Chapter 11 above: "When an army has penetrated deep into enemy territory, and has many of the enemy's walled cities and towns at its back, it is on critical terrain." Master Sun is explicit in his injunction, "Plunder the enemy's resources on critical terrain."

by many of the enemy's cities and towns. Our supply lines have been cut off and stopped. If we try to go back now, there is no way we will make it. If we try to feed off of the enemy, he is sure to put up a fight. What then are we to do?"

Sun Wu replied: "Generally when an army has occupied critical terrain, the officers and men rely on courage in pressing ahead. If the supply lines are broken, they plunder to provision themselves. If the rank and file get grain or cloth, it is all handed over to the superiors. When many receive rewards, the men will have no thought of going back. If we intend to launch another attack, we must be thoroughly prepared with deep ditches and high barriers, giving the enemy the impression it will be a long and protracted battle. If the enemy doubts our capacity to move on his roads, he himself will recall his troops from guarding vital arteries. Under a cloak of silence we can then dispatch a detachment of light chariots at the quick. Under the cover of a cloud of dust, we can use horses and cattle to bait him. If the enemy sends his troops out, sound the drums and go after him. Conceal our troops, and when the enemy has walked into the ambush, fall on him from all sides. His defeat is assured."

又問曰：吾入圮地，山川險阻，難從之道，行久卒勞，敵在吾前而伏吾後，營居吾左而守吾右，良車驍騎，要吾隘道，則如之何？武曰：先進輕車，去軍十里，與敵相候，接期險阻。或分而左，或分而右，大將四觀，擇空而取，皆會中道，倦而乃止。

The King of Wu enquired of Sun Wu, saying: "We have entered difficult terrain and, with the mountains and

★The topic of this passage, "difficult terrain," is defined in Chapter 11 above: "Mountains and forests, passes and hazards, wetlands and swamps, and any such roads hard to traverse constitute difficult terrain." Master Sun is explicit in his injunction, "Press ahead on difficult terrain."

rivers, passes and natural hazards, the road is hard to follow. We have been pressing on for a long time, and our troops are exhausted. The enemy occupies the ground ahead, and has also set an ambush behind us. He has established camp to the left of our forces, and has set up defenses against our right flank. His fine chariots and elite mounted troops threaten our precarious route. What are we to do?"

Sun Wu replied: "First dispatch our light chariots to advance about ten *li* in front of the main force to keep an eye on the enemy. Prepare to engage the enemy in battle amid the passes and natural hazards of this difficult terrain. Divert the troops to the left and to the right. On the signal of the high command, select vulnerable targets and take them, with all of the men regrouping back at the main road. Break off the operation once the troops are exhausted."

(viii)★

又問曰：吾入圍地，前有強敵，後有險難，敵絕我糧道，利我走勢，敵鼓噪不進，以觀吾能，則如之何？武曰：圍地之宜，必塞其闕，示無所往，則以軍為家，萬人同心，三軍齊力。并炊數日，無見火烟，故為毀亂寡弱之形。敵人見我，備之必輕。告勵士卒，令其奮怒；陣伏良卒，左右險阻，擊鼓而出。敵人若當，疾擊務突，前鬭後拓，左右犄角。又問曰：敵在吾圍，伏而深謀，示我以利，縈我以旗，紛紛若亂，不知所之，奈何？武曰：千人操旌，分塞要道，輕兵進挑，陣而勿搏，交而勿去，此敗謀之法。

★The topic of this passage, "terrain vulnerable to ambush," is defined in Chapter 11 above: "Ground that gives access through a narrow defile and where exit is tortuous, allowing an enemy in small numbers to attack our main force, is terrain vulnerable to ambush." Master Sun is explicit in his injunction, "Devise contingency plans on terrain vulnerable to ambush."

The King of Wu enquired of Sun Wu, saying: "We have entered terrain vulnerable to ambush. Directly in our path is a formidable enemy, and to our back are natural hazards and rough terrain. The enemy has cut off our supply lines, and wants us to think our best advantage lies in flight. He sounds his drums and raises a hue and cry, yet does not advance on us, trying to gauge our battle strength. What are we to do?"

Sun Wu replied: "On terrain vulnerable to ambush, we must seal off the passes. If we show the men there is nowhere to go, they will take their fellows-at-arms as family, everyone will be united in spirit, and the entire army will fight as one. Prepare several days' provisions at once, but do not let the enemy see the fire and smoke, thus creating the impression that our forces are run-down, disorderly, and few in number. The enemy forces will take our measure, and in preparing against us are sure to think we are of little consequence. Arouse the officers and men, and rally them to rise up in fury against the enemy. Detail our superior fighting men in attack formation and in ambush. With defiles and natural hazards on all sides, sound the battle drums and launch the attack. If the enemy forces offer resistance, lash out at them suddenly and in full fury. Those on the front line carry the fight and those behind buttress them, working together to ram the enemy position."

The King of Wu again enquired: "The enemy has fallen into our ambush, but takes cover and plans his strategy carefully. He offers us some concessions, encircles us with his standards, and mills about as though his ranks are in disorder. We do not know what to make of it. What are we to do?"

Sun Wu replied: "Dispatch a thousand men to take care of the standard bearers, send a detachment to block off the main arteries, and send the light chariots ahead to harass the enemy. Deploy our main force in battle formation, but do not pounce on him. Join him in battle and do not withdraw. This is the way to defeat his strategy."

1. Arrow indicates site of Han tombs numbers 1 and 2 at Silver Sparrow Mountain, Lin-i, Shantung Province.

2. *Han Tombs numbers 1 (a) and 2 (b) Silver Sparrow Mountain. See the appendix for detail.*

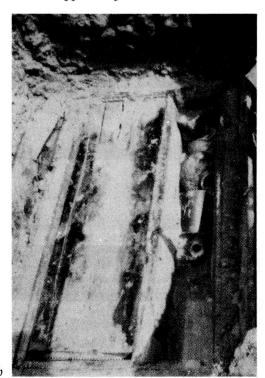

a

b

a

3. Tomb goods useful in attempting to identify the occupants and to date the finds: (a) an ear-shaped cup from Tomb No. 1 bearing the characters "Ssu-ma" engraved on the inside; (b) pan-liang coins, the upper found in Tomb No. 1, the lower in Tomb No. 2; (c) a san-chu coin from Tomb Number 1.

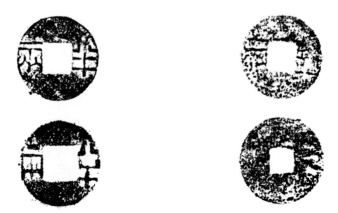

b   *c*

4. The state of the texts found at Silver Sparrow Mountain: *a*
(a) as found; (b) after initial separation; (c) after cleaning.

c

5. For comparison, note the state of texts excavated from the roughly contemporary Han Tomb No. 3 at Ma-wang-tui: (a) compartmented lacquer box containing (b) wooden slips at top and a folded silk text at center left, (c) medical texts written on wood.

b

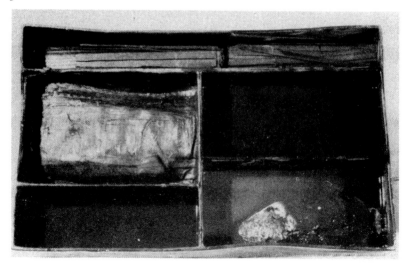

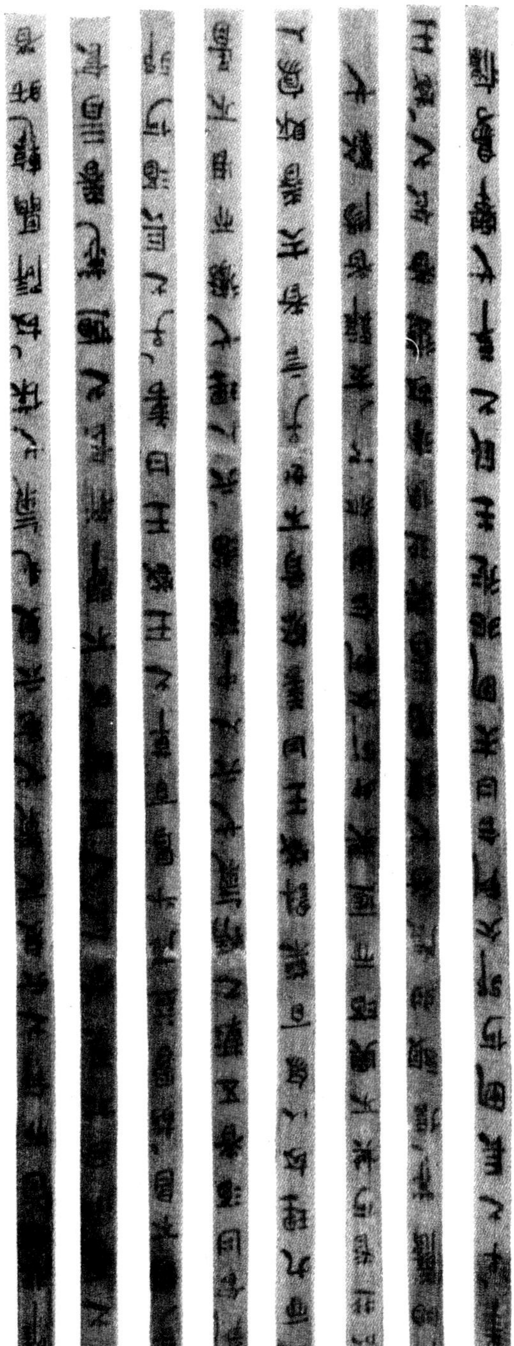

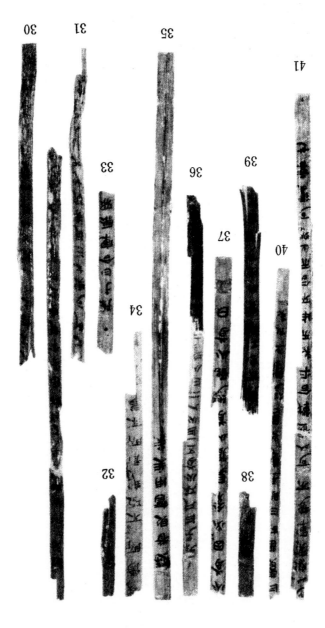

6. Restored wooden slips found at Silver Sparrow Mountain:
(a) part of Sun-tzu: The Art of Warfare; (b) fragments of a
wood slat bearing a table of contents of the traditional thirteen-
chapter text; (c) transcription of the table of contents.

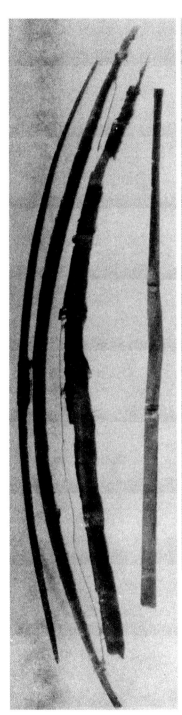

12. *Several bows and a wooden sword from Ma-wang-tui Han Tomb No. 3. On the right are a quiver and arrows from the same tomb.*

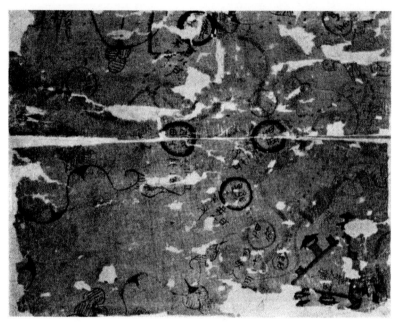

13. *Detail from a map of troop positions. Note walled city at lower righthand corner. The map was buried in Han Tomb No. 3 at Ma-wang-tui in 168 B.C.*

吳王問孫武曰：吾師出境，軍於敵人之地。敵人大至，圍我數重，欲突以出，四塞不通。欲勵士激衆，使之投命潰圍，則如之何？武曰：深溝高壘，示爲守備，安靜勿動，以隱吾能。告令三軍，示不得已。殺牛燔車，以饗吾士。燒盡糧食，填夷井灶，割髪捐冠，絶去生慮。將無餘謀，士有死志。於是砥甲礪刃，并氣一力，或攻兩旁，震鼓疾譟，敵人亦懼，莫知所當。鋭卒分行，疾攻其後。此是失道而求生。故曰：困而不謀者窮，窮而不戰者亡。吳王曰：若吾圍敵，則如之何？武曰：山峻谷險，難以踰越，謂之窮寇。擊之之法，伏卒隱廬，開其去道，示其走路，求生透出，必無鬬意。因而擊之，雖衆必破。

The King of Wu enquired of Sun Wu, saying: "Our army has moved across our own borders and has entered enemy territory. The enemy arrives in force, and throws a cordon around us several times over. We want to break through his lines and escape, but the enemy has blocked off the roadways in all directions. We want to arouse the officers and inflame the rank and file so our men are willing to sacrifice their lives in bursting through the blockade. What are we to do?"

Sun Wu replied: "Gouge out deep ditches and pile up high barriers, showing the enemy we are prepared to defend our ground. Lie still and motionless, thereby concealing our strength from the enemy. Solemnly inform the entire army that our situation is a last-ditch fight to the death. Slaughter the oxen and burn the wagons to feast our troops, cook up all of the remaining provisions, and fill in and flatten our wells and cooking holes. Shave your head, throw away your official cap, and give up any thought of living. The commander has no further strategies; the officers and men are armed with their death resolve. At this, wipe down the armor, sharpen the blades, unite the men in spirit and strength, and launch the attack on two flanks. With the thundering of our drums and our ferocious battle cries, the enemy will be terrified, and will not know how to stop us. Divide our crack troops into two divisions to smash through enemy lines and launch a stinging attack on his rear lines. This is what is called snatching life from a disaster of our own making. Thus it is said:

> To fail to think fast when surrounded by the enemy
> is to have your back pressed to the wall;
> And to fail to take the battle to the enemy when
> your back is to the wall is to perish.

King Wu again enquired: "What do we do if it is we who have surrounded the enemy?'

Sun Wu replied: "Our mountains and valleys, high crags and defiles, are difficult for the enemy to traverse. His predicament is called the invader with his back to the wall. As for how to attack him: Conceal our troops in unlikely

218

hiding places, and give the enemy a way out so he thinks there is a road to safety. He will pass through the corridor in an effort to save himself, and is sure to have no heart for battle. Take this opportunity and attack him, and even though he may be more numerous, you are sure to smash him."

又問曰：吾在死地，糧道已絕，敵伏吾險，進退不得，則如之何？武曰：燔吾蓄積，盡我餘財，激士勵衆，使無生慮。鼓呼而衝，進而勿顧，決命爭強，死而須鬭，順而勿抗，陰守其利，絶其糧道，恐有奇伏，隱而不睹，使吾弓弩，俱守其所。

(x)★

★The topic of this passage, "terrain from which there is no way out," is defined in Chapter 11 above: "Ground on which you will survive only if you fight with all your might, but will perish if you fail to do so, is terrain with no way out." Master Sun is explicit in his injunction, "On terrain from which there is no way out, take the battle to the enemy."

The King of Wu enquired of Sun Wu, saying: "We occupy terrain from which there is no way out, and our supply lines have already been cut. The enemy ambushes us on the rough terrain, and we can neither advance nor retreat. What are we to do?"

Sun Wu replied: "Put our stores to the torch and use up whatever goods we have left. Inflame the officers and incite the rank and file so they have no thought of living. With war drums and battle cries mounting to the heavens, advance on the enemy without looking back. Enter the fray having resolved to win or die, being fully aware that the only alternative to death is to do what is needed in the struggle.

"If it is the enemy who is on terrain from which there is no way out, and the morale and courage of his officers and men is at its height, the way to attack him is this: Be responsive to the enemy's moves and do not take him head on. Secretly deploy troops to safeguard our advantages, cut off the enemy's supply lines, and watch out for the surprise ambush. Go into hiding where we cannot be seen, dispatch the archers and crossbowmen, and have them all hold their ground."

吳王問孫武曰：敵人保據山險，擅利而處之，糧食又足，挑之則不出，乘間則侵掠，爲之奈何？武曰：分兵守要，謹備勿懈。潛探其情，密候其怠。以利誘之，禁其樵牧。久無所得，自然變改。待離其固，奪其所愛。敵據險隘，我能破之也。

The King of Wu enquired of Sun Wu, saying: "The enemy occupies the mountains and passes, and constantly uses his terrain advantage against us. He moreover has all he needs of supplies and provisions, and though we harass him he does not come out. And as soon as he sees an opening, he breaks through and pillages. What can we do about this?"

Sun Wu replied: "Divide up and deploy the army to

222

safeguard our critical points, and prepare against the enemy thoroughly and with utmost vigilance. Covertly explore the enemy's situation, and wait in readiness for the least sign of negligence. Try to tease him out with seeming opportunities, and put an end to his herding and gathering so that for an extended period he brings in nothing. He will change his posture of his own accord. Wait for him to leave his stronghold, and then snatch what he covets the most. Though the enemy might occupy strategic passes and terrain, we are still able to smash him.''

(i)

孫武兵書云：軍井未達，將不言渴；軍灶未炊，將不言飢。

The military treatise of Sun Wu says: "Before the army's watering hole has been reached, the commander does not speak of thirst; before the fires have food on them, the commander does not speak of hunger."[244]

(ii)

孫子曰：將者：智也，仁也，敬也，信也，勇也，嚴也。是故智以折敵，仁以附眾，敬以招賢，信以必賞，勇以益氣，嚴以一令。故折敵則能合變，眾附則思力戰，賢智則陰謀利，賞罰必則士盡力，氣勇益則兵威令自倍，威令一則惟將所使。

Master Sun said: "The traits of the true commander are: wisdom, humanity, respect, integrity, courage, and dignity. With his wisdom he humbles the enemy, with his humanity he draws the people near to him, with his respect he recruits men of talent and character, with his integrity he makes good on his rewards, with his courage he raises the morale of his men, and with his dignity he unifies his command. Thus, if he humbles his enemy, he is able to take

226

advantage of changing circumstances; if the people are close to him, they will be of a mind to go to battle in earnest; if he employs men of talent and wisdom, his secret plans will work; if his rewards and punishments are invariably honored, his men will give their all; if the morale and courage of his troops is heightened, they will of themselves be increasingly martial and intimidating; if his command is unified, the men will serve their commander alone."[245]

孫子兵法曰：人效死而上能用之，雖優游暇譽，令猶行也。

Sun-tzu: The Art of Warfare states: "Where men are committed to fight to the death, their superiors are able to make good use of them. Even when they are taking it easy and are at their leisure, commands will still be carried out."[246]

孫子兵法云：貴之而無驕，委之而不專，扶之而無隱，危之而不懼。故良將之動也，猶璧玉之不可污也。

Sun-tzu: The Art of Warfare states: "Exalt him and he is not arrogant; commission him and he does not act autocratically; support him and he does not conspire; threaten him and he is not afraid. Thus the actions of the able commander are as incorruptible as a jade insignium."[247]

(v)

孫子兵法秘要云：良將思計如飢，所以戰必勝，攻必取也。

Sun-tzu: The Secret Essentials of the Art of Warfare[248]
states: "Because the able commander plans and calculates
like a hungry man, he is invincible in battle and uncon-
querable in the attack."[249]

孫子兵法云：非文無以平治，非武無以治亂。善用兵者有三略
焉：上略伐智，中略伐義，下略伐勢。

Sun-tzu: A Discussion of the Art of Warfare[250] states: "It takes a person of civil virtue to bring peace to the empire; it takes a person of martial virtue to quell disorder in the land. The expert in using the military has three basic strategies that he applies: The best strategy is to attack the enemy at the level of wisdom and experience; the second is to expose the injustice of the enemy's claims; and the last is to attack the enemy's battle position (*shih*)."[251]

231

(vii)

孫子曰：將者，勇，智，仁，信。

Master Sun said: "The traits of the true commander are: courage, wisdom, humanity, and integrity."[252]

孫子曰：將必擇其福厚者。

Master Sun said: "The commander will surely choose those who are most fortunate."[253]

(i)

孫子曰：天隙之地，丘墓故城，兵不可處。

Master Sun said: "On marching through terrain with natural defiles, grave mounds, and the ruins of old walls, the army cannot tarry."[254]

孫子兵法曰：林木蘙薈，草樹蒙籠。

Sun-tzu: The Art of Warfare states: "The forests lie thick and tangled, the vegetation is lush and overgrown."[255]

孫子曰：故曰：深草蓊穢者，所以逃遁也；深谷險阻者，所以止禦車騎也；隘塞山林者，所以少擊衆也；沛澤杳冥者，所以匿其形也。

Master Sun said: "Therefore it is said: Terrain covered with thick brush and lush foliage is used for escape and for hiding; ground marked with deep valleys, defiles, and natural hazards is used to ward off chariots and mounted troops; narrow passes and mountain forests are used for the few to attack the many; terrain covered with marshy jungle and dark thickets is used to conceal one's position."[256]

237

(iv)

孫子曰：凡地多陷曲，曰天井。

Master Sun said: "Lowlands covered with quagmires and labyrinths, are called natural wells."[257]

(i)

孫子占曰：三軍將行，其旌旗從容以向前，是爲天送，必亟擊之，得其大將。三
軍將行，其**旍**旗墊然若雨，是爲天霑，其帥失。三軍將行，**旍**旗亂於上，東西南
北，無所主方，其軍不還。三軍將陣，雨甚，是爲浴師，勿用陣戰。三軍將戰，
雲其上而赤，勿用陣，先陣戰者，莫復其跡。三軍方行，大**風**飄起於軍前，右周
絕軍，其將亡，右周中其師，得糧。

The Prognostications of Sun-tzu says: "The combined
army is about to set off. When the standards and banners
are unfurled, they flutter in the direction the army is to go.

239

This means Heaven is sending it on its way. It must strike quickly and will capture the enemy's high command.

The combined army is about to set off, and the standards and banners droop limply as though rain-soaked. This means Heaven has opened up a deluge on them, and its officers will be lost.

The combined army is about to set off, and the standards and banners flap around every which way on their staffs, without blowing in any particular direction. This army will not return.

The combined army is about to assume battle formation, and it rains in torrents. This is an army awash. It should not go to battle in formation.

The combined army is about to enter battle. Clouds gather above that are flaming red in color. Do not use battle formation in engaging the enemy. The first one to deploy in battle formation will not retrace his steps.

The combined army has just set off. Strong winds blow up in front of the troops. If the winds sweep to the right and cut off the advancing forces, the army's commanders will perish; if the winds sweep to the right behind the troops, the army will capture provisions."[259]

(ii)

孫子稱司雲氣，非雲非煙非霧，形似禽獸，客吉，主人忌。

Master Sun said of those cloudlike vapors that govern a situation that they are neither cloud nor smoke nor mist. Where they take the shape of birds or animals, it is auspicious for the aggressor and a bad omen for the defending forces.[260]

(i)

孫子八陣，有蘋車之乘。

Master Sun's "eight-division formation" includes the armored personnel–style chariots.[262]

(ii)

孫子兵法曰：長陣爲甄。

The *Sun-tzu: The Art of Warfare* states: "The extended battle formation deploys winged flanks."[263]

八陣圖曰：以後爲前，以前爲後；四頭八尾，觸處爲首；敵衝其中，首尾俱救。

The *Eight-Division Formation Diagrams*[264] states: "In deploying in this formation, make the rear the front line, and the front line the rear. It has four heads and eight tails, so wherever the enemy strikes is its head. And when the enemy bursts through the lines, the head and tail can both come to the rescue."[265]

移軍移旗，以順其意。銜枚而陣，分師而伏。後至先擊，以戰則克。

Redeploy the army and redistribute the banners in response to the enemy's intentions. Move the troops under a cloak of silence into their battle formation, and lay detachments in ambush. If the enemy is last to arrive at the battlefield, be first to launch the attack. If you use this battle strategy, you will defeat him.

(i)

Master Sun said: "As for these thirteen chapters . . .[268]

(ii)

相
勝
奈
何
？
孫
子
曰
：

"How do we take the victory?" Master Sun replied, ". . .

(iii)

軍
鬪
令

孫
子
曰
：
能
當
三
□
……

Cited in *Battle Ordinances*, Master Sun says: "To be able to face three . . ."

(iv)

合戰令孫子曰：戰貴齊成，以□□

Cited in *Ordinances for Joining the Enemy in Battle*, Master Sun says: "On the battlefield exalt concerted achievement, thereby . . ."

(v)

□令孫子曰：軍行患車轄之，相……

Cited in [. . .] *Ordinances*, Master Sun says: "As the army advances concern yourself if the war chariots break ranks, and . . . each other . . ."

(vi)

子曰：軍患陣不堅，陣不堅則前破，而□……

The Master said: "In deploying the troops concern yourself if the formation is not solid, for if the formation is not solid, the front line will be crushed, and . . ."

(i)

孫子兵法曰：其鎮如岳，其渟如淵。

The *Sun-tzu: The Art of Warfare* states: "Stable, it is like a mountain peak; at rest, it is like a deep abyss."[269]

(ii)

孫子曰：強弱長短雜用。

Master Sun said: "Weak and strong, short and long, are mixed together in their use."[270]

又曰：遠則用弩，近則用兵，兵弩相解也。

[Master Sun] went on to say: "At a distance, use your crossbow; at close quarters, use your hand weapons. Hand weapons and crossbow are of mutual aid."[271]

(iv)

又曰：以步兵十人擊騎一匹。

[Master Sun] went on to say: "Use a ratio of ten infantry to each mounted soldier in attacking."[272]

(v)

孫子曰：金城湯池而無粟者，太公、墨翟不能守之。

Master Sun said: "A city might have walls of iron and be surrounded by moats of boiling water, but if it is inadequately provisioned, even a Chiang T'ai-kung or a Mo Ti would be unable to defend it."[273]

259

APPENDIX

BACKGROUND TO THE EXCAVATION AT YIN-CH'ÜEH-SHAN

Lin-i is a city and prefecture some 120 miles southwest of Ch'ing-tao (Tsingtao) in Shantung province. The mountain, Meng-shan, stands to the north of Lin-i city. To the south of the city, there are flat farmlands which the I river traverses from north to south. The prefecture of Lin-i takes its name from the fact that in its eastern reaches, it "meets" (*lin*) the I river.

Prevailing opinion has located Lin-i in what was, during the Warring States period, the southern portion of the state of Ch'i—the state that Sun Pin served as military adviser. It is also very near to the border of what was Confucius' home state of Lu. Approximately two thirds of a mile south of the old city wall, there are two small rises that run east and west, the eastern hill being called Chin-ch'üeh-shan (Gold Sparrow mountain) and the western hill, Yin-ch'üeh-shan (Silver Sparrow mountain).

In April 1972, during a construction project, two

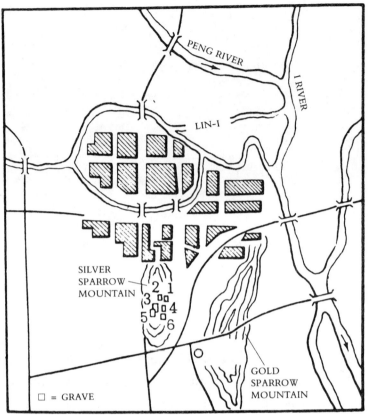

The Yin-ch'üeh-shan excavation site at Lin-i city in Shantung province

major finds dating from the Western Han dynasty (202 B.C.–
A.D. 9), designated Tomb #1 and Tomb #2, were discov-
ered at Yin-ch'üeh-shan. They were excavated under the
direction of the Shantung Provincial Museum. Three insti-
tutions took responsibility for the find: The Institute of
Scientific Technology for the Preservation of Artifacts, The
Shantung Provincial Museum, and the Forbidden Palace
Museum. From 1972 to 1974, a team of scholars including
Lo Fu-i, Ku T'ieh-fu, and Wu Chiu-lung did initial recon-
struction work on the texts found in the tombs. In 1974,

the preliminary results of the find were published under the name of the Committee for the Reconstruction of Yin-ch'üeh-shan Han Dynasty Bamboo Strips (hereafter, the Yin-ch'üeh-shan Committee). The committee, having focused first on the texts of the *Sun-tzu* and *Sun Pin*, completed a preliminary editing and annotation of all of the strips. The translations in this book are based on the ongoing published work of this committee.

The crypts in both tombs are rectangular pits dug out of the rock. Tomb #1, running north and south, is 3.14 meters long and 2.26 meters wide; Tomb #2, also running north and south, is 2.91 meters long and 1.96 meters across. Tomb #1 ranges from 2 to 3 meters in depth, and Tomb #2 is from 3.5 to 4 meters deep. Over the course of time, the upper covering of both of the tombs suffered breakage and water collected within them.

The tombs are divided lengthwise into two sections, one section as a crypt to contain a coffin, and the other to contain the various burial effects. The coffin crypts are intact, and between the pit and the wooden coffin, there is a very fine grayish clay. The structure of the coffin crypts in both tombs is approximately the same: Tomb #1 is 2.64 meters long, 1.76 meters wide, and 1 meter deep; Tomb #2 is 2.41 meters long, 1.56 meters wide, and .88 meters deep. In each of the coffin areas, there are skeletal remains that have decomposed to the extent that sex is impossible to determine, but the extension and direction of the corpse can be discerned. Both tombs contain a wealth of burial effects (see diagrams).

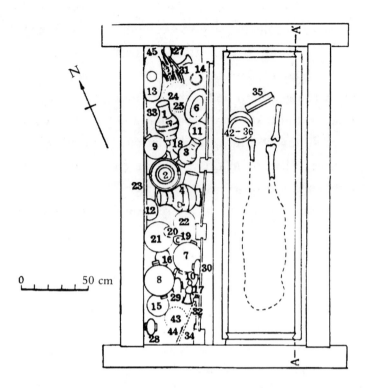

Diagram of Tomb #1 at Yin-ch'üeh-shan

1–4	earthenware pots	31	wooden vessel
5, 6	earthenware bowls	32	wooden gameboard
7–10	earthenware tripods	33–34	wooden canes
11, 12	earthenware containers	35	lacquered pillow
13	cocoon-shaped earthenware pot with four legs	36	lacquered toilet case
14–16	earthenware jars	37	coarse wooden comb
17–20	earthenware figurines	38–40	fine wooden combs
21	earthenware vessel with cover	41	comb stand
22–23	earthenware containers	42	bronze mirror
24–25	lacquered plate with colored ornamentation	43	bamboo basket
26	wine goblet	44	chestnuts
27–30	lacquered ear-shaped cups	45	35 *pan-liang* (half tael) coins

264

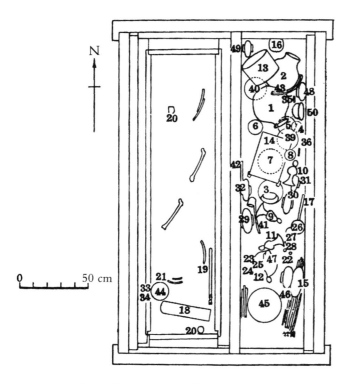

Diagram of Tomb #2 at Yin-ch'üeh-shan

1	earthenware jar with characters	23–25	lacquered bowls with colored ornamentation
2	earthenware jar	26	small lacquered bowl
3–4	earthenware pots with colored ornamentation	27–32	lacquered ear-shaped cups
5–6	earthenware containers with colored ornamentation	33	coarse wooden comb
7–8	earthenware tripods with colored ornamentation	34	fine wooden comb
9–12	earthenware figurines with colored ornamentation	35–38	small wooden heads
13	lacquered toilet case	39–40	lacquered bowls
14	lacquered tube	41	lacquered ladle
15	oval wooden container	42	wooden gate
16	remains of a wooden owl	43	broken piece of a lacquered circular box
17	wooden cane	44	lacquered toilet case
18	wooden pillow	45	plain lacquered bowl
19	wooden handle	46–47	lacquered ear-shaped cups with colored ornamentation
20	small lacquered container	48–49	lacquered ear-shaped cups
21	bronze mirror	50	bronze pot
22–38	*pan-liang* (half-tael) coins		

DATING THE TOMBS AND
IDENTIFYING THE OCCUPANTS

There are several factors that shed light on the basic questions: when and who? From the shape, ornamentation, and style of the vessels contained in the tombs, and from the tombs themselves, we can determine they date from early Western Han. The pottery burial vessels still preserve the legacy of Warring States ritual vessels.

The seventy-four ancient coins found in the tombs are important clues, and enable us to make a closer estimate of the dates. Wu Chiu-lung speculates these coins might have been used to secure the thin silk cords that bound the bamboo strips of the manuscripts together.[274] From Tomb #1, thirty-six coins—thirty-five *pan-liang* (half-tael) coins and one *san-chu* (three-*chu*) coin—were recovered. In Tomb #2, thirty-eight of the *pan-liang* coins have been found.

According to the "Chronicle of Emperor Wu" in the *History of the Han Dynasty*,[275] the *san-chu* coin was first minted in 140 B.C. and then discontinued shortly thereafter in 136 B.C. Thus, neither tomb could be earlier than 140 B.C. Again, although so many *pan-liang* coins were found in the tombs, not one *wu-chu* (five-*chu*) coin minted under Emperor Wu from 118 B.C. was found. One can thus speculate that both tombs date from between 140 and 118 B.C. during the Western Han reign of Emperor Wu (r. 141–86 B.C.).

This date can be further refined, at least in the case of Tomb #2. In addition to the *pan-liang* coins, a calendar was recovered that begins in 134 B.C. and covers a thirteen-month period. This narrows the date of Tomb #2 to 134–118 B.C.

266

As to *who* was buried in these tombs, engraved on the bottom of two lacquer cups from Tomb #1 in clerical script (*li-shu*) are the two characters, *"Ssu-ma."* From its appearance we can determine it is not the imprint of the craftsman who made the vessel, but rather the surname of the owner engraved onto the vessel at some later date. *"Ssu-ma,"* then, was probably the name of the occupant of Tomb #1. *Ssu-ma* could also have been this person's official title. The *History of the Han Dynasty* states that "the militarist school possibly derives from the ancient office of *Ssu-ma*, the royal office of military preparations."[276] According to this same source, "for seventy years from the beginning of the reign of Emperor Wu," there was the custom of "taking the name of one's office as one's surname."[277] Taking into account the collection of specifically military books found in the tomb together with this custom, it has been speculated that the occupant or his family had taken this military office as a surname. However, it is perhaps more likely that a person would engrave his name than the title of his office on to a cup, and by this time, "Ssu-ma" had already become a popular surname. If "Ssu-ma" was the name of the occupant's office, it is also likely it was the surname of the occupant.[278]

Burial effects were customarily things in daily use or of some particular value. From the large collection of military works found in Tomb #1, we can assume the occupant was someone who knew about the art of warfare or who was connected with the military in some way. The absence of weapons of any kind might suggest this interest stopped somewhat short of the occupant's being an active military man.

On the shoulder of an earthenware jar found in Tomb #2 there are the four characters *Shao-shih shih tou*—"ten pecks of the Shao family." This would suggest the occupant of Tomb #2 was surnamed Shao.[279]

The sum of this rather limited evidence has led to speculation that the occupants of Tombs #1 and #2, dated 140–118 B.C. and 134–118 B.C. respectively, were husband and wife, perhaps surnamed Ssu-ma and Shao. Even though the actual burials date from this period, it should be remembered that the texts themselves may have been copied considerably earlier.

The texts with which we are concerned were discovered among the lacquerware, pottery, bronzeware, coins, and various other burial effects. The bamboo strips constituting these early documents were found in both tombs.

THE FIRST PUBLISHED REPORTS

After the initial find, the Yin-ch'üeh-shan Committee devoted some two years of research to the 4,942 strips and fragments before making the preliminary results of this research known to the world in the February 1974 issue of the academic journal, *Cultural Relics* (*Wen-wu*). In addition to the partial texts of the *Sun-tzu: The Art of Warfare* and the *Sun Pin: The Art of Warfare*, portions of the following texts were tentatively identified and published:[280]

1. *Six Strategies* (*Liu-t'ao*)—illustrated *Wen-wu* (*Cultural Relics*) (hereafter, *WW*) 1974:2; transcribed in *WW* 1977:2, pp. 21ff.—54 pieces

2. *Master Wei-liao (Wei-liao-tzu)*—illustrated *WW* 1972:2; transcribed in *WW* 1974:2, pp. 30ff.—36 pieces

3. *Master Kuan (Kuan-tzu)*—shown *WW* 1974:2 and 1976:12; transcribed in *WW* 1976:12, pp. 36ff.—10 pieces

4. *Master Yen (Yen-tzu)*—shown *WW* 1974:2—112 pieces

5. *Master Mo (Mo-tzu)*—shown *WW* 1974: 2—1 piece (plus 42 additional pieces resembling lost chapters)

To a greater or lesser extent these partial texts all seem to deal with military affairs. Another group of textual materials, although primarily dealing with *yin-yang* theory and prognostication, also relates in some way to military affairs. There is speculation that these materials might in some part be divination texts from the lost *Miscellaneous Prognostications of Sun-tzu: The Art of Warfare*, [281] or perhaps treatises on divination originally included in *Sun Pin: The Art of Warfare*. These materials include:

6. *Yin-Yang of Master Ts'ao (Ts'ao-shih yin-yang)*—24 pieces

7. *Wind Direction Divination (Feng-chiao-chan)*—51 pieces

8. *Portent and Omen Divination (Tsai-i-chan)*—53 pieces

9. unknown textual material concerning divination—82 pieces

There is also one veterinary text dealing with the physiognomic examination of dogs:

10. *The Classic on Examining Dogs (Hsiang-kou-ching)*—11 pieces

From Tomb #2 was unearthed the oldest and most complete ancient calendrical record we have to date, which, as such, has considerable value for the study of calendrical methods during the ancient period:

11. *A Calendrical Record for the First Year of the yüan-kuang Reign Period of Emperor Wu of Han: 134 B.C. (Han Wu-ti yüan-kuang yüan-nien li-p'u)*—32 pieces

Perhaps the most significant and exciting textual material uncovered in Tomb #1 is the additional text of the extant *Sun-tzu: The Art of Warfare* and the portions of the long-lost *Sun Pin: The Art of Warfare*. The initial description of these materials in a report of the Yin-ch'üeh-shan Committee published as *Yin-ch'üeh-shan Han-mu chu-chien* I in July 1975[282] contains the following information:

12. *Sun-tzu: The Art of Warfare (Sun-tzu ping-fa)*—196 pieces: 11 complete ones, 122 partial slips, and 63 fragments, totaling 3,160 characters. Fragments from all 13 chapters of the received text have been identified, together with 68 pieces from what seem to be 6 previously unknown chapters.

13. *Sun Pin: The Art of Warfare (Sun Pin ping-fa)*—364 pieces: 187 complete ones, 109 partial slips, and 68 fragments, totalling 8,700 characters.

Considering for comparison that the *Lao-tzu* is approximately 5,000 characters in length and the thirteen-chapter *Sun-tzu* is about 6,000, the supplement to the *Sun-tzu* of over 1,200 characters and the newly recovered *Sun Pin*, though it has been revised downward to about half of this initial 8,700 figure, are substantial documents.

The updated report of the Yin-ch'üeh-shan Committee is summarized in the Introduction.

THE BAMBOO STRIP MANUSCRIPTS
AND THEIR DATES

In ancient China, "books" were generally written on bamboo, wood, or silk. From the extant classical records, it would seem that bamboo strips were already in use during the Shang dynasty (traditionally, 1751–1112 B.C.). The character *ts'e*, a graph depicting symbolically "rolls of strips," is frequently seen on the oracle-bone inscriptions that date from the Shang dynasty.

Certain material factors have contributed to a situation in which, after two thousand years, these strips have been recovered in a still legible condition. The strips in these tombs were buried quite deep and out of the sunlight, and hence kept at a low and relatively constant temperature. The tombs themselves were carved out of the rock from the top down, and, as a consequence, were relatively easy to seal tightly. The fine, gray glutinous clay must have functioned as a relatively water-tight sealant. The combination of these factors certainly has had a bearing on the condition of the strips. Still, after such a long time immersed in the muddy water that eventually did leak in, the strips were much discolored, had become very fragile, and are now easily fragmented.

Most of the strips came from Tomb #1. A total of more than 7,500 strips and fragments were found in the northern corner of the burial-effects pit between the lacquerware and pottery. Few of these are whole; most are fragments; many have only one or two characters. Of the 7,500 strips, then, 4,942 constitute the working core of the reconstructed texts. Physically, the complete strips divide into long and short strips. The long ones are about 27.5 cm with most having a width of 0.5 to 0.7 cm and a thickness of 0.1 to 0.2 cm. Almost all of the texts are copied on the long strips. Only the divination texts seem to be found on the shorter ones. All of these shorter strips are fragmentary, but the estimated length is about 18 cm with a width of about 0.5 cm. The bamboo strips were originally bound into scrolls or *ts'e* and tied with cords, but the cords rotted away long ago, and hence were not in place to preserve the order when the strips were recovered. Most of the long strips were originally joined with three cords, with those at the top and bottom about 2 cm from the ends, and one in the center. The shorter strips and some of the long strips were joined with only two cords, with the cords at the top and bottom being about 2 cm from the ends.

Tomb #2 produced a total of 32 bamboo strips found in the southeastern corner with other burial effects. These strips constitute the calendrical register for the first year of the *yüan-kuang* reign period, the seventh year of Emperor Wu of the Han dynasty (134 B.C.). They are about 69 cm long, 1 cm wide, and 0.2 cm thick, and were joined together with three cords.

The characters on the strips from Tomb #1 are all in clerical script (*li-shu*), which had become the standard style with the unification of Chinese states under the state of Ch'in in 221 B.C. Given that the strips belong to an early period in the standardization of the clerical script (*li-shu*), they are a substantial resource for investigating developments in the construction of the character and the style of writing during the process of transition from the seal-style (*chuan-shu*) to the clerical-style script. They were written with a brush using black ink. The immediate observation that some of the characters are well formed and symmetrical while others are more crude leads to the assumption that they are not the product of one hand. Because they were not written by one person or at one time, there is some variation in the written form of the characters and in the length of the lines of text. In the written form of the characters, for example, the strips divide into the two large categories of standard and cursive, with each of these including several different hands. Most complete strips have over thirty characters, but some of those written with characters close together have over forty, while those written with some space between the characters have only twenty-odd. There is not always internal consistency within the texts. The same text can include several different hands and may vary in the length of lines.

The basic unit of text is the chapter (*p'ien*). Some of the chapter titles are written on the back of the first strips, some are written on strips by themselves, and some are written at the end of the chapter. This variation can be explained if we understand the physical structure of the classical Chinese "scroll," or *ts'e*. Most *ts'e* would have the last strip of text as its core, and then be rolled up from left to right (from the end of the text to the beginning) with the characters facing inward to protect them. Once a *ts'e* was rolled up in this manner, the outer surface of the first strip in the text could then be used for recording the title of the first chapter on the scroll as a way of facilitating easy reference.

In some cases a scroll would contain only the one

chapter with the title written on the outer surface of the first strip, that is, the back of the first strip. But if it contained more than one chapter, typically the title of the first chapter in the scroll would be written on the outer surface of the first strip, and the titles of the remaining chapters would be written either on separate strips at the beginning of each chapter, or at the end of the chapters. Several of the shorter chapters of the reconstructed Yin-ch'üeh-shan bamboo scrolls have the titles on both the back of the first strip and at the end, while some of the others just have the title at the end. The former were probably the first chapters in a scroll, while the latter chapters were contained somewhere within the scroll.

For example, on the strips that constitute "The Eight-Division Formation" and "Terrain as Treasure" chapters of the *Sun Pin: The Art of Warfare*, there is a similarity in the form of the characters and in the length of the lines, suggesting that they belong to the same scroll. But "The Eight-Division Formation" chapter has its title on both the back of the first strip and at the end of the chapter. This chapter then was probably the first chapter of the scroll. "Terrain as Treasure" has its title at the end, but not on the back of the first strip, and hence was probably a chapter following "The Eight-Division Formation" within the scroll.

In the Yin-ch'üeh-shan bamboo scrolls, each chapter that has a title on an individual strip has no title on either the back of the first strip or at the end. For example, the fragments of the thirteen chapters of the *Obeying Ordinances* (*Shou-fa*) are like this. We can surmise that in these bamboo scrolls, those chapters that have their titles on individual strips, and those that have them on the back of the first strip, did not belong to the same scroll.

In addition to the bamboo strips found in Tomb #1, several slats of wood were found with what seems to be a listing of the titles of the chapters on them. A wooden slat was probably bound to the outside of each scroll as a table of contents.

Li Hsüeh-ch'in describes four wooden slats that list the chapter titles: #1 has the thirteen core chapters of *Sun-tzu: The Art of Warfare*; #2 has the thirteen chapters of the *Obeying Ordinances and Orders* (*Shou-fa shou-ling*); #4 has the *Yin-Yang of Master Ts'ao* (*Ts'ao-shih yin-yang*). Wooden slat #3 has only a few characters remaining, but at least two lines, "Fatal Weaknesses of the Commander" (*chiang-pai*) and "Common Mistakes of the Military" (*Ping chih heng-shih*), seem to refer to chapters that have been included in the supplemental Part II of *Sun Pin: The Art of Warfare*.[283] The style of the characters is similar to those strips that we can be sure belong to *Sun Pin: The Art of Warfare*. Some of the other titles on this slat seem to refer to discussions on government. This does not preclude the possibility that slat #3 was originally part of the table of contents for *Sun Pin: The Art of Warfare*. As Li Hsüeh-ch'in observes, the other military texts—*Sun-tzu*, *Six Strategies*, and *Master Wei-liao*—all include discussions of government.[284] The fact that there is no fuller table of contents for the *Sun Pin: The Art of Warfare*, however, makes the process of reconstructing this particular text more difficult.

NOTES

References to *Sun Pin: The Art of Warfare* are to the *Yin-ch'üeh-shan Han-mu chu-chien* Collection I, prepared by Yin-ch'üeh-shan Han-mu chu-chien cheng-li hsiao-tsu (Committee for the Reconstruction of the Yin-ch'üeh-shan Han strips) and published in 1985. For those chapters originally included in the *Sun Pin* but excluded from the 1985 publication, I refer to the *Sun Pin ping-fa* published by Yin-ch'üeh-shan Han-mu chu-chien cheng-li hsiao-tsu (Committee for the Reconstruction of the Yin-ch'üeh-shan Han strips) in 1975.

1. The Chinese expression for China, *"chung-kuo,"* often translated as "Middle Kingdom," dates back to pre-imperial days, and refers to a plurality of "central states," not one unified political entity. The English name, "China," is reportedly taken from the state of Ch'in, which was the ultimate victor in establishing a unified empire in 221 B.C.

2. For a short history of the *Sun-tzu* in European languages, see Appendix III in Samuel B. Griffith (1963), *"Sun-tzu* in Western Languages."

3. I retain the untranslated title *Lao-tzu* throughout for two reasons. Firstly, there is an ambiguity with respect to its meaning: It could reasonably be translated as either "Master Lao" or "the old Master." Secondly, there is the recognition factor.

4. D. C. Lau (1982).

5. *Wen-wu (Cultural Relics)* 1981.8:11–13. Ting-hsien Tomb #40 dating from the Han dynasty has yielded bamboo strips totaling approximately half of the received *Analects*. Although the *Ana-*

277

lects was one of the earliest texts to find its canonical form, several alternative versions circulated until it was edited into its present form by Ho Yen (A.D. 190–249). It is reported that there are some important differences between this Han dynasty version and our present text. The sectioning of passages is often not the same, and if we take grammatical particles into account, there are variants in almost every passage.

6. The *Wen-wu* (*Cultural Relics*) 1981.8:11–12 report on the *Master Wen* recovered from the Ting county tomb sheds important new light on the *Master Wen*. Reasons for taking the Han strips text as more authoritative than the received text are several. Firstly, of course, is its incontrovertible presence in a tomb that can be dated back to the Han dynasty.

Secondly, the structure of the Han strips text is consistent with the *Master Wen* as described in the library catalog of the Han dynasty court. The *History of the Han Dynasty* lists "*Master Wen* in nine chapters" in the "Record of Literary Works" (*Yi-wen chih*) of the *History of the Han Dynasty*, a catalog of the imperial library completed during the first century A.D. A commentary is appended, identifying Master Wen as a disciple of Lao-tzu who lived as a contemporary of Confucius, and who was asked questions by King P'ing of Chou. Some passages of the Han strips text are similar in content to the received Master Wen; some of them are entirely different. On the passages in the Han strips text that parallel the received *Master Wen*, the occurrences of "Master Wen" have been changed in the received text to read "Lao-tzu," and Master Wen has become the student asking the questions. On the Han strips, consistent with the description in the *History of the Han Dynasty* account, King P'ing asks the questions, and Master Wen answers them.

Thirdly, it would seem likely that the text would be named for Master Wen the teacher rather than Master Wen the disciple.

The discovery of the *Master Wen* from the Ting county tomb not only gives this text new status as an indisputably ancient work, but further, for the history of early Chinese thought, adds new textual material that has previously been unknown to us.

7. A great deal of scholarly attention is being invested in these four documents. Robin Yates is presently working on an annotated translation that is forthcoming in this same *Classics of Ancient China* series. These documents have, in recent scholarship, notably by R. P. Peerenboom, been used to articulate a definition of "Huang-

Lao" Taoism, a specific mixture of Taoist and Legalist thought that emerged in the early Han dynasty. This clarification is particularly important, because many scholars continue to use the "Huang-Lao" category as a catch-all for any and all early Han philosophical works that make reference to Taoism. See Peerenboom (1993).

8. I am working on an annotated translation of *Sun Pin: The Art of Warfare* that will appear in this same *Classics of Ancient China* series.

9. Wu Chiu-lung (1985):9.

10. Chang Chen-tse (1984):2 (preface).

11. Wu Chiu-lung (1985):13.

12. *Historical Records* (1959): Chapter 65.

13. See *Intrigues of the Warring States* (1920):4/6b; cf. Crump (1979):154; 7/8b, 380; and *Historical Records*(1959):279, 1845–1846, 1962, 2343, 2351, 3300.

14. See *Lü-shih ch'un-ch'iu* (1935):802.

15. *History of the Sui Dynasty* (1973):1012–1013.

16. Su Ch'in is frequently found in the list of commoners who became high ministers of state. Although Su Ch'in figures frequently in the *Historical Records* and the *Intrigues of the Warring States* that chronicle events of this period, there has been considerable speculation concerning the historicity of these accounts. See J. I. Crump (1979):13–15. For traditional views on Su Ch'in's dates, see Ch'ien Mu (1956):306 who, following Ssu-ma Ch'ien, places him as having died in 321 B.C.

The discovery of the *Documents of the Warring States Strategists (Chan-kuo tsung-heng-chia shu)* in Tomb #3 at Ma-wang-tui in 1973 has provided us with textual materials not available to China's earliest historians that are enabling scholars to revise significantly the historical profile of Su Ch'in, and the dates of his life. This text, dating from 195–188 B.C., was initially thought to be a version of the *Intrigues of the Warring States*, but since the *Intrigues of the Warring States* was not compiled by Liu Hsiang until the late first century B.C., further study has shown that the *Documents of the Warring States Strategists* was copied from at least three independent sources. See Blanford (1991):198n12. It consists of twenty-seven passages, ten of which in some form appear in Liu Hsiang's *Intrigues of the Warring States* and eight of which appear in Ssu-ma Ch'ien's *Historical Records*. Discounting the overlap between these two records, sixteen passages are new.

279

In his 1976 article, "Precious Historical Materials Unseen by Ssu-ma Ch'ien," T'ang Lan asserts that Ssu-ma Ch'ien never saw any firsthand historical materials recounting the thoughts and ideas of Su Ch'in and, as a consequence, confused the order of persons and events, introduced various errors concerning these same events, and even invented some episodes. Chronologically, Ssu-ma Ch'ien inadvertently pushed those events of Su Ch'in's life that occurred at the beginning of the third century B.C. back into the end of the fourth century B.C. T'ang Lan suggests that the *Historical Records* account of Su Ch'in is more like a historical novel than a chronicle of events. It is clear that these newly recovered documents will be of inestimable value in sorting out the sequence of events during the key era when the Warring States period was drawing toward its climax, and in reevaluating the role played by Su Ch'in.

17. Samuel B. Griffith (1963):3–11.

18. See Joseph Needham *et al.* and Robin Yates (forthcoming). Jerry Norman and Mei Tsu-lin (1976):293–294 make a case for an Austroasiatic origin of the crossbow and the term for it, *nu*, on philological and historical grounds, suggesting that the Chinese acquired this weapon from the proto-Tai and Vietnamese sometime in the third or fourth century B.C.

19. D. C. Lau (1982): 134.

20. *Sun-tzu* 3:111.

21. *Sun Pin* (1985):50–51.

22. *Sun Pin* (1975):115–116, "Male and Female Fortifications."

23. *Historical Records* (1959): 2161–2162.

24. *Historical Records* (1959):1466.

25. See J. J. L. Duyvendak (1928).

26. See particularly Chapter 10, "The Method of Warfare"; also, Chapters 11 and 12. Duyvendak (1928):244–252.

27. See John Knoblock (1990):211–234.

28. *Han Fei-tzu so-yin* (1982):49.12.25. See Burton Watson (1964):110.

29. See *Historical Records* (1964):2162.

30. See Li Ling (1983):552–553.

31. Pan Ku (1962):1731. The military writers are listed under the Taoist school.

32. See John Fairbank in Frank A. Kierman, Jr. (1974):7; H. G. Creel (1970) Chapter 10, especially pp. 247–257.

33. See for example *Analects* 9/26, 13/29, 13/30, and 16/7.

34. See Mark Lewis (1990): chapters 2 and 3 for a thorough discussion of this changing situation in classical China.

35. See Lai Hai-tsung (1984) for a discussion of the changing role of the military in early China.

36. The concept *shih*, translated as "strategic advantage," for example, can be traced in the Legalist, Confucian, and even Taoist philosophical sources back to a specifically militarist notion of battle advantage. See Roger T. Ames (1983): Chapter 2.

37. See *Analects* 2/12 and 13/23. See also 1/12, 2/14, and 15/22. An explication of this one passage is really the central theme of Hall and Ames (1987), *Thinking Through Confucius*.

38. *Analects* 15/29.

39. Michel Foucault's *The Order of Things: An Archaeology of the Human Sciences* is a self-conscious response to Borges's category. See Foucault (1973):xv.

40. *Analects* 13/23.

41. Hsü Wei-yü (1935):540.

42. *Discourses of the States (Kuo-yü)* 16/4a–b.

43. Wing Tek Lum (1987):105.

44. Graham (1981):275.

45. See Paul Demiéville's essay, "Philosophy and Religion from Han to Sui" in Denis Twitchett and Michael Loewe (1986).

46. *Analects* 19/21.

47. See John Fairbank (1987):83–94.

48. *Analects* 2/1 and 15/5.

49. John Fairbank, "Introduction: Varieties of the Chinese Military Experience" in Frank A. Kierman, Jr. (1974):8.

50. *Shih* is written as *chih* in the ancient texts.

51. For an exploration of the later political implications of this term, see Ames (1983):Chapter 3 *passim*.

52. *Sun Pin* (1985):62–63.

53. *Sun-tzu* 5:120–121.

54. *Sun-tzu* 5:120.

55. *Sun-tzu* 1:104.

56. *Sun-tzu* 11:158.

57. See for example *Lao-tzu* 36, 40, 50, 57, and 78. This same understanding of the nature of change can be found in such disparate sources as the *Book of Changes* and the Confucian *Analects*.

58. *Sun Pin* (1975):121.

59. *Sun-tzu* 5:120.

60. *Sun Pin* (1975):121.

61. *Sun Pin* (1975):121.

62. *Sun Pin* (1975):121.

63. *Sun Pin* (1985):48. See also *Sun-tzu* 6:126–127.

64. *Sun-tzu* 6:127.

65. *Sun Pin* (1975):122.

66. See Lau (1965):332–333 and Ames (1983):67.

67. *Sun-tzu* 6:125.

68. *Sun-tzu* 4:116.

69. *Sun-tzu* 6:125.

70. *Sun-tzu* 1:105.

71. *Master of Huai Nan* (1968):15/8a–b.

72. *Sun-tzu* 6:127.

73. *Sun-tzu* 2:108.

74. *Sun-tzu* 12:165.

75. *Sun-tzu* 6:127.

76. *Sun-tzu* 2:107–108.

77. *Sun Pin* (1985):58.

78. *Sun Pin* (1985):59.

79. *Sun Pin* (1985):48.

80. *Sun-tzu* 3:111.

81. *Sun Pin* (1985):59.

82. *Sun-tzu* 1:103.

83. *Sun-tzu* 3:111–112.

84. *Sun-tzu* 4:115.

85. *Sun-tzu* 6:123.

86. *Sun-tzu* 8:136.

87. *Sun-tzu* 11:157.

88. *Sun-tzu* 6:125.

89. *Sun-tzu* 2:107.

90. *Sun Pin* (1985):48.

91. *Sun-tzu* 10:150.

92. *Sun-tzu* 1:103. See also *Sun-tzu* III:2:ii, p. 226.

93. *Sun-tzu* 3:112.

94. *Sun-tzu* 2:109.

95. *Sun-tzu* 3:113. Compare *Sun Pin* (1985):58:
    There are five conditions that ensure constant victory: to have the full confidence of one's ruler and full authority over the army will lead to victory; . . .

96. *Sun-tzu* 8:135.
97. *Sun-tzu* 10:150.
98. *Sun-tzu* 13:171.
99. *Sun-tzu* 6:125.
100. *Sun-tzu* 13:169.
101. *Sun-tzu* 5:120.
102. *Sun-tzu* 13:169.
103. *Sun-tzu* 13:171.
104. *Sun-tzu* 3:111.
105. *Sun-tzu* 3:111.
106. *Sun-tzu* 4:116.
107. *Sun-tzu* 4:116.
108. *Sun-tzu* 1:105.
109. See D. C. Lau (1965):331–332.
110. *Sun-tzu* 8:135.
111. *Sun-tzu* 6:125.
112. *Sun-tzu* 6:126.
113. *Sun-tzu* 1:104–105.
114. *Sun-tzu* 3:113.

115. The basic meaning of the character *ping* translated here as "war" is "arms" or "weapons." By extension in different contexts it means "soldiers," "army," and "war" itself.

116. The Han strips text has an additional phrase here:

Complying with or defying these conditions will determine military victory.

117. I have followed Wu Chiu-lung (1990) in adding this phrase from the Han strips.

118. *Chiang* can be read as "commander" rather than as a particle indicating futurity. An alternative translation, then, would be:

If a commander heeds my assessments, to employ him is certain victory. Keep him. If a commander does not heed my assessments, to employ him is certain defeat. Dismiss him.

119. I have adapted this passage from D. C. Lau's review of Samuel B. Griffith's translation. Lau (1965):332 points out that the key to understanding this passage is *suan*: "counters or, more precisely, counting rods which are used to form numbers. . . . In the final calculation, the number of rods is totted up, and for the side that has scored more rods victory is predicted."

120. The character *fan*, conventionally translated "in general" or "generally speaking," is taken care of here and elsewhere through the text by treating this kind of introductory phrase as a caption. See D. C. Lau (1965):323–324.

121. A thousand *li* amounts to several hundred miles.

122. I read the *ku* here—often translated inferentially as "therefore"—as simply a passage marker. This is a familiar usage of *ku* in the classical corpus, and there is a real danger if we insist on a formulaic translation that suggests linear inference where there is none.

123. There is an ambiguity in this passage. D. C. Lau (1965):334–335 uses contemporaneous texts to construct a persuasive argument that the "*ch'üan*" as it occurs in *ch'üan kuo* and the other parallel binomials is a technical term meaning "to preserve intact." I have followed his reading of this passage. The more standard interpretation would be:

> It is best to preserve the enemy's state intact; to crush the enemy's state is only a second best. It is best to preserve the enemy's army, battalion, company, or five-man squad intact; to crush the enemy's army, battalion, company, or five-man squad is only a second best.

Mark Lewis (1990):116 has this reading. Another possible reading would be:

> It is best to preserve a state intact, and only second best to crush it; it is best to preserve an army, battalion, company, or five-man squad intact, and only second best to crush it.

124. I follow D. C. Lau (1965):334–335 in his reading of "*chüan*" as a technical term here.

125. I follow the arguments of Wu Chiu-lung *et al.* (1990):42 in reversing these two phrases, which originally read:

> . . . when double, divide him; when you and the enemy are equally matched, be able to engage him . . .

126. Many of the commentators reconstrue the grammar here in imaginative ways to arrive at the alternative reading:

> Thus, if a small force simply digs in, it will fall captive to a larger enemy,

I have opted for a more literal translation that seems to make perfect sense.

127. Mark Lewis (1990):109 identifies this guard as "the pole mounted on the side of a chariot to keep it from overturning."

128. See note 122 above for *ku* as a passage marker.

129. Several texts have "in every battle will be defeated," but both the rhyme and the meaning recommend "be at risk *(tai)*" over "be defeated *(pai)*."

130. See D. C. Lau (1965):332–333, for a discussion of the various meanings of *hsing*, here translated "strategic positions." See also Ames (1983):Chapter 3 for a discussion on the relationship between *hsing* and *shih*, "strategic advantage/political purchase."

131. Compare the *Master of Huai Nan* (1968):15/14a.

132. Many of the commentators have an alternative reading of this passage: "He who cannot win takes the defensive; he who can win attacks."

133. I follow the word order on the Han strips here. All of the received texts have an alternative reading:

> If one assumes a defensive posture, it is because one's strength is deficient; if one launches the attack, it is because one's strength is more than enough.

Both versions make good sense. The Han strips version is familiar in the Han dynasty histories; see, for example, the *History of the Han Dynasty*, Pan Ku (1962):2981, and the *History of the Later Han Dynasty*, Fan Yeh *et al.* (1965):650. However, the version found in the received texts also occurs in the *History of the Later Han Dynasty*, Fan Yeh *et al.* (1965):2305, and the commentary of Ts'ao Ts'ao (155–220) on the *Sun-tzu* is based upon the received text version. It would appear the change in the transmission of *Sun-tzu* had already been made in the later Han dynasty. See Yin-ch'üeh-shan Committee (1985):8n7.

134. I am following the Han strips version here. The Sung edition reads:

> Therefore, in the battle victory for the expert neither wins him reputation for wisdom nor credit for courage.

135. See note 122 above for *ku* as a passage marker.

136. Compare the *Master of Huai Nan* (1968):15/6b.

137. The "way" is defined in *Sun-tzu* 1:103 in the following terms:

> The way *(tao)* is what brings the thinking of the

people in line with their superiors. Hence, you can
send them to their deaths or let them live, and they
will have no misgivings one way or the other.

"Regulation" is also defined in the same chapter 1:103:

And regulation entails organizational effectiveness,
a chain of command, and a structure for logistical
support.

138. I follow the Han strips version here. There is corroboration for it in *Lao-tzu* 47 and *Kuan-tzu* 2:75–130. The alternative reading is ". . . and thus is able formulate policies governing the outcome of the war."

139. It is difficult to be certain about these classical measures because of regional and temporal disparities, but the units referred to in this passage probably indicate about a 600 to 1 differential.

140. The Han strips text has two drafts of this particular chapter that, each written in a different hand, can be separated into "A" and "B" texts. I follow both "A" and "B" versions of the Han strips text here in substituting the phrase "the army that has this weight of victory on its side" for "the victorious army" in the received texts. Compare the *Master of Huai Nan* (1968):15/11b.

141. This passage reads literally:

. . . it is the dividing and counting of numbers that
makes managing many soldiers the same as managing a few.

142. The expression here is literally "forms and names" rather than "flags and pennants." I follow Robin Yates (1988):220–222 who makes his argument on the basis of the following passage which he translates from the *Mo-tzu*:

The standard method/procedure for defending
cities is: Make gray-green flags for wood; make
red flags for fires; make yellow flags for firewood
and fuel; make white flags for stones; make black
flags for water; make bamboo flags for food; make
gray goshawk flags for soldiers that fight to the
death; make tiger flags for mighty warriors; make
double rabbit flags for brave [?] soldiers; make youth
flags for fourteen-year-old boys; make grasping
arrow flags for women; make dog flags for crossbows; make forest flags for *ch'i* halberds; make
feather flags for swords and shields; make dragon

286

flags for carts; make bird flags for cavalry. In general, when the name of the flag that you are looking for is not in the book, in all cases use its form and name to make [the design on the flag].

See also Robin Yates (1980):387–390.

Yates argues persuasively that many expressions such as "forms and names (*hsing-ming*)" that were to become central political terms in the fourth and third centuries B.C. originated with often more concrete military terminology in centuries prior to it. "Forms and names" in later Legalist doctrine came to mean "accountability," where one's actual performance would be carefully weighed against what one had promised as a result. I have made the same connection between military terminology and later political vocabulary with respect to "strategic advantage (*shih*)"—see Ames (1983):65–107.

143. I follow the Han strips text here that corroborates the commentarial emendation.

144. These terms are commonly translated as "regular" and "irregular," but this does not capture their correlativity. In military language, "regular" and "irregular" conjures forth a distinction between "regular army" and "irregular militia." The distinction here is between what can be anticipated by the enemy and what catches him off guard—the element of surprise. Importantly, it might be an otherwise "regular" action that surprises an enemy using guerrilla tactics.

145. The Han strips version has "rivers and seas," where the Sung text has "rivers and streams." It is their flowing that makes the rivers and seas inexhaustible.

146. All of the received texts have "like going around a ring without beginning or end," but this seems to entail a later emendation.

147. I follow Wu Chiu-lung *et al.* (1990):75 in this reading. The alternative more common version is:

... that the velocity of a bird of prey can even smash its victim to pieces is due to its timing.

148. I follow the Han strips text here. The alternative is "He tempts the enemy ..."

149. I take the *ku* at the beginning of this passage as a passage marker. See note 122 above.

150. Compare the *Master of Huai Nan* (1968):15:11b.

151. I am following Yang Ping-an (1985):73–75 and Wu

Chiu-lung *et al.* (1990):85 in reconstructing this passage on the basis of the Han strips, the received text, and the encyclopedic works. This reading is more consistent with the demands of context. D. C. Lau (1965):321, prior to the discovery of the Han text, argued for the unemended received text that would translate:

> Thus being able to wear down a well-rested enemy, to starve one that is well-provisioned, and to move one that is settled lies in going by way of territory that the enemy does not make for, and making for places where it never occurred to him you would go.

152. Compare *Sun Pin* (1985):51.

153. Compare the *Master of Huai Nan* (1968):15/15a, and *Lao-tzu* 68.

154. The order of this passage is reversed and somewhat corrupt in the Han strips. Yang Ping-an (1985):79 makes the point that in Sun Wu's own world, his state of Wu compared with Ch'u and Yüeh could be fairly described as small and weak.

155. I am following the Han strips version here. Most of the other redactions read "what good is this to them in determining the outcome?"

156. The Han strips does not have *ku* here—commonly translated as "therefore." Even if we retain it, it only functions as a passage marker.

157. I am following the Han strips text here. The Sung edition has:

> . . . just as it is the disposition (*hsing*) of water to avoid high ground and rush to the lowest point, so in dispositioning (*hsing*) troops, avoid the enemy's strong points and strike where he is weak.

158. I follow the Han strips redaction here. Many of the traditional texts have:

> Thus an army does not have constant strategic advantages (*shih*); water does not assume a constant form (*hsing*).

This change might have been made to avoid the character *heng* (translated here as "invariable") that was the given name of Emperor Wen of the Han (r. 179–157 B.C.), and hence taboo. The presence of *heng* in the Han strips might suggest the text was copied before Emperor Wen came to the throne, although during the

Western Han, the taboo on the emperor's name was not always strictly observed.

159. The Han strips text has:

> To be able to transform oneself according to the
> enemy is called being inscrutable.

I translate *shen*—"spiritual, godlike, divine"—as "inscrutable" here, taking this sense of *shen* from the *Chou I* (*Book of Changes*) (1978):41/ *hsi shang*/5: "What cannot be fathomed with *yin* and *yang* is called *shen*."

160. The Han strips text concludes with a round dot and an additional two characters, *shen yao*—"the essentials of inscrutability." This could be an alternative chapter title, or possibly a reader's summary of the contents of the chapter.

161. I read *ku* here as a passage marker. See note 122 above.

162. This passage seems out of place. Yang Ping-an suggests it belongs to the following chapter, and has been mistakenly interpolated here. The same passage appears again in *Sun-tzu* 11:161, where it also seems out of context.

163. An alternative reading for this phrase is:

> Use flags and pennants to divide up your num-
> bers . . .

164. Although this phrase seems out of place here, its location is corroborated by the Han strips text.

165. The Han strips redaction begins this passage with "for this reason" while most other versions do not. Most commentators take this expression "*chün cheng*" to refer to a lost text entitled *The Book of Military Policies*, similar to a text called *Military Annals* (*chün chih*) cited in the *Tso-chuan* (Duke Hsi 28 and Duke Hsüan 12).

166. I have followed the arguments of the Yin-ch'üeh-shan Committee (1985):16 in retaining the order of the Han strips text in reorganizing this passage, inserting this sentence here instead of its location a few lines later in the received texts.

167. On the basis of the Han strips text, I have replaced *jen* with "the men" (*min*) here and below.

168. The *Master of Huai Nan* (1968):15/9b–10a has a similar passage:

> Thus the skilled commander in using the troops
> makes them of one mind and unifies their strength,
> so that the courageous will not have to advance

alone, and the cowardly will not get to retreat alone.

169. I read *ku* here as a passage marker rather than as "therefore." See note 122 above. Several redactions omit it altogether.

170. Yang Ping-an interprets the "day" metaphor here to refer to the progress of battle. Hence, his reading would be:

> . . . at the outset of battle, the enemy's morale is high; as the battle continues, it begins to flag; by battle's end, it has drained away.

D. C. Lau's interpretation of the text is persuasive. See Lau (1965):321–322.

171. This tally appears on the last strip. The Sung edition has a total of 477 characters, which is close.

172. Literally, this chapter is entitled "Nine Contingencies (*chiu pien*)." There has been a debate among the commentators whether or not to take the number "nine" literally, given that this passage seems to enumerate ten contingencies. Some suggest that as the largest primary number, "nine" should be construed in this text as "all of the various."

I take "nine" literally. The "[Four Contingencies]" chapter recovered in the Yin-ch'üeh-shan find is a commentary on this chapter. Having elaborated on four of the contingencies, it then states:

> . . . if the commands of the ruler are contrary to these four contingencies, do not obey them.

Thus it excludes this concluding summary proscription from its tally of four. If we do the same here and take the phrase "and commands from the ruler not to be obeyed" as a summary proscription, we arrive at the tally of nine. Other examples of this usage are "nine heavens (*chiu t'ien*)" and "nine kinds of terrain (*chiu ti*)."

173. The opening passage of Chapter 7 is identical, and commentators speculate that it has been erroneously interpolated here in the process of transmission. The uncharacteristic brevity of this chapter would suggest some substantial textual problem.

174. This particular kind of terrain, *yi ti*, is defined in *Sun-tzu* 11:153 in the following terms:

> Mountains and forests, passes and natural hazards, wetlands and swamps, and any such roads difficult to transverse constitute difficult terrain.

175. This kind of terrain, *ch'ü ti*, is defined in *Sun-tzu* 11:153:

> The territory of several neighboring states at which their borders meet is a strategically vital intersection. The first to reach it will gain the allegiance of the other states of the empire.

See D. C. Lau (1965):328 for a discussion of this passage.

176. This type of terrain, *chüeh ti*, is defined in *Sun-tzu* 11:160:

> When you quit your own territory and lead your troops across the border, you have entered cut-off terrain.

See D. C. Lau (1985):327–328.

177. The kind of terrain called *wei ti* is described in *Sun-tzu* 11:153–155:

> Ground that gives access through a narrow defile, and where exit is tortuous, allowing an enemy in small numbers to attack our main force, is terrain vulnerable to ambush.

178. This kind of terrain, *szu ti*, is described in *Sun-tzu* 11:155:

> Terrain in which you will survive only if you fight with all your might, but perish if you fail to do so, is terrain with no way out.

See D. C. Lau (1965):328.

179. In the "[Four Contingencies]" chapter recovered in the Yin-ch'üeh-shan find and translated below (Part II:2 p. 179), it elaborates on this passage:

> That there are roadways not to be traveled refers to a roadway where if we penetrate only a short distance we cannot bring the operations of our vanguard into full play, and if we penetrate too deeply we cannot link up effectively with our rearguard. If we move, it is not to our advantage, and if we stop, we will be captured. Given these conditions, we do not travel it.

180. In the "[Four Contingencies]" chapter recovered in the Yin-ch'üeh-shan find and translated as Part II:2 p. 179, it elaborates on this passage:

> That there are armies not to be attacked refers to a

situation in which the two armies make camp and face off. We estimate we have enough strength to crush the opposing army and to capture its commander. Taking the long view, however, there is some surprise advantage (*shih*) and clever dodge he has, so his army . . . its commander. Given these conditions, even though we can attack, we do not do so.

181. In the "[Four Contingencies]" chapter recovered in the Yin-ch'üeh-shan find and translated as Part II:2 p. 179–180, it elaborates on this passage:

That there are walled cities not to be assaulted refers to a situation in which we estimate we have enough strength to take the city. If we take it, it gives us no immediate advantage, and having gotten it, we would not able to garrison it. If we are [*lacking*] in strength, the walled city must by no means be taken. If in the first instance we gain advantage, the city will surrender of its own accord; and if we do not gain advantage, it will not be a source of harm afterwards. Given these conditions, even though we can launch an assault, we do not do so.

182. In the "[Four Contingencies]" chapter recovered in the Yin-ch'üeh-shan find and translated as Part II:2 p. 180, it elaborates on this passage:

That there is territory not to be contested refers to mountains and gorges . . . that are not able to sustain life. . . . vacant. Given these conditions, do not contest it.

183. In the "[Four Contingencies]" chapter recovered in the Yin-ch'üeh-shan find and translated as Part II:2 p. 180, it elaborates on this passage:

That there are commands from the ruler not to be obeyed means that if the commands of the ruler are contrary to these four contingencies, do not obey them. . . . obey them. Where affairs . . . contingencies, one understands how to use troops.

184. It is not clear what the "five advantages" are, although the commentaries are ready to speculate that they refer to five contingencies listed at the beginning of this chapter. The shortness of

this chapter suggests that much of the original text is missing, and perhaps with it, a more conclusive explanation.

185. I read *ku* ("therefore") here as a passage marker. See note 122 above.

186. I read *ku* ("therefore") here as a passage marker. See note 122 above.

187. This passage is problematic. I am following most of the commentaries with this reading. Alternative interpretations of this passage are (1) "do not ascend high ground that stands alone" (because you can then be surrounded), and (2) "descend rather than ascend to engage the enemy."

188. Many of the commentators simply read this as "low ground to your front and high ground to your rear," and while this is generally true, it is also to simplify the insight. If your position forces the enemy to have mountainous terrain to his rear, you thereby disadvantage him by cutting off his retreat. If you have an exit to your rear that can be easily defended in the case of retreat, this is to give yourself advantage at the rear.

189. This passage reads literally, "the four emperors," but the reference has been unclear in the legend surrounding the Yellow Emperor, symbolic ancestor of the Han peoples. Commentators have speculated that "four Emperors" should read "four regions," or "four armies." In the newly recovered chapter, "The Yellow Emperor Attacks the Red Emperor," it states:

> [to the south he attacked the Red Emperor] . . . to the east he attacked the [Green] Emperor . . . to the west he attacked the White Emperor . . . to the north he attacked the Black Emperor . . . and having defeated the four Emperors, he ruled over all under heaven.

Hence "the four Emperors" is not an error, but might refer to the ancestors of those peoples occupying the territory in each of the four directions.

Compare an alternative account of these battles attributed to Chiang-tzu in the *T'ai-p'ing yü-lan* (1963):79/369–370.

190. Although this passage seems out of place, it does occur here in the Han strips text. Several commentators suggest that it has been erroneously interpolated here from the passage near the beginning of this chapter where it describes "positioning an army when near water."

191. Compare *Sun Pin* (1985):61.

192. A popular alternative reading of this phrase is "if he has no treaty yet sues for peace," but it would seem unnecessary to sue for peace if a treaty had in fact already been completed.

193. The Sung text has "military vehicles" instead of "troops," but I follow the Han strips text here.

194. I have not translated the *ku* at the beginning of this passage as "therefore," taking it to be simply a passage marker. See note 122 above.

195. Compare *Sun Pin* (1985):51.

196. I follow Sun Hsing-yen (1965) in emending this passage for the rhyme. The unemended text reads:

> Know the natural conditions, know the ground,
> and the victories will be inexhaustible.

197. I am relying on D. C. Lau (1965):321 here.

198. I follow the Han strips here in omitting "his troops," thereby preserving the pattern of four character rhymed phrases.

199. Ts'ao Kuei was a native of Lu who in 681 B.C., disregarding his own life, succeeded in recovering lands lost to the state of Ch'i by grabbing Duke Huan of Ch'i and holding him at knifepoint. Chuan Chu was an assassin in the state of Wu who disregarded the certainty of his own death to take the life of King Liao of Wu in 515 B.C. These stories are recounted in *Historical Records* (1959):2515–2518.

200. In the received texts, Mount Heng is written as Mount Ch'ang, but given that the Han strips text has *"heng,"* ch'ang was probably substituted for *heng* by scribes following the convention of avoiding the given name of the emperor—in this case, Emperor Wen of the Han (r. 179–157 B.C.). See note 158 above.

201. See *Intrigues of the Warring States* (1920):7/33b; cf. Crump (1979):412–413.

202. This passage suggests that the commander takes such measures as tying up the legs of the horses and rendering the chariots inoperable to show his troops there is no retreat, and to make plain his resolve to fight to the death.

203. A common alternative reading of this ambiguous phrase is:

> The principle of exploiting terrain is to get value from both your shock units and your weaker troops.

That is, a commander can maximize his effectiveness by coordinating the quality of his troops with the features of the terrain.

204. The received texts have "keeping the enemy [literally, "others" (*jen*)] in the dark," but I follow the Han strips text here that has "keeping people (*min*) in the dark." It would appear that throughout this passage, scribes made this substitution to avoid the personal name of Li Shih-min, first emperor of the T'ang.

205. Most of the received texts include an additional phrase here:

> He sets fire to his boats and smashes his cooking
> pots.

I follow the Han strips text in omitting it.

206. The Han strips version reads "On contested terrain, I would not allow them to remain."

207. The Han strips version reads ". . . on intermediate terrain, I would make sure of my alliances."

208. The Han strips version reads ". . . at a strategically vital intersection, I would pay particular attention to reliability."

209. The Han strips version reads ". . . on critical terrain, I would hurry up our rear divisions."

210. The Han strips text reads "Therefore, the psychology of the [feudal] lords is: . . ."

211. I treat the *shih ku*—conventionally, "for this reason"—as a passage marker. See note 122 above.

212. This passage occurs almost word for word in Chapter 7:130, but seems as out of place there as it does here.

213. I follow the Han strips text in reversing the order of hegemon and king to restore what is a familiar classical expression.

214. I follow the Han strips version of the text here, which seems more consistent with the passage that follows. The received texts read ". . . get them to make the gains, but do not reveal the dangers."

215. There is an alternative interpretation of this passage, but it is not responsible to the syntax of the text:

> Therefore, the business of waging war lies in the pre-
> tence of accommodating the designs of the enemy.

216. The text at this point is clearly corrupt, and any translation can only be tentative.

217. I follow the Han strips version here, which repeats "fuel" in the second phrase rather than "smoke" or "sparks."

218. The Winnowing Basket (four stars), the Wall (two stars), the Wings (twenty-two stars), and the Chariot Platform (four stars) are four of the twenty-eight constellations called "lunar mansions" (*hsiu*), equatorial divisions that constitute segments of the celestial sphere. See Needham (1970):229–283.

219. Yang Ping-an (1986):192 recommends emending this text to read:

> If the wind blows in the daytime, follow through;
> if it blows at night, do not.

His argument is that the unemended interpretation of this passage is not consistent with what follows.

220. I read the *ku*—conventionally, "therefore"—that begins this sentence as a passage marker. See note 122 above.

221. Yang Ping-an (1986):193 suggests an emendation that would reinforce the parallel structure:

> Water can be used to cut the enemy off;
> Fire can be used to deprive him of his supplies.

222. Compare *Lao-tzu* 68.

223. I read *ku*—conventionally, "therefore"—as a passage marker. See note 122 above.

224. I follow the similar passage in *Lao-tzu* 14 in interpreting this phrase.

225. I have emended this on the basis of the Han strips text. In the received Sung text, it reads:

> Thus, in the operations of the combined forces, no
> one should have more direct access than spies, . . .

226. I follow Yang Ping-an here, but the more popular reading with the traditional commentators is:

> It is necessary to search out the enemy's agents
> who have been sent to spy on us, take care of them
> with generous bribes, and provide them with a
> place to live.

227. The same passage in the Han strips version can be reconstructed as:

> [The rise of the] Yin (Shang) dynasty [*was because
> of Yi Yin*] who served the house of Hsia; the
> rise of the Chou dynasty was because of Lü Ya
> who served [*in the house of Shang*]; [*the rise of the
> state of . . .*] was because of Commander Pi who
> served the state of Hsing; the rise of the state of

Yen was because of Su Ch'in who served the state of Ch'i. Thus only those farsighted rulers and their superior [*commanders who can get the most intelligent people as their spies are destined to accomplish great things.*].

The implication here is that Yi Yin was a minister of Chieh, the classically diabolical last ruler of the Hsia, and led troops against the throne to install T'ang, the first ruler of the Shang dynasty. Lü Ya was a minister of the equally evil Chou, the last ruler of the Shang dynasty, and was instrumental in overthrowing his sovereign and founding the Chou dynasty. These are examples of historical figures who, having inside information, could effectively topple the power at the center.

The mention of Su Ch'in here, a historical figure who lived many generations after Sun Wu, introduces the problem of dating the *Sun-tzu*. See the discussion in note 16, above.

228. I have followed the Yin-ch'üeh-shan Committee (1985) for the order of these additional chapters.

229. "Six commanders" refers to the six high ministers of Chin: Han, Chao, Wei, Fan, Chung-hang, and Chih-po.

230. The *yüan* and the *chen* are classical units of land measure. The point here is that a commander's tenure as ruler was related in inverse proportion to the taxes exacted from his people. Each household was allowed a fixed parcel of land, and the commander whose "square foot" was the smallest could exact the most taxes. Fan and Chung-hang taxed their people at 150 percent the rate of Chao.

231. This section elaborates four of the contingencies discussed in Chapter 8, "Adapting to the Nine Contingencies," above. See note 172, which suggests an explanation for why five situations are addressed as "four contingencies."

232. This passage is unclear on the Han strips, and the Yin-ch'üeh-shan Committee's reconstruction is only tentative. If an army's strength is insufficient, it would seem too obvious that siege as a strategy must be ruled out.

233. See the reference to the Yellow Emperor's attack on the Four Emperors in Chapter 9, "Deploying the Army," above. This fragmentary chapter seems to be a later commentary on "Deploying the Army."

234. In other sources, the battle site is identified as "the fields of the Pan Springs." See, for example, Ssu-ma Ch'ien (1959):3.

235. The terminology in this chapter is somewhat obscure. Some commentators suggest this passage uses terminology associated with the prognostications of the Yin-yang Five Phases School that arose under Tsou Yen (c. 305–240 B.C.)—"right/left," "*yin/yang,*" "facing/to the back," "complying/going against." According to this school, all natural phenomena and events in the processes of the world are defined in terms of their place relative to the changing conditions of their context. The description of the conquest of the Yellow Emperor also seems to refer to the "five processes" (*wu hsing*). The *Master Han Fei* 19.1.43 refers rather impatiently to such beliefs:

> Thus it is said: Divining to the gods and spirits on tortoise shells is not going to give you the victory; calculating your position "right or left," "facing or to the back" is not going to decide the battle. There is no greater stupidity than, in spite of the irrelevance of such factors, to still rely upon them.

The *Master Wei-liao (1977)*:1–4 has a similar reference:

> Master Wei-liao replied: "The Yellow Emperor's dispatching the military to punish the disorderly and showing his generosity in taking care of the people had nothing to do with calculating the auspicious days, the *yin* and *yang* relations or his relative direction described in the *Heavenly Almanac*. The Yellow Emperor was the Yellow Emperor because of his ability to use people, and nothing else."

However, the *Historical Records (1959)*:2617 has the following reference to taking practical advantage of the terrain:

> *The Art of Warfare* recommends that the right flank of the army have its back to the mountains and hills, and the left flank have the water and swamplands to its front.

This *Historical Records* description is certainly consistent with the language of Chapter 9, "Deploying the Army," which describes the advantages of maintaining high ground to the rear of the right flank and keeping to the sunny side, and also refers explicitly to the conquest of the Yellow Emperor over the four quarters. In addition, *Sun-tzu* is rather practical in tone, and unsympathetic to divinatory "revelation." In Chapter 13 above it states explicitly:

> Thus the reason the farsighted ruler and his superior commander conquer the enemy at every move and achieve successes far beyond the reach of the common crowd is foreknowledge. Such foreknowledge cannot be had from ghosts and spirits, educed by comparison with past events, or verified by astrological calculations. It must come from people—people who know the enemy's situation.

If we insist that the terminology here reflects the influence of a Yin-yang Five Phases School, it would mean a relatively late date not only for this fragmentary commentarial chapter, but for the thirteen-chapter *Sun-tzu* itself.

236. Of the fragments assigned to this chapter, I have tentatively translated those strips which provide us with additional content.

237. Compare Chapter 9:141 above, and *Sun Pin* (1985):61. "The natural net is dense forest and underbrush, the natural well is a box canyon, and the natural prison is terrain that is closed on all sides."

238. This is similar to a passage in Chapter 11:159, "The Nine Kinds of Terrain."

239. I follow the order of the 1985 Yin-ch'üeh-shan Han strips edition. See Hattori Chiharu (1987) for a revised ordering of these strips. I have tentatively translated those remaining fragments where they provide us with additional content—for example, the explicit references to the "thirteen-chapter" text.

240. I have followed the reconstruction of Hattori Chiharu (1987) in inserting this passage from the remaining fragments at this point in the text.

241. I have followed the reconstruction of Hattori Chiharu (1987) in inserting this passage from the remaining fragments at this point in the text.

242. These eight passages have been reconstructed from treatise 159 of a T'ang dynasty encyclopedic work in two hundred books, the *T'ung-tien*, compiled by Tu Yu (735–812). See *T'ung-tien* (1988):4076–4079.

243. The *T'ung-tien* (1988):4076 text does not have the first portion of this paragraph. It is restored on the basis of the (Sung) Ho Yen-hsi commentary. See Sun Hsing-yen (1965):226.

244. See the K'ung Ying-ta (574–648), (1931):57/4a commentary to *Tso-chuan* (Duke Ai 1).

245. See Wang Fu's (76–157) *Ch'ien-fu-lun* (1928):5/8b (Advice to the Commander). It is difficult to tell what is being cited from *Sun-tzu*, and what is Wang Fu's own commentary. The first sentence adds one additional trait ("respect") of the commander to a list found in Chapter 1:103 above of the original thirteen-chapter text. But what follows this one sentence appears to be Wang Fu's own elaboration.

246. See the Li Shan (d.689) commentary to *Wen-hsüan* (1931):9/97.

247. See *Pei-t'ang shu-ch'ao* 115/2a.

248. This title does not appear in any of the early court catalogs, and might be an apocryphal text from some later period.

249. See *Pei-t'ang shu-ch'ao* 115/3a.

250. This title does not appear in any of the early court catalogs, and might be an apocryphal text from some later period. Pi I-hsün (1937):10 states that in later times, many descendants of Sun Wu wrote on military affairs. This work might well have been the product of one of them.

251. See the *Pei-t'ang shu-ch'ao* 116/1a.

252. See *T'ai-p'ing yü-lan* (1963):273/4b. Compare the list of traits in Chapter 1:103.

253. Cited in Yang Ping-an (1986):216.

254. Cited in Huang K'uei (1989):251. In chapter 9:141 above, it states that in "encountering . . . natural defiles, quit such places with haste. Do not approach them. In keeping our distance from them, we can maneuver the enemy near to them; in keeping them to our front, we can maneuver the enemy to have them at his back."

255. See the Li Shan commentary to *Wen-hsüan* (1931):3/89. Chapter 9:000 above has a similar passage that states:

> If the army is flanked by precipitous ravines, stagnant ponds, reeds and rushes, mountain forests and tangled undergrowth, they must be searched carefully and repeatedly, for these are the places where ambushes are laid and spies are hidden.

256. See *T'ung-tien* (1988):4074.

257. In Chapter 9:141 it states: "Encountering . . . natural wells, . . . quit such places with haste." This passage is cited in Pi I-hsün (1937):8 as coming from *T'ai-p'ing yü-lan*.

258. The court catalog of the *History of the Sui Dynasty* has the entry, "*The Miscellaneous Prognostications of Sun-tzu* in four scrolls."

Sun-tzu Chapter 11:158 explicitly rejects prognostication as a positive source of military information: "proscribe talk of omens and get rid of rumors, and even to the death they will not retreat." This makes any direct attribution of this work problematic.

259. See *T'ai-p'ing yü-lan* (1963): 328/3b.

260. See *T'ai-p'ing yü-lan* (1963):8/7a.

261. *Sun Pin* (1985):60 describes this deployment in a chapter entitled "The Eight-Division Formation:"

> Master Sun Pin said, "When putting the eight-division formation into battle operation, turn whatever advantages the terrain permits to account, and adapt the formation to meet these conditions. Divide your main body in three with each of these detachments having a vanguard force, and each vanguard having reinforcements to its rear. All should move only upon command. Commit one detachment to the fray while holding the other two in reserve. Use one detachment to actually assault the enemy, and the other two to consolidate your gains. Where the enemy is weak and in disarray, commit your elite troops first to gain a quick advantage. But where he is strong and tight in formation, commit your weaker troops first to bait him. Divide the chariots and cavalry that will be used in combat into three detachments: one on either flank and one at the rear. On flat and easy ground, make greater use of the war chariots; on rugged terrain use more cavalry; on terrain that is sheer and closes in on both sides, use more crossbowmen. Taking into account both the rugged and the easy terrain, you must distinguish between safe ground and terrain from which there is no way out. And you must occupy the safe ground yourself while attacking the enemy where he has no way out."

262. Pi I-hsün (1937):9 attributes this passage incorrectly to the Cheng Hsüan (A.D. 127–200) commentary to the *Chou-li*. I do not know where he found it. Such chariots used screens to conceal the occupants and protect them from bolts and other projectiles.

263. See the Li Shan commentary to *Wen-hsüan* (1931):9/93.

264. The commentary to the court catalog of the *History of the*

Sui Dynasty (Sui-shu) (1973):1012 records that the *Eight-Division Formation Diagrams of Sun-tzu* in one scroll has been lost.

265. This passage is cited in the Chang Yü commentary to Chapter 11 of the Sung edition of *Sun-tzu with Eleven Commentaries (Shih-i chia chu Sun-tzu)* (1978):274.

266. There is no record of this text in the court catalogs until the *Former History of the T'ang Dynasty*, which might suggest its vintage.

267. In addition to the Han dynasty strips found in the Yin-ch'üeh-shan tombs, another cache of strips dating from the late Western Han dynasty was discovered in 1978 in Tomb #115 of the Sun family compound in Ta-t'ung county, Ch'ing-hai province, and reported in the *Wen-wu (Cultural Relics)* 1981 no. 2. Six strips had "Master Sun" on them, suggesting some relationship with the *Sun-tzu*.

268. This corroborates the received "thirteen-chapter" text referred to both in the Yin-ch'üeh-shan Han strips and the *Historical Records*.

269. See the Li Shan commentary to *Wen-hsüan* (1931):9/99. It is reminiscent of Chapter 7:130 above:

> Thus, advancing at a pace, such an army is like the wind; slow and majestic, it is like a forest; invading and plundering, it is like fire; sedentary, it is like a mountain; unpredictable, it is like a shadow; moving, it is like lightning and thunder.

270. Cited from the *T'ung-tien* in Pi I-hsün (1937):9.

271. Cited from the *T'ung-tien* in Pi I-hsün (1937):9.

272. Cited from the *T'ung-tien* in Pi I-hsün (1937):9.

273. See *Feng-su t'ung-yi* (1980):403. If "Master Sun" here refers to Sun Wu, the mention of Mo Ti (Master Mo) is an anachronism, and makes the relationship of this passage to the historical Sun Wu suspect.

274. See Wu Chiu-lung (1985):12.

275. *History of the Han Dynasty (Han-shu)* (1962):156, 1164.

276. *History of the Han Dynasty (Han-shu)* (1962):1762.

277. *History of the Han Dynasty (Han-shu)* (1962):1135–1136.

278. I am grateful to my colleague Tao Tien-yi for helping me think this through.

279. See Lo Fu-i (1974):35.

280. Compare Michael Loewe (1977).

281. See *History of the Sui Dynasty* (1973):1013.

282. Yin-ch'üeh-shan Han-mu chu-chien cheng-li hsiao-tsu (1975b).

283. In the first assessment of the Yin-ch'üeh-shan find in 1975, the *Sun Pin* was reconstructed in thirty chapters. After another decade of study, the committee in its 1985 publication reconsidered this attribution, and reduced the number of chapters to fifteen of these original thirty, and added one new one to make a total of sixteen chapters. The fifteen chapters excluded from the *Sun Pin* in the 1985 publication can be regarded as "supplemental."

284. See Li Hsüeh-ch'in's preface to Li Ching (1990):4 (preface).

BIBLIOGRAPHY
OF WORKS CITIED

Ames, Roger T. *The Art of Rulership: A Study in Ancient Chinese Political Thought.* Honolulu: University of Hawaii Press, 1983.

Blanford, Yumiko F. "A Textual Approach to *Zhanguo zonghengjia shu*: Methods of Determining the Proximate Original Word among Variants" in *Early China* 16, 1991.

Calthrop, Captain E. F. *The Book of War.* London: John Murray, 1908.

Carson, Michael F. (comp.). *A Concordance to Lü-shih ch'un-ch'iu*, 2 volumes. San Francisco: Chinese Materials Center, Inc., 1985.

Chan-kuo-ts'e. Peking: Shang-wu shu-chü. Ssu-pu ts'ung-k'an edition, 1920.

Chang Chen-tse. *Sun Pin ping-fa chiao-li.* Peking: Chung-hua shu-chü, 1984.

Chang-sun Wu-chi (d. 659), (comp.). *History of the Sui Dynasty (Sui-shu).* Peking: Chung-hua shu-chü, 1973.

Ch'i Kuang. *Sun Wu ping-fa chu-shih.* Peking: Pei-ching ku-chi ch'u-pan-she, 1988.

Ch'ien Mu. *Hsien-Ch'in chu-tzu hsi nien* (revised edition). Hong Kong: Hong Kong University Press, 1956.

Chih Wei-ch'eng (editor). *Sun-tzu ping-fa shih-cheng.* Peking: Chung-kuo shu-tien, 1988.

Chou I (Book of Changes). Reprint of Harvard–Yenching Institute Sinological Index Series. Taipei: Nan-yü ch'u-pan-she, 1978.

Chu Chun. *Sun-tzu ping-fa shih-yi.* Peking: Hai-ch'ao ch'u-pan-she, 1988.

Cleary, Thomas. *The Art of War: Sun-tzu.* Boston: Shambhala, 1988.

Creel, H. G. *The Origins of Statecraft in China*, Vol. I. Chicago: Chicago University Press, 1970.

Crump, James (trans.). *Chan-kuo ts'e* [*Intrigues of the Warring States*]. San Francisco: Chinese Materials Center, Inc. Second revised edition, 1979.

Discourses of the States (Kuo-yü). Shanghai: Chung-hua shu-chü. Ssu-pu pei-yao edition, 1928.

Duyvendak, J. J. L. (trans.). *The Book of Lord Shang*. London: Arthur Probsthain, 1928.

Fairbank, John. *China Watch*. Cambridge, MA: Harvard University Press, 1987.

Fan Yeh *et al.*, (comp.). *History of the Later Han Dynasty* (*Hou-Han-shu*). Peking: Chung-hua shu-chü, 1965.

Foucault, Michel. *The Order of Things: An Archaeology of the Human Sciences*. New York: Vintage Books, 1973.

Fu Chen-lun. *Sun Ping ping-fa shih-chu*. Ssu-ch'uan: Pa-shu shu-she, 1986.

Giles, Lionel. *Sun Tzu on the Art of War*. London: Luzac & Co., 1910.

Graham, A. C. *Chuang-tzu: The Inner Chapters*. London: George Allen & Unwin, 1981.

Griffith, Samuel B. *Sun Tzu: The Art of War*. Oxford: Oxford University Press, 1963.

Guisso, Richard W., and Stanley Johannesen (eds.). *Women in China: Current Directions in Historical Scholarship*. Youngstown, NY: Philo Press, 1981.

Hall, David L., and Roger T. Ames. *Thinking Through Confucius*. Albany, NY: State University of New York Press, 1987.

Han Fei-tzu so-yin. Peking: Chung-hua shu-chü, 1982.

Hattori, Chiharu. *Sun-tzu ping-fa chiao-chieh*. Peking: Chün-shih k'o-hsüeh ch'u-pan-she, 1989.

Henricks, Robert G. *Lao-tzu Te-tao Ching: A New Translation Based on the Recently Discovered Ma-wang-tui Texts*. New York: Ballantine Books, 1989.

Hou Yin-chang. *Sun Pin ping-fa ch'ien-shuo*. Peking: Chieh-fang-chün ch'u-pan-she, 1986.

Hsiao T'ung (501–531) (comp.). *Wen-hsüan*. Shanghai: Shang-wu yin-shu-kuan, 1931.

Hsü P'ei-ken and Wei Ju-lin. *Sun Pin ping-fa chu-shih*. Taipei: Li-ming wen-hua shih-yeh kung-szu, 1976.

Hsün-tzu. Harvard-Yenching Institute Sinological Index Series, Supplement 22. Peking: Harvard-Yenching, 1950.

Hsü Wei-yü. (ed.). *Lü-shih ch'un-ch'iu.* Taipei: Shih-chieh shu-chü, 1935 (1955 reprint).

Huang K'uei. *Sun-tzu tao-tu.* Ch'eng-tu: Pa-shu shu-she ch'u-pan, 1989.

Kanaya Osamu. *Sonbin heiho.* Tokyo: Toho shuten, 1976.

Kierman, Frank A., Jr. (editor). *Chinese Ways in Warfare.* Cambridge, MA: Harvard University Press, 1974.

Knoblock, John. *Xunzi: A Translation and Study of the Complete Works,* Vol. II, Books 7–16. Stanford: Stanford University Press, 1990.

Kuan-tzu. *A Concordance to the Kuan-tzu.* Compiled by Wallace Johnson. Taipei: Ch'eng-wen ch'u-pan-she, 1970.

K'ung Ying-ta (574–648). *Tso-chuan chu-su (Commentary on the Tso-chuan).* Shanghai: Chung-hua shu-chü. Ssu-pu pei-yao edition, 1931.

Kuo Hua-jo. *Sun-tzu shih-chu.* Shanghai: Shang-hai ku-chi ch'u-pan-she, 1984.

Lai Hai-tsung. *Chung-kuo wen-hua yü Chung-kuo ping.* Taipei: Li-jen shu-chü, 1984 (Taiwan reprint).

Lau, D. C. "Some Notes on the *Sun-tzu.*" *Bulletin of the School of Oriental and African Studies* 1965:28:2:318–335.

—— (trans.). *Chinese Classics: Tao Te Ching.* Hong Kong: Chinese University Press, 1982.

—— (trans.). *Chinese Classics: Mencius.* Hong Kong: Chinese University Press, 1984.

Le Blanc, Charles. *Huai-nan-tzu: Philosophical Synthesis in Early Han Thought.* Hong Kong: Hong Kong University Press, 1985.

Lei Hai-tsung. *Chung-kuo wen-hua yü Chung-kuo te ping.* Taipei: Li-jen shu-chü, 1984.

Lewis, Mark Edward. *Sanctioned Violence in Early China.* Albany, NY: State University of New York Press, 1990.

Li Ching. *Ch'i Sun-tzu fa-chieh.* Peking: Chung-kuo shu-tien, 1990.

Li Fang (925–996) (comp.). *T'ai-p'ing yü-lan.* Peking: Chung-hua shu-chü, 1963.

Li Ling. "Ch'ing-hai Ta-t'ung-hsien shang Sun-chia-chai Han-chien hsing-chih hsiao-i [A brief discussion of the nature of the Han dynasty strips recovered in the Ch'ing-hai Ta-t'ung county Sun family compound dig]" in *K'ao-ku (Archaeology)* 1983:6:549–553.

Liu An (editor). *Huai Nan-tzu (Master of Huai Nan)*. Taipei: Yi-wen yin-shu-kuan. Ssu-pu ts'ung-k'an edition, 1968.

Liu Chung-p'ing. *Wei-liao-tzu chin-chu chin-shih* (trans. and commentary). Taipei: Commercial Press, 1975.

Liu Hsiang (attributed). *Intrigues of the Warring States (Chan-kuo ts'e)*. Peking: Shang-wu shu-chü. Ssu-pu ts'ung-k'an edition, 1920.

Liu Hsin-chien (editor). *Sun Pin ping-fa: hsin-pien chu-shih.* Honan: Honan University Press, 1989.

Lo Fu-i. "Lin-i Han-chien kai-shu." *Wen-wu (Cultural Relics)*, 1974:2.

Loewe, Michael. "Manuscripts found recently in China: A preliminary survey." *T'oung Pao* Vol. 63, no. 2–3:99–136, 1977.

Lum, Wing Tek. *Expounding the Doubtful Points.* Honolulu: Bamboo Ridge Press, 1987.

Mencius (Meng-tzu). Harvard–Yenching Institute Sinological Index Series, Supplement 17. Peking: Harvard–Yenching, 1941.

Needham, Joseph. *Science and Civilisation in China*, Vol. III. Cambridge: Cambridge University Press, 1970.

Needham, Joseph, *et al.*, and Robin D. S. Yates. *Science and Civilisation in China* Vol. 5, Part VI. Cambridge: Cambridge University Press (forthcoming).

Nei Meng-ku ta-hsüeh chung-wen-hsi. *Sun Pin ping-fa yen-chiu.* Hu-ho-hao-t'e: Nei Meng-ku ta-hsüeh chung-wen-hsi, 1978.

Norman, Jerry, and Tsu-lin Mei. "The Austroasiatics in Ancient South China: Some Lexical Evidence" in *Monumenta Serica* Vol. XXXII, 1976, 274–301.

Pan Ku (32–92). *History of the Han Dynasty (Han-shu)* Peking: Chung-hua shu-chü, 1962.

Peerenboom, R.P. *Law and Morality in Ancient China. The Silk Manuscripts of Huang-Lao.* Albany, NY: State University of New York Press, 1993.

Pi I-hsün. *Sun-tzu hsü-lu (Citations from Sun-tzu)*. Shanghai: Shang-wu yin-shu-kuan, 1937.

—— (trans.). *Kuan-tzu: A Repository of Early Chinese Thought.* Hong Kong: Hong Kong University Press, 1965.

Rickett, W. A. (trans.). *Guanzi: Political, Economic, and Philosophical Essays from Early China.* Princeton, New Jersey: Princeton University Press, 1985.

Ssu-ma Ch'ien *et al. Historical Records* (*Shih-chi*). Peking: Chung-hua shu-chü, 1959.

Sun Hsing-yen. *Sun-tzu shih-chia chu.* Taipei: Shang-wu yin-shu-kuan, 1965.

Sun-tzu shih-i-chia chu. Taipei: reprint of the Central Library's Sung edition in the *Chung-kuo tzu-hsüeh ming-chu chi-ch'eng* series, 1978.

T'ang Lan. "Ssu-ma Ch'ien so mei-you chien-kuo-te chen-kuei shih-liao" in *Chan-kuo tsung-heng-chia shu.* Ma-wang-tui Han-mu po-shu cheng-li hsiao-tsu (ed.). Peking: Wen-wu ch'u-pan she, 1976.

T'ao Han-chang. *Sun-tzu ping-fa kai-lun.* Peking: Chieh-fang-chün ch'u-pan-she, 1989.

Teng Tse-tsung. *Sun Pin ping-fa chu-shih.* Peking: Chieh-fang-chün ch'u-pan-she, 1986.

Tu Yu (735–812). *T'ung-tien.* Peking: Chung-hua shu-chü, 1988.

Twitchett, Denis, and Michael Loewe (editors). *The Cambridge History of China, Vol. I: The Ch'in and Han Empires 221 B.C.–A.D. 220.* Cambridge: Cambridge University Press, 1986.

Wang Fu (76–157) (comp.). *Ch'ien-fu-lun.* Shanghai: Chung-hua shu-chü. Ssu-pu pei-yao edition, 1928.

Wang Jen-chün. *Sun-tzu i-wen* (unpublished text preserved in the archives of the Shanghai Library).

Wang Yin-chih. *Ching-chuan shih-tsu.* Hong Kong: T'ai-p'ing shu-chü, 1966.

Watson, Burton (trans.). *Han Fei Tzu: Basic Writings.* New York: Columbia University Press, 1964.

Wei Cheng. *History of the Sui Dynasty* (*Sui-shu*). Peking: Chung-hua shu-chü, 1966.

Wu Chiu-lung. *Yin-ch'üeh-shan Han-chien shih-wen.* Peking: Wen-wu ch'u-pan-she, 1985.

Wu Chiu-lung *et al.* (editors). *Sun-tzu chiao-shih.* Chün-shih k'o-hsüeh ch'u-pan-she, 1990.

Yang Kuan. "Ma-wang-tui po shu *Chan-kuo tsung-heng-chia shu* te shih-liao chia-chih" in *Wen-wu* (*Cultural Relics*) 1975.2.

Yang Ping-an. *Sun-tzu hui-chien.* Chung-chou: Chung-chou ku-chi ch'u-pan-she, 1986.

Yates, Robin D. S. *The City Under Siege: Technology and Organization as Seen in the Reconstructed Text of the Military Chapters of Mo-tzu.* Unpublished Ph.D. dissertation, Harvard University, 1980.

Yates, Robin D. S. "New Light on Ancient Chinese Military Texts: Notes on Their Nature and Evolution, and the Development of Military Specialization in Warring States China." *T'oung Pao*, 1988:64:211–248.

Yin-ch'üeh-shan Han-mu chu-chien cheng-li hsiao-tsu (Committee for the Reconstruction of the Yin-ch'üeh-shan Han strips). (1975a). *Sun Pin ping-fa*. Peking: Wen-wu ch'u-pan-she, 1975(a).

Yin-ch'üeh-shan Han-mu chu-chien cheng-li hsiao-tsu (Committee for the Reconstruction of the Yin-ch'üeh-shan Han strips). *Yin-ch'üeh-shan Han-mu chu-chien* I, 10 *ts'e* (1–4 *Sun-tzu: The Art of Warfare*: 5–10 *Sun Pin: The Art of Warfare*). Peking: Wen-wu ch'u-pan-she, 1975(b).

Yin-ch'üeh-shan Han-mu chu-chien cheng-li hsiao-tsu (Committee for the Reconstruction of the Yin-ch'üeh-shan Han strips) *Yin-ch'üeh-shan Han-mu chu-chien* Collection I. Peking: Wen-wu ch'u-pan-she, 1985.

Ying Shao (fl. 189–220). *Feng-su t'ung-yi* (*Comprehensive Meaning of Customs*). Peking: T'ien-chin jen-min ch'u-pan-she, 1980.

Yü Shih-nan (558–638) (comp.). *Pei-t'ang shu-ch'ao*. Blockprint edition re-cut from traced Sung edition, 1888.

INDEX

according with the enemy (yin) 83, 84, 127, 162, 165
advantage. See strategic advantage (shih)
alliances 111, 153, 160, 161, 208, 209
ambush 141, 200, 201, 203, 205, 207, 211, 213, 215, 247
Ames, Roger T. 281, 282, 287
amnesty 183
amputation 70
An, Lo-che 58
anachronism 22
Analects of Confucius 10, 25, 39, 41, 280, 281
  recovered at Ting-hsien 277
analogy 73
  categorization by 53
analysis
  categorization by 52
ancestral temple 162
appropriateness (yi) 67, 68
archaeological excavations
  importance to the study of early China 9
  two most important 13
archers 74, 221
Aristotle 59
armor 24, 107, 218, 243
army
  allegiance of the 144
  deploying the 254
  divided in purpose 203
  as family 200, 215
  fearful 203
  flexibility in maneuvering the 159
  in formation 187, 193, 194, 195, 216, 240, 243, 244, 245, 247
  functioning as one person 131, 159, 161, 209, 215, 226, 227, 289
  keeping intact 85, 111, 112, 166
  of a king or hegemon 161
  like herding a flock of sheep 159
  on the march 235
  not to be attacked 135, 179, 291
  numerical strength of 112, 119, 125, 126, 144, 155, 157, 207, 214, 237
  operations for an invading 157, 159
  positioning in the mountains 139
  positioning near water 139, 293
  positioning on the flatlands 139
  positioning on the salt marshes 139
  provisioning the 157
  redeploying the 247
  thinking of home 202, 203
  training the 144
  which will not return 240
art of contextualizing 59, 60, 62
  and warfare 67

assessments 104
assumptions
  Chinese cultural 49
  uncommon 43
  Western cultural 43
astrological calculations 169
attack 115, 123
  incendiary 165
  by water 166
authoritativeness 67
authority 64, 65, 195
autogenerative (tzu-jan) 50

baiting the enemy 120, 129, 132
bamboo strip manuscripts
  bound into scrolls (ts'e) 272
  dating the 271
  divided into chapters 273
  number of characters on the 273
  order of the 273
  a physical description of 271
  reconstructing the 271
  style of the characters on the 272
  table of contents for the 275
  titles of chapters on the 274
battle 56, 89, 90, 109, 220
  anticipating the 126
  and counting rods 94
  determining the outcome of 162
  difficulty of the 129
  the expert in 123
  no heart for 219
  short duration of 86
  temple rehearsal of 94, 105
  tumult and clamor of 120
battle cries 218, 221
battle line 90
Battle Ordinances 251
battlefield 108, 252
Being 48
Bill of Rights 69
Black Emperor 183, 293
Blanford, Yumiko F. 279
body 61
Book of Changes (I Ching) 10, 54, 281, 289
Book of Lord Shang 35, 39
The Book of Military Policies 130, 289
Borges, Jorge Luis 54
box canyons 141, 299
burial effects 271
  in the tombs of Yin-ch'üeh-shan 265, 267
"burning of the books" 26

calendar
  recovered at Yin-ch'üeh-shan 14, 266, 269, 270, 272

311

Calthrop, Captain, E. F.
  his translation of the *Sun-tzu* 8
categorization (lei) 52, 53
cattle 211
cavalry 258, 287, 306. See also
    mounted troops
  equipped with crossbows 29, 205
center
  centripetal 62, 64, 66, 88
Chan-kuo ts'e. See *Intrigues of the
    Warring States (Chan-kuo ts'e)*
Chang, Chen-tse 15, 279
Chang, Shou-chieh 37
Chang, Yü 302
change 52, 54, 131
  inexhaustability of 126
  the irrespresibility of 80
  as movement between polar
      opposites 76
  reality of 50
  the rhythm of 81
changing conditions 131
Chao 175, 176. See Chin: six high
    ministers of
Chao, Ch'i 38
chaos 46, 149
chaos theory 90
chapter titles 99
Chariot (constellation) 165
chariots 29, 109, 142, 159, 203, 209,
    213, 237, 301
  armored personnel-style 243
  four-horse 107
chen
  differing measurements of 175, 176
Ch'en Chen-sun 20
Cheng Hsüan 301
ch'i
  psychophysical energy 50, 55, 241
Ch'i, state of 261
Chiang, T'ai-kung 259
Chieh, King of Hsia 184
Ch'ien, Mu 20, 279
Chih (Chih-po) 175, 176 See Chin: six
    high ministers of
Chin
  six high ministers of 297
  the state of 22, 175
Ch'in dynasty (221–206 B.C.) 16
Ch'in Shih Huang Ti. See First
    Emperor of the Ch'in Dynasty
Chin-ch'üeh-shan (Gold Sparrow
    mountain) 261
China
  material culture of 9
"China," the word
  comes from the state of Ch'in 277
Chinese gods
  as ancestors and dead cultural heroes
      72
"Chinese Hot Pot" 61
Ch'ing-tao (Tsingtao) 261
Chou I (Book of Changes). See *Book of
    Changes (I Ching)*
Chou, King of Shang 184

Chou-li 301
Chuan, Chu 158, 294
Ch'uan, Tsu-wang 20
Chuang-tzu 65
Chung-hang 175, 176. See Chin: six
    high ministers of
chung-kuo "central states," not "Middle
    Kingdom" 277
*Classic on Examining Dogs
    (Hsiang-kou-ching)* 269
Cleary, Thomas
  his translation of the Sun-tzu 8
clerical script (li-shu) 267
climate 103, 104
cloak of silence 203, 211, 247
coherence 53, 56, 57
coins
  pan-liang (half-tael) 266
  san-chu (three-chu) 266
  used to secure silk cords 266
  wu-chu (five-chu) 266
command 103
commander 89, 90, 91, 96, 104, 111,
    131, 144, 225, 233, 240
  controlling of events 92
  and correlativity 94
  and defeat 93
  employing spies 169, 170, 171
  the enemy 143, 179
  as an exemplary person (chün-tzu)
      87, 88
  exploiting the situation 166
  as final arbiter 88, 109
  five criteria of 103
  five dangerous traits of 136
  humane and just 170
  inciting battle 166
  incorruptibility of 229
  and integrity 85
  keeping his forces intact 85, 111,
      112
  and knowing the enemy 144, 151,
      169, 170, 171
  in the *Master of Huai Nan* 83
  and the nine contingencies 135
  receiving orders from the ruler 129,
      135
  relationship with his men 144, 150
  relationship with the ruler 86, 87,
      88, 113
  and selecting the right person for
      intelligence 91
  as side-guard on the carriage of state
      88, 112
  and the six guidelines governing the
      use of terrain 149
  and the six ways to certain defeat
      150
  slaying the enemy 162
  three basic strategies of 231
  traits of the consumate 87, 135, 150,
      155, 169, 171, 226, 229, 230,
      231, 232
  urgent business of the 159
  and victory 93

312

the way of the 195
and wisdom 89, 90, 108
Commander Pi, who served the state
of Hsing 23
commands
obeying 32, 33, 34, 194, 195
of the ruler not to be obeyed 88, 89,
113, 135, 150, 179, 180, 192,
292
commentaries 198
*Commentary of Master Tso
(Tso-chuan)* 20, 289, 299
communication on the battlefield 130,
131, 155
conditions 57, 60
casual 56
focal 56, 57
local 56
local field of 76
site-specific 90
Confucianism 67
and Han dynasty syncretism 66
as state ideology 65
Confucius 32, 59, 72
contemporary of Sun Wu 18
and warfare 41
conscription 108
Constant Hall 187
constellations 165
contextualizing. See art of
contextualizing
correlativity 52, 62, 77, 78, 81, 94,
120, 135, 287
and circumstances 89
and the commander 94
of time (chou) and space (yü) 82
cosmogony 48
courage 158, 211, 221, 226, 227, 232
covert operations 171
creativity
classical Chinese conception of 58
classical Western conception of 59
Creel, H. G. 280
cross-cultural understanding 44
crossbow, 74, 75, 120, 221, 257, 301
Austroasiatic origins of the 280
introduction into China 24
use by cavalry 29
culinary arts, 59, 60, 61, 62
Crump, J. I. 279, 294
Cultural Relics (Wen-wu) 98, 268, 269,
277, 278, 302

deceit 95, 104, 130
decoys 203
defeat 92, 93, 104, 139, 191
six ways to certain 150
turned to victory 161, 218
warfare is always 85, 93
defense 115, 123, 160
defenses 213
consolidating 200
reinforcing 205, 207, 218
deference
patterns of 64, 67

Deity
Judaeo-Christian 48, 69
transcendent 46, 72
deliberation 93, 94
Demiéville, Paul 281
dialogue format 6, 37
dignity 226
discipline 144, 157, 158
discourse
levels of 58
Discourses of the States (Kuo-yü) 60,
281
dispositions (hsing) 76, 77
no invariable 80
uniqueness of 79
ditches 218
divination 269, 298
Documents of the Warring States Strategists
and the *Intrigues of the Warring States*
279
drums 194, 205, 209, 211, 215, 218,
221
dualistic thinking 45, 47, 52, 56
Duke Huan of Ch'i 294
Duyvendak, J.J.L. 280

eight-division formation 243
"The Eight-Division Formation"
274, 301
Eight-Division Formation Diagrams
245
*Eight-Division Formation Diagrams of
Sun-tzu 302*
embodying (t'i) 71
emissaries
enemy 144, 162
Emperor Ching of the Han 15, 16
Emperor Hui of the Han 15
Emperor Wen of the Han 15, 16,
288
Emperor Wu of the Han 15, 16, 267
Empress Lü of the Han 15
encyclopedias 97, 197, 198, 288
mention of Sun-tzu in the 5
enemy 95
an angry 144
anticipating the 81
assessing the 141, 142, 143, 144,
149, 150, 161
breaking through his lines 217, 245
capturing its high command 240
cornering the 136, 213, 218
cutting his supply lines 221
cutting off the 206
demoralizing the 131
the design of the 161
a desperate 143
disciplined in its formation 131
in disorder 143
emissary of the 144, 162
feeding off of the 211
fragmented 95
harassing the 216, 222
and intelligence 90
killing the 108

313

enemy (continued)
   occupying the strategic ground of
      the 223
   proactive attitude toward 78
   responding to intentions of the 83,
      84, 127, 162, 165, 247
   taking the battle to the 155, 218,
      220, 221
   with the terrain advantage 222, 223
enemy commander 143, 179
espionage 84, 92, 170. See also spies
essentialism 51, 52, 53, 54, 56, 57, 58
evidence 73

Fairbank, John K. 66, 68, 280, 281
Fan 175, 176. See Chin: six high
   ministers of
Fan, Yeh 285
"female" fortifications 28
Feng-chiao-chan. See Wind Direction
   Divination (Feng-chiao-chan)
Feng-su t'ung-yi 302
fighting to the death 143, 155, 157,
   158, 160, 161, 217, 218, 221,
   228, 294
fire. See incendiary attack
First Emperor of the Ch'in Dynasty 12
five phases (wu-hsing) 77, 80, 127
flags and pennants 109, 119, 131, 143,
   205, 286, 289
flatlands 139
flexibility 80, 84
  in maneuvering the army 159
flight 149
focal order 56, 57, 65
focus-field 65
Forbidden Palace Museum 262
force-marching 129
foreknowledge (chih) 89, 94, 169, 170,
   171, 299
  the commander's 92
formation 244, 254
  army 187
  assuming battle 193, 194, 195, 216,
    240, 247
  attack 215
  eight-division 243, 245, 301
  the extended battle 244
Former Kings 61
fortifications
  "male" and "female" 28
four Emperors 293
fuel
  inflammable 165

generalization 45
geometry 54, 55
ghosts and spirits 169, 298, 299
gifts 209
Giles, Lionel
  commentary on Calthrop's Sun-tzu
   translation 8
"givenness" 50, 57, 58, 59, 62
gorges, river 141
Graham, A. C. 281

Greek philosophy
  centrality of metaphysics in 46
  classical 45, 55
[Green] Emperor 183, 293
Griffith, Samuel B. 277, 280, 283
  translation of the Sun-tzu 8, 24

Hall, David L., and Ames
  Thinking Through Confucius 281
Han 175. See also Chin: six high
  ministers of
Han dynasty
  intellectual and political order
   during 65
Han Fei 35
Han Fei-tzu. See Master Han Fei (Han
   Fei-tzu)
Han Fei-tzu so-yin 280
Han dynasty strips,
  dating of 15, 266
Han-shu. See History of the Han Dynasty
   (Han-shu)
hand weapons 257
harmony (ho) 43, 55, 58, 59, 60, 61,
   62, 66, 67, 119, 120
  centripetal 62, 63, 64, 66, 67, 88
  Chinese model of 42
  and unique particularity 73
  unmediated 89
Hattori, Chiharu 299
heart-and-mind 131
Heaven (t'ien) 67, 240
Heaven's mandate 68
Henrick, Robert G.
  translation of Lao-tzu: Te-tao-ching
   10
herding and gathering 223
high ground 139, 141, 147, 187, 188,
   293, 298
historians 53
Historical Records (Shih-chi) 18, 19, 32,
   34, 36, 38, 191, 279, 280, 294,
   298
historiography 53
History of the Han Dynasty (Han-shu)
   18, 30, 37, 39, 266, 278, 285,
   302
History of the Later Han Dynasty
   (Hou-Han-shu) 19, 285
History of the Sui Dynasty (Sui-shu) 20,
   279, 300, 301, 302
Ho, Yen 278
Ho, Yen-hsi 299
holograph 65, 76
honor 136
horses 209, 211
Hou-Han-shu. See History of
   the Later Han Dynasty
   (Hou-Han-shu)
Hsiang-kou-ching. See Classic
   on Examining Dogs
   (Hsiang-kou-ching)
Hsiang-p'ing 183
hsing. See strategic positioning
hsing. See punishments

314

Hsü, Wei-yu 281
Hsün-tzu. See Master Hsün
    (Hsün-tzu)
Huai Nan-tzu. See Master of Huai Nan
    (Huai Nan-tzu)
Huang, K'uei 98, 300
"Huang-Lao" Taosim 278
Huang-ti po-shu. See Silk Manuscripts of
    the Yellow Emperor
    (Huang-ti po-shu)
human being
    classical Chinese conception of 58
    classical Western conception of 48
    irreducibly communal 64
    as roles and relationships 58
human spirituality/divinity (shen) 72
humanity 226, 232
Hundred Schools 65
hunger 225

I Ching. See Book of Changes
    (I Ching)
identity 51
image 73, 74
immanence 49, 75, 76
imperial names, taboo on use of 15,
    288
incendiary attack 165, 166, 296
infantry
    ratio to mounted troops 258
information 90, 91, 94, 170, 171
    use of false 171
inscrutability (shen) 80, 84, 127
Institute of Scientific Technology for
    the Preservation of Artifacts
    262
insubordination 149
integrity 85, 95, 226, 232
intelligence 90, 91, 92. See espionage,
    spies
interdependence 52
interregnum 66
intersection
    strategically vital 135, 153, 155,
    160, 208, 209, 291, 295
Intrigues of the Warring States
    (Chan-kuo ts'e) 10, 19, 279, 294
invincibility 86, 115, 224

Juan, Hsiao-hsü 38
Judaeo-Christian tradition 45, 59

Kao Yu (fl. 205–212) 19
keng (millet gruel) 59
Kierman, Frank A, Jr. 280, 281
King Ho-lu of Wu 32, 36, 191, 195,
    217
    enquiring of Sun Wu 202, 204, 206,
    209, 210, 212, 215, 221, 222
    an interview with the 191
    and Master Sun 175, 199
Knoblock, John 280
knowledge 49, 57
    as comprehensiveness 56
    aural vocabulary of 55

performative 59, 92
visual vocabulary of 54
vocabulary of 57
Ku, T'ieh-fu 262
Kuan-tzu. See Master Kuan (Kuan-tzu)
K'ung, Ying-ta 299
Kuo-yü. See Discourses of the States
    (Kuo-yü)

labyrinths 238
Lai, Hai-tsung 281
Lao-tzu 39, 270, 277, 281, 286, 288,
    296
    copy found in Ma-wang-tui
    Tomb #3 10
Lau, D. C. 82, 277, 280, 282, 283,
    284, 285, 288, 290, 291, 294
    commentary on Griffith translation 8
    examination of the Lao-tzu 26
    on the canonization of texts 26
    translation of the Lao-tzu 10
lei. See categorization (lei)
Leonardo 63
Lewis, Mark 281, 284, 285
Li, Ching 303
Li, Hsüeh-ch'in 275, 303
Li, Ling 38, 98, 280
Li, Shan 300, 301, 302
Li, Shih-min 295
Li, Ssu 26
Liang, Ch'i-ch'ao 20
Liao, King of Wu 294
life and death 103
light chariots 211, 213, 216
light infantry 200
Lin-i 261
Liu, Hsiang (77–6 BC) 19, 22, 38, 279
Liu, Hsin (d. AD 23) 38
Liu, Pang
    taboo on characters used in name of
    15
Liu t'ao. See Six Strategies (Liu-t'ao)
Lo, Fu-i 262, 302
Loewe, Michael 281, 302
logistics 116, 120, 166
Lü, Ya 23, 171, 296, 297
Lü-shih ch'un-ch'iu. See Spring and
    Autumn Annals of Master Lü
    (Lü-shih ch'un-ch'iu)
Lum, Wing Tek 61, 281

Ma-wang-tui
    discovery of the Documents of the
    Warring States Strategists 279
    Tomb #3 9, 11
    Western Han tombs discovered at 13
    basis for D.C. Lau's translation of
    the Lao-tzu 10
    "male" fortifications 28
Mao, Tse-tung 42, 43, 67
marches 123, 129
Master Han Fei (Han Fei-tzu) 26, 39,
    298
Master Hsün (Hsün-tzu) 39
    "Debate on Warfare" 35

315

316

power
  balance of 116
precipitous defile 147
predicament 218
prescription 53
prestige 161
principle
  determinative 48
prognostications 240
The Prognostications of Sun-tzu 239
protest 69
provisions 107, 108, 157, 160, 200,
    209, 211, 215, 218, 222, 240,
    259
psyche 49, 52
psychology 160, 295
punishments (hsing) 70, 88, 104, 143,
    144, 195, 227
purpose 58

quagmires 141, 238
"The Questions of Wu" chapter 22

radial order 64
rationality 51, 54, 55
ravines, precipitous 141
reality 54
"reality-appearance" distinction
    46
rearguard 155, 160, 179
reconnaissance 92
Red Emperor 183, 293
regulations 103, 104, 116
rehearsal 94, 105, 162
relationships 58
  hierarchical complex of 51, 64
religiousness
  Chinese 72
retreat 158, 160
rewards 104, 108, 143, 161, 170, 171,
    195, 211, 226, 227
ritual practices and role playing (li) 64,
    71
roadways
  not to be traveled 135, 179, 291
rout 149, 150
route
  the circuitous 159
  the direct 129
  the tortuous 129
ruin 149
ruler 88, 91, 104
  arrogant 175, 176
  disobeying the 88, 89, 113, 135,
    150, 179, 180, 192, 292
  employing spies 169, 170, 171
  failings of the 112
  farsighted 166, 169, 171
  frugal 176
  giving orders to the commander
    129, 135
  mobilizing his armies 166
  as pole star 67
  relationship with the able
    commander 86, 87, 88, 113

thinking through the situation
    166
rumors 158, 301

sage
  as virtuoso 55
salt marshes 139
scales 74
scouts
  employing local 161
select troops 205, 209, 218
self-interest (li) 67, 68
Shantung Provincial Museum 262
shen. See human spirituality/divinity,
    inscrutability
shih. See strategic advantage (shih)
shih. See strong points (shih)
Shih-chi. See *Historical Records
    (Shih-chi)*
Shih-i chia chu Sun-tzu. See *Sun-tzu with
    Eleven Commentaries (Shih-i chia
    chu Sun-tzu)*
Shou-fa shou-ling. See *Obeying
    Ordinances and Orders
    (Shou-fa shou-ling)*
Shu-sui 184
siege 27, 107, 111, 161, 170, 297
  as a viable strategy 28
*Silk Manuscripts of the Yellow Emperor
    (Huang-ti po-shu)* 11, 39
single-ordered universe 54
Six Strategies (Liu-t'ao) 10, 14, 31,
    275
  transcribed in Wen-wu (Cultural
    Relics) 268
snake
  "sudden striker" 158
soldiers
  treatment of captured 109
Son of Heaven (t'ien tzu) 67
speaking (yen) 71
speed 87, 95, 107, 109
  and warfare 86
spies 84, 126, 141, 169
  and the able commander 170
  direct access for 170
  as double agents 169, 170, 171
  executing 170
  expendable 169, 170, 171
  five kinds of 169, 171
  held in secrecy 170
  importance of 169
  as inside agents 169, 170
  local (yin) 169, 170
  rewarding 170
  and the sagacious ruler 170
  unexpendable 169, 170, 171
spirituality/divinity (shen) 73
*Spring and Autumn Annals of Master
    Lü (Lü-shih ch'un-ch'iu)* 39, 60,
    279
*Spring and Autumn Annals of Master Yen
    (Yen-tzu ch'un-ch'iu)* 10, 19
Spring and Autumn period
    (c. 772–481 B.C.) 3, 18

317

318

vanguard 150, 155, 179, 301
vehicles
  armored personnel 111
victory 103, 104, 105, 115, 250
  by according with (yin) the enemy
    84, 127
  commander as final arbiter of 88, 116
  the complete 115, 151, 205
  creating the 126, 150
  from out of defeat 161
  is defeat 85, 93
  the easy 116
  factors which anticipate 113
  the highest 111
  inevitability of 81
  master of 92, 169
  possibility of 116
  as a predetermined certainty 93
  the quick 87, 107, 109
  throwing away the 113
  water as metaphor for 127
  the way of battle guarantees 150
vital points 205
vocabulary
  aural and visual 55
vulnerability 115, 160, 213

wagons 218
  four-horse leather-covered 107
walled cities 200, 203, 207, 210, 259
  assaulting 111
  fortifying 200
  not to be assaulted 135, 179, 292
  reinforced 203
Wang Fu
  Ch'ien-fu-lun 300
Wang Jen-chün 98
war
  declaration of 162
war chariots 253
warfare
  and advantage 191
  as applied philosophy 41
  the art of 107, 111, 112, 116, 129
  as an "art" 41
  as the art of deceit 95, 104, 130
  as the art of contextualizing 67
  from art to industry 3
  association with punishment 70
  burden on the people 108
  and chaos 149
  and character 42
  Chinese attitude compared with
    Greek and Roman 40
  and Confucius 41
  correlative vocabulary of 78
  cost of 107, 108, 169
  always defeat 92, 191
  the evils of 108
  and flight 149
  frequency of 175, 176
  general attitudes toward 68
  importance of 103
  and insubordination 149
  intelligence as the essence of 171

  as last resort 40, 85
  and morality 68, 191
  not glorified 40
  on the borders 70
  proactive attitude toward 86
  and prognostication 269
  relationship to philosophy in China
    39
  righteous 70
  and rout 149
  and ruin 149
  ruler's attitude toward 191
  and speed 86, 157
  as sport 191, 193
  in Spring and Autumn China 40
  and timing 86
  and troop numbers 112, 119, 125,
    126, 144, 214, 237
  using the enemy against himself 108,
    109
  in Warring States China 41
  the way of 193, 195
  and yin-yang theory 269
Warring States period (403–221 B.C.)
  3, 64, 65, 75
water 84
  attack by 166
  fording 141
  on the left 187
  as metaphor 127
  positioning an army when near 293
  on the right 187
water supply 28
watering hole 225
way. See tao
weak points (hsü) 119, 123, 125
weapons 107, 108, 112, 218
Wei 175. See Chin: six high ministers of
Wei-liao-tzu. See Master Wei-liao
  (Wei-liao-tzu)
Wen-hsüan 300, 301, 302
Wen-tzu. See Master Wen (Wen-tzu)
Wen-wu. See Cultural Relics
  (Wen-wu)
Western Han (202 B.C.–A.D. 8) 13
White Emperor 183, 293
Wind Direction Divination
  (Feng-chiao-chan) 11, 269
winds 240
winged flanks 244
wisdom 226, 232
world view
  classical Confucian 66
Wu, Chiu-lung 16, 97, 262, 266, 279,
  283, 284, 287, 302
  summary of the content of the Han
    strips by 13
Wu, Emperor of Han 266
Wu, King of Chou 184
Wu, the King of 200
Wu-kang 183
Wu-sui 183

Yang, Ping-an 97, 287, 288, 289, 290,
  296, 300

320

Yao, Nai 20
Yates, Robin 24, 278, 280, 286, 287
Yeh, Shih 20
Yellow Emperor 183, 293, 297, 298
  defeating the emperors of the four
    quarters 139
Yen, Shih-ku (581–645)
  commentary on *Sun-tzu of Chi: The
    Art of Warfare* 19
  commentary on *Sun-tzu of Wu: The
    Art of Warfare* 19
Yen-tzu ch'un-ch'iu. See *Spring and
    Autumn Annals of Master Yen
    (Yen-tzu ch'un-ch'iu)*
Yi, Yin 23, 171, 296, 297
yin. See according with the enemy

yin conditions 183, 184
Yin-ch'üeh-shan 27, 97
  background to the excavation at 261
  excavations at 5, 8, 13
Yin-ch'üeh-shan Committee 13, 14,
    36, 263, 285, 289, 297
  first published reports of 30, 268
yin-yang 14, 52, 77, 94, 298
Yin-yang Five Phases School 298, 299
*Yin-Yang of Master Ts'ao (Ts'ao-shih
    yin-yang)* 269, 275
yüan
  differing measurements of 175, 176
Yüan-kuang reign period (134 B.C.)
  calendar for the first year of 14, 266,
    269, 270, 272

321

ABOUT THE TRANSLATOR

Roger T. Ames is one of the leading interpreters of Chinese philosophy in America today. He received his Ph.D. from the School of Oriental and African Studies, University of London in 1978, under the supervision of Professor D. C. Lau. He is presently Professor of Comparative Philosophy and Director of the Center for Chinese Studies at the University of Hawai'i. He edits the journal *Philosophy East & West*, and is Executive Editor of *China Review International*. His major publications include *The Art of Rulership: Studies in Ancient Chinese Political Thought* (1983); *Thinking Through Confucius* (with David L. Hall) (1987); *Nature in Asian Traditions of Thought: Essays in Environmental Philosophy* (edited with J. Baird Callicott) (1989); *Interpreting Culture Through Translation: A Festschrift in Honor of D. C. Lau* (edited with Ng Mausang and Chan Sin-wai) (1991).